THE COMPLETE YORKSHIRE TERRIER

Jeanne Grimsby

The Yorkshire Terrier is alone among purebred dogs in its demand of metallic colors of gleaming radiance displayed through hairs of lustrous spun silk. Pictured is Irish and Am. Ch. Gleno Playboy, bred by Eugene Weir (N. Ireland).

THE COMPLETE
Yorkshire Terrier

by Joan B. Gordon
and Janet E. Bennett

First Edition

HOWELL
BOOK HOUSE
New York

Howell Book House
Macmillan Publishing Company
866 Third Avenue, New York, NY 10022

Collier Macmillan Canada, Inc.
1200 Eglinton Avenue East, Suite 200
Don Mills, Ontario M3C 3N1

Library of Congress Catalog Card No. 75-30417
ISBN 0-87605-360-6

Macmillan books are available at special discounts for bulk purchases for sales promotions, premiums, fund-raising, or educational use. For details, contact:

Special Sales Director
Macmillan Publishing Company
866 Third Avenue
New York, NY 10022

20 19 18 17 16 15 14 13 12

Printed in the United States of America

This book is dedicated to

*the patience and good humor of Stu Gordon,
Joan's husband, who has had to trip over
books, pictures and papers for many days.
His encouragement and help have kept us
dedicated to rearing and showing Yorkshire
Terriers, and to writing of them.*

*The Wildweir Yorkies are also grateful to
Stu, for the many good pats and back
scratchings he has given them. They are
grateful, too, as are their owners, to
their veterinarians for without their
help and care there would not be a
Wildweir Yorkshire Terrier.*

OUT HUNTING.

Mother love —
2-day-old puppy and dam.

Contents

W<small>E WOULD</small> like to express our sincere thanks to:

Sally Summerfield, who struggled through our squiggles to type this book.

Nancy Donovan, for her help and courier service.

Jeanne Grimsby, for the lovely original illustrations that grace this book.

Elissa Taddie, for her fine sketches and charts of the Yorkie coat pattern.

Goldie Stone for her constant encouragement.

Mary Mills, Kay Finch, Bette Trudgian, Ron Thompson, Merrill Cohen and Ruby Erickson for all their invaluable help.

And very importantly - all the Yorkshire Terrier exhibitors who have cooperated in sending us pictures.

The authors pictured at the first sanction match of the current Yorkshire Terrier Club of America in 1952. Left, Mrs. L. S. (Joan) Gordon, Jr. with Ch. Golden Fame. Right, Miss Janet Bennett with Fame's uncle, Eng. & Am. Ch. Sorreldene Honeyson of the Vale. Judge, Miss Violet Boucher. Fame was Best in Match.

The Authors:

If awards such as those given annually on Broadway were to be given for outstanding performance with Yorkshire Terriers, there would be no question as to which twins deserve the "Tony."

No American kennel has ever registered an impact upon the Yorkshire Terrier to match that made by the Wildweir Kennels, owned by our authors—the twin sisters, Mrs. L. S. (Joan) Gordon, Jr. and Miss Janet Bennett. The records established since the finish of their first champion in 1950 are simply staggering. Consider:

Wildweir has bred or owned 169 AKC champions, over a hundred of which have been homebred.

One of these homebreds stands as the all-time top sire of the breed with 95 champion offspring (fantastic in a breed noted for small litters). Dogs bred by Wildweir Kennels have been finished to championships in Canada, Mexico, Bermuda, Colombia, Brazil and Argentina.

As winners, they have been overpowering. Of the 30 Yorkshire Terriers that have won Best in Show all-breeds in the United States to date, 11 have been owned by Wildweir. (Two, owned by others, were bred by Wildweir.) A Wildweir dog was the first of the breed to win an all-breed BIS in this country, and another stands as the top winning Yorkie of all time. A current representative is a third generation Best in Show winner.

Thirty-one Yorkies owned or bred by the sisters have have won 365 Toy Groups at shows from coast to coast, including the most prestigious—Westminster, Chicago International, Harbor Cities, etc. Of 22 Specialties held by the parent Yorkshire Terrier Club of America, 16 have been won by Wildweir entries.

What's more, all of these dogs have been owner-handled.

In addition, Joan and Janet have finished to championship: 3 Scottish Deerhounds (of which 2 were BIS winners), 4 Italian Greyhounds and a Pomeranian.

From the beginning, they have been as one. Even close friends will be hard put to distinguish just which chapters in this book were written by Joan, and which by Janet.

Both are charter members of the current Yorkshire Terrier Club of America (formed in 1951) and each has served on its Board of Directors. They have scrupulously compiled a record of every champion, every important win, and every important doing in the breed, and their treasure of books, photos and miscellany on the Yorkshire Terrier is probably unexcelled in the world.

Happily, all of this is now reflected in this book. The reader who comes to these pages for guidance in breeding, raising, judging, or simply knowing the Yorkshire Terrier, is in the best possible hands.

—*Ab Sidewater*
Editor

Ch. Little Sir Model   Eng. Ch. Kelsbro Quality Boy

Quality and type mirrored through the generations. Ch. Wildweir Reluctant Dragon, owned by G. Olerich, Tenn., is the great-grandson of Model, and the great, great grand-nephew of Quality Boy.

Preface

IN 1891, Mr. P. H. Coombs in *The American Book of the Dog* wisely cautioned: "It is quite an undertaking to breed a Yorkshire combining the proper colors, texture of coat and Terrier type; and no amount of care or attention on the part of the owner can turn a badly-bred, ill-formed specimen into a good one."

Coat texture and hair colors are inherited. Bred in, the wrong coat texture can be counted on to arrive on a well-composed Yorkie as readily as on an ill-composed one. Similarly, wrong hair colors—bred in—find their way on to well-formed and ill-formed specimens alike.

Well-bred Yorkies are obtainable; breeders with knowledge and experience offer Yorkies that will grow into adults that are as sound as possible in all features. But it is important that the well-bred Yorkie be wisely bred in turn, and spared such indiscriminate matings as suffered by the dog of whom Philipp Gruening wrote in *The Dobermann Pinscher* "They took this great mansion and tore it down to build hovels."

Thankfully, all across the country there are breeders that are holding the line and producing Yorkies that meet the standard—lovely gold and blue dogs. Sound dogs, too—of fine health and disposition—with well-proportioned bodies that enable them to show, to enjoy their owner's lives and to produce in top flight style. And because they model the AKC-approved standard, they are correct in type.

If this book helps new judges, new exhibitors, and particularly new breeders, to recognize them and to seek them out, it will have served our aim.

—JOAN B. GORDON
JANET E. BENNETT

"Badger Baiting", 1804 painting by H. B. Chalon.—*Photo courtesy of The Sporting Gallery, Middleburg, Va.*

1

Manufacture of
The Yorkshire Terrier

THOUGH many breed histories would make it appear so, the Yorkshire Terrier is not a breed drawn from thin air.

Too many of these histories are, alas, no more than folklore gleaned from pages of other books, whose authors did little research. Contrary to their claims, the origins, early history and cultivation of the Yorkshire terrier are not lost in the mists of time. Nor do they lie buried in the cunning, crafty minds of the Yorkshire weavers. The warp and woof of how this silken terrier came into the world of purebred dogs *can* be traced.

Included in the theories offered regarding the production of the Yorkshire Terrier are that he was bred from a large dog like an Airedale, from a smooth-coated dog like a Manchester, or from a short-legged, long-backed uneven toplined dog such as a Dandie Dinmont. The reasoning given for these breeds is that they are born black and tan, and some change color to blue and tan. But if that be the basis, why not say the Doberman Pinscher, or even add a dash of the Chow?

These authorities then throw in the Maltese, to explain how the Yorkshire acquired a silky coat. In this, their reasoning is more understandable, but hardly solid. For the Maltese and Yorkshire merger, if it did happen, came into the picture after the Yorkshire had already taken his place in The Kennel Club stud book.

That there are certain genetic factors that these breeds hold in common with the Yorkshire Terrier, is undeniable. But easy as it might be to do so, this is no cause to make them the genetic ancestors of the Yorkie. For all dogs originally came from the same stock, and so carry the same factors to an extent—dependent upon what was sought to form the required animal.

Color in dogs, for example, is formed by various genes. The two basic colors are yellow or dark brown (or black). They are controlled by other genes to allow the color pattern, color distribution and the depth or dilution of the color. The hair texture is controlled by another set of genes. The size of the dog is controlled by other genes, as are his head shape, ear shape, carriage of his tail, and so on.

With this in mind, how could the Yorkshire have been developed in a few short years? The answer lies in study of the history of the dogs of his birthland, Great Britain, with search for a dog who had the basic factors required by the first Yorkshire Terrier breeders.

TRACING THE FACTORS

The Waterside Terrier

In the early years of dogs in Great Britain almost all hunting land was denied to the serfs. To keep them from poaching with hunting dogs, laws were written that date as far back as The Canons of Canute in the 11th century. However, the serfs were allowed "the little dogs" because "it stands to reason that there is no danger in them."

These insignificant little Toy dogs were not of any Spaniel breed, for Spaniels could not be kept in a forest without a special grant. The determinant as to whether or not a serf might keep a dog was size. The foresters were provided with a fixed gauge, a hoop, and only the little dogs that could pass through the seven-inch diameter of the hoop could be owned by the serfs.

These little dogs went into the fields with the mowers to kill the rats. They killed the rabbits in the vegetable patch, and in general kept the poor man's home safe from rats and other varmints, as well as supplying small game from the fields and hedgerows for his table.

By the time of King William IV (1765-1835) the Waterside Terrier, a small, longish-coated dog, occasionally grizzly (bluish-gray) in color, was common in Yorkshire. In an article in *The English Stockkeeper* (1887), G. H. Wilkinson reported:

I have been at some trouble looking up several old fanciers, one of whom is Mr. John Richardson of Halifax who is now in his 67th year, and very interesting it was to hear this aged man go back to "the good old days" of over half a century ago. Fifty years ago, there was in Halifax, and the immediate neighborhood, a type of dog called at that time (and even within

Waterside Terriers, from a painting c.1820, artist unknown.

"Ratcatchers", from a painting believed done by Edwin Landseer in 1821, showing Scotch Terriers "Vixen", "Brutus" and "Boxer".

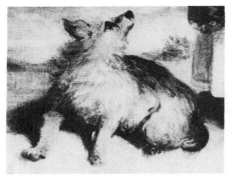

Scotch Terrier. Detail from a painting by Sir Joshua Reynolds, 1776.

Drawing (1821) by Edwin Landseer of his pure-bred Scotch Terrier "Vixen"—a famous ratter—at 14 years.

Otter Terrier, from a steel engraving, 1858.

Scotch Terriers. *Left,* detail of an oil painting, circa 1835, attributed to S. J. E. Jones. England, Dog in rear: medium steel with tan points, white on chest, cropped ears, appears 15–20 lbs. *(Photo, courtesy Jeanne Grimsby). Right,* from an 1846 engraving.

these last twenty years) a "Waterside Terrier", a game little dog, varying in weight from six to twenty pounds, mostly about ten pounds weight—a dog resembling the present Welsh and Airedale Terrier on a small scale. At this period, these dogs were bred for the purpose of hunting and killing rats. They would go into the river with a ferret, and were just in their element when put into a rat pit. An almost daily occurrence at that time was to back them to kill a given number of rats in a given time.

It seems a pity that such a breed should have become extinct. Mr. Richardson himself owned a little bitch 'Polly', who weighed six pounds and she was frequently put into a rat pit with a dozen rats, the whole of which she would speedily kill against time. She would also swim the river and hunt with the ferret. This little bitch, I am told, had four or five inches of coat on each side of her body, with a white or silver head.

These little Waterside Terriers, with their ratting ability, more than likely traveled all the rivers, backwaters and canals along which early commerce, from the Shires to Scotland, moved prior to railroads and roadways.

In fact, the little Terrier journeyed down around the Horn to the vast Australian continent. Along with his ratting abilities, this small Terrier's faculties as a watchdog made him invaluable to the free settlers of the frontier lands of the vast Crown Colonies in the Southern Pacific. *The Australian Terrier and the Australian Silky Terrier*, by W.A. Wheatland, contains the following:

In discussing the breed with Mr. Scott, of Ross, Tasmania, whose family have resided in the district for over hundred years, he stated:

"It is known that sometime prior to 1820, the free settlers of the Midlands of Tasmania in the areas of Campbelltown and Ross successfully bred Broken-Coated Terrier Dogs of a blue-sheen body colour, with tan legs and face and weighing approximately seven to ten pounds. In those days, marauding Aboriginals, bushrangers, and escaped convicts were prevalent in these districts. It was the unerring and uncanny instinct of these Blue and Tan Terriers to detect the approach of strangers at great distances that made them a prized possession as watchdogs and safeguards around the home. They were extremely hard to come by, the individual strains being most jealously guarded."

By 1872, Mr. J. Spink, one of the original Yorkshire Terrier breeders, had exported "Punch", a grandson of "Old Sandy" out of a Halifax bitch, to Norman D'Arcy, Brisbane, Queensland, Australia. Old Sandy was also the grandsire of Huddersfield Ben, the first dog to receive the designation of Yorkshire Terrier. "Punch" is listed as having won prizes at 13 shows in England prior to his exportation to Australia.

Here, in the Waterside Terrier, lay a supply of genes for silky coats, small size, blue and tan pattern. It is in this ancient breed, too, that we find the reason that the Airedale has been mistakenly theorized to be an ancestor of the Yorkie.

Children play a game at parties where one whispers something into another's ears, and it is repeated from ear to ear until the last child tells the version he's heard—and it is always strangely removed from the original. An old breeder of Yorkies may well have said, "Well, we used the Waterside Terrier in their origin," and that statement may have been repeated down the line. Some years later—in about the late 1890s—a writer, searching for the breed's origin, hears that it was made from a Waterside Terrier, and immediately conceives it to be descended from the Airedale. For when the Yorkshire men living in the dale of the river Aire had wanted a dog with the virtues of the Waterside Terrier, but larger—a dog with the ability to hunt larger game along the riverbank and in the water—they found their answer in combining their Terrier with the Otter Hound. The resulting dog was, at first, still called a Waterside Terrier and classes were provided at early dog shows. At last, at Birmingham in 1883, the classes were for Waterside or Airedale Terriers. Soon, he officially became the Airedale Terrier and the little Waterside Terrier, as such, vanished from the scene. Thus, the writer of the late 1890s, knowing that in its early days the Airedale Terrier had been called a Waterside Terrier, puts his facts back to front, and identifies the Airedale as the Yorkie's unknown factor.

The Clydesdale and the Paisley Terriers

With the beginnings of the Industrial Revolution in the later years of the 1700s, the displaced crofters of Scotland, their clans broken, went south to Yorkshire, England's largest shire. In fact, Yorkshire was so large that, in the days of horse transport, it was divided into Ridings— East, North, and West; each an area that could be covered on a horse in a given time. The West-Riding included the large industrial towns of Halifax and Bradford. Nearby, across the county border in Lancashire, was the manufacturing city of Manchester. There, these displaced men and women found work as weavers and brought with them their little dogs, unwittingly adding confusion to the facts of the Yorkshire's origin.

Rawdon B. Lee, speaking of Yorkshire Terriers in *Modern Dogs (Terriers)* says: "How the name of Scotch Terrier became attached to a dog which so thoroughly had its home in Yorkshire and Lancashire is somewhat difficult to determine, if it can be determined at all, but a very old breeder of the variety told me that the first of them came from

Scotland, where they had been accidently produced from a cross between the silk-coated Skye (the Clydesdale) and the black and tan Terrier. One could scarcely expect that a pretty dog, partaking in a degree after both its parents, could be produced from a smooth-coated dog, a long-coated bitch or vice versa. Maybe, two or three animals so bred had been brought by some of the Paisley weavers into Yorkshire and there, suitably admired, pains were taken to perpetuate the strain.'' Though Mr. Lee helps here to add confusion, at least it's nice to see one early skeptic of a smooth-coated breed being a factor.

Scotland with its mountain highlands limited the communication between the dwellers in their highland fastness and their lowland counterparts. The isolation and the segregation of the Scottish clans and Scottish people gave each room to develop a dog to fit his requirements: the Scotchman of the Isles bred one type, the Highlander another, and the man of the heath and moor developed yet another.

These Terriers acquired their names from their work, their area of origin, or the estates of individual owners. Names included Aberdeen, Highland, Cairn, Skye, Short-Coated Skye, Lowland, Roseneath, Paisley, Clydesdale, Diehard, Otter Terrier, Sorty Terrier, and so on. But *all* were also catalogued as Scotch Terriers.

In 1822, *The History of Quadrupeds* describes the Scotch Terrier as: ''rough; short-legged; long-backed; very strong and most commonly of a yellow color mixed with black and white.''

It would have been a considerable help in unraveling canine history if breed names had been standardized when language was first invented. If dog shows have done nothing else for the different breeds, they have at least given them distinctive names and standards which belong to no other breed. Certainly the early Scotch Terriers could have benefited by an earlier sorting.

These Terriers, all coming into England from Scotland, were all referred to in the 1800s as Scotch Terriers. The Aberdeen Terrier finally grabbed the title closest to this nomenclature by becoming the Scottish Terrier. The first Scottish Terrier standard called for a weight between 15 to 20 lbs. The first volume of the Scottish Terrier Club of Scotland, published in 1895, almost ten years after the breed's finding a place in the Kennel Club Stud Book, registers the dogs under the following colors: black-brown on legs; black face and legs brown; dark, steel gray; steel gray, white on chest; red-gray brindle; black, brown of face and legs; plus the usual colors.

The Scotch Terrier that has the most interesting factors for the Yorkshire Terrier is the early Skye Terrier. From *Terriers, Their Points and Management* (F.T. Barton, 1918), we get: ''What are sometimes described as Roseneath (Roseneath being in the Island of Bute) Terriers appear to have been the original type of Skye. These Terriers are

Prize dogs of the second Islington show, from an engraving in *The Illustrated London News*, 1864. Note contrast of size of Skye Terrier with Fox Terrier and Pomeranian.

Paisley Terrier. Mr. John King's "Lorne of Paisley."

Clydesdale Terrier, with drop ears.

described as of a fawn or silver gray and from 10 to 16 lbs." Also, in describing the early Skye, the same author says:"The small size of these Terriers and their handsome appearance has had a great deal to do with these little dogs being so much sought after." Their weight is given as dogs 16 to 20 lbs.; bitches, 16 lbs.; height at shoulders, 9 inches for dogs, 8½ inches for bitches; length from the back of the head to tail set-on, 22½ inches. The coat was not to be silky.

The fanciers of the Skye had a problem in settling the breed to type. The early Skyes, before standards were set, produced what was called a soft-coated, prick-eared Skye. Sometimes it was called a Linty or a Glasgow Silky. Out of this confusion came the Skye Terrier — a dog with a long, hard, flat coat and an undercoat — and two breeds that have been swept from sight, the Clydesdale Terrier and the Paisley Terrier.

Much confusion remains today in articles written of the Clydesdale and Paisley. Most authors conceive them to be one and the same breed, which they probably were until fanciers started selecting and breeding them to a fixed standard. In *The Dogs of Scotland* (1891), the author, D. J. Thomson Grey, gives the following on the Paisley or Clydesdale Terrier:

Blackhall writing in the *Scottish Terrier* for June, 1884 says: "It will be in the recollection of many readers that nine or ten years ago this Terrier exercised breeders of the Skye Terrier considerably, and week after week was the occasion of, shall I say, interesting? friendly? or interested? correspondence in *The Country and Fancier's Chronicle* or *Livestock Journal*, when behind the unsicklier shelter of nom de plumes, our Skye Terrier friends wrote up their own dogs and decried those of the opposition.

"This paper warfare was continued with increasing acrimony, fresh combatants being enlisted on the various sides, until in the interest of general readers, who were doubtless beginning to grumble at the flat, stale, and unprofitable character of their threepence worth, the editors added their quota to the subject — viz: This correspondence must now cease. *Ed.*

"There being no separate classes for fancy Terriers, they were exhibited in the Skye Terrier classes and very frequently carried off the honors. However, the aforesaid correspondence served at least one good purpose in deciding once and for all, that the Skye Terrier must have a hard coat, thus ousting one of the 'Dromios' from a false position.

"That decision was well-nigh the death of the silky-haired Terrier, as at no show, even under the new arrangement, with exception of one or two in the west country, were the boycotted Terriers provided for. The only opening left being the unsatisfactory 'any other variety class'. It is therefore, no cause for wonder that, under these adverse circumstances, interest in the breed rapidly waned, and but for the effort made by a very few admirers to keep them on their legs, this popular dog would soon have degenerated into a mongrel and have been deposited upon the silent shore of memory."

The Clydesdale Terrier did not get washed ashore but kept afloat as late as the 1900s, having a place in The Kennel Club and the AKC stud books. The Paisley stayed afloat long enough to have a standard drawn up in 1884. These two Terriers probably were the result of breeding soft-coated, prick-eared Skyes and were both developed in the vale of the Clyde river, one of whose river markets is Paisley. Their breed standards and descriptions show them to have had somewhat different requirements, though the wording of their standards should have given a clue as to where they ultimately came to rest.

Mr. Freeman Lloyd in the AKC publication, *Pure-Bred Dogs-American Kennel Gazette*, March 31, 1934, described the Paisley Terrier in an article on "Many Dogs in Many Lands":

One of the handsomest of Scottish breeds was the Clydesdale or Paisley Terrier, which has unfortunately died out. At least, I have not seen one for years. This dog was sometimes known as the Glasgow Terrier. It came into prominence in the middle '80s of the last century. Of all the "fancy dogs," this creature, in full coat, was easily the most delightful. Imagine a dog of the same build in body and head as a first-class, 18 lb. Skye Terrier. Visualize it with the same prick-ears. Think of such a dog covered with long hair often trailing on the ground; the hair being of the same color and fibre as the silk or spun-glass-like quality, of that carried by a real exquisite specimen of the Yorkshire Terrier at its very best. That was the Paisley Terrier from the Dale of the Clyde.

The author says further on:

Were it possible to bench a row of representative dogs of this kind at a Westminster Show, the animal would attract great attention, even among the luxurious class that visit Madison Square Garden. To give a word picture of the breed is difficult. One of the most attractive points was the heavily-fringed, upright ears. The silky hair hung like the mantilla of a Spanish senorita. The body and headcoat was perfectly flat and free from any trace of curl or waviness; very glossy and silky in texture (not linty) and without any pily undercoat as is found in the Skye Terrier.

The colors ranged from dark blue to light fawn. The most desired were the various shades of blue. Dark blue was preferred, but without any approach to blackness. The color of the head was best liked when of a beautiful silvery blue, which became darker on the ears. The back, or body coat varied in its shades of blue, inclining to silvery on the lowest parts of the body and legs. The tail was generally of the same shade, or a little darker than the back.

Some day, perhaps, we shall again see the Clydesdale, Paisley, or Glasgow Terrier. If he be but a soft-coated Skye Terrier, he will be like some attractive exotic amid the sterner dogs of the land of Burns and of Scott, both dog lovers to the core.

24

The Paisley Terrier standard drawn up in 1884 called for color to be; "various shades of blue, dark blue for preference. The hair on head and lower extremities slightly lighter than the body color, but it should not approach a linty shade." (Lint in this case signified flax, therefore a light straw color).

Unfortunately, the Paisley Terrier fanciers threw in their lot with the Skye Terrier club and disappeared from view. A few Glasgow fanciers formed themselves into a club and resolved to change their breed name from Paisley to Clydesdale Terrier. It would seem that the Glasgow fanciers had dogs that carried strong factors for that "linty" shade.

Capt. W. Wilmer in *The Book of the Dog*, writes: "The Clydesdale may be described as an anomaly. He stands as it were upon a pedestal of his own; and unlike other Scotch Terriers he is classified as Non-Sporting. Perhaps his marvelously fine and silky coat precludes him from the rough work of hunting vermin, though it is certain his game-like instincts would naturally lead him to do so. Of all Scotch dogs he is perhaps the smallest; his weight seldom exceeding 18 lbs."

The breed standard described him as:

A long, low, level dog, with heavily fringed erect ears and a long coat like the finest silk or spun glass, which hangs quite straight and evenly down each side, from a parting extending from the nose to the root of the tail. *Color:* A level, bright steel blue extending from the back of the head to the root of tail, and on no account intermingled with any fawn, light or dark hairs. The head, legs and feet should be a clear bright golden tan, free from grey, sooty or dark hairs. The tail should be very dark blue or black. *Coat:* as long and straight as possible, free from all trace of curl or waviness, very glossy and silky in texture with an entire absence of undercoat.

Thus the blue and silver Paisley had become a blue and golden tan Clydesdale who found a place in The Kennel Club stud book and, for a few years, in the American Kennel Club stud book.

From the North Sea, the Scottish border marches westward with the border of the shire of York, forming the northern boundary line of England. The Yorkshire border turns southward to end and turns east at the Cathedral City of York. To the west, in the shire of Lancaster, is the large manufacturing city of Manchester and this area holds another factor that was needed to produce the Yorkshire Terrier.

The old English working Terriers of Manchester area were first described in 1771 in a book called *The History of Manchester*, by Whitaker: The dogs of that area are described as: "Little Terrars of black and tan and sometimes white and red, with crooked legs and shaggy hair."

From these shaggy haired dogs was developed the smooth silky-coated old black and tan Terrier or Manchester Terrier. At a show in Holburn in 1862, there were 42 benched, divided equally in two classes, one for animals over 5 lbs., the other for dogs and bitches under 5 lbs.

In *The Dog in Health and Disease,* "Stonehenge" (nom-de-plume of J. H. Walsh) describes the black and tan Terrier's color as: "The only true color is black and tan . . . but many puppies are marked with white, even so much as to predominate in white and sometimes, but rarely, they are blue". Mr. Rawdon Lee says, "Before closing the chapter (black and tan Terriers), allusion must be made to the 'blue' or slate-colored Terriers which are occasionally obtained from this variety, though the parents may be correctly marked themselves. Such 'sports' are in reality as well bred as the real article and are found in all sizes, perhaps most commonly amongst the 'toys' and the small-sized specimens, than amongst the larger ones. Some are entirely 'blue' or slate-colored, others have tan markings."

There were many other English Terriers in the Yorkshire and Lancashire area that were rough-coated and of a black and tan pattern. They were small enough to be carried in a hunter's pouch. But without popular support they have passed from the scene or have been lost in some recognized terrier breed. Like the Terriers from Scotland, the old English Terriers were named for their ability, color or place of origin. Though there were many Terriers from Manchester, the black and tan smooth-coated became so indentified with Manchester that he became officially the Manchester Terrier. There were also in the area, dogs that were black and tan with white markings, grizzle and tan, rough, wire-haired, broken-haired and silky-coated. Plenty of factors to choose from.

All of the aforementioned dogs obviously carried the genes to produce coat patterns of black and tan; the genes to dilute the black to blue or grizzle. Dogs, in some strains, carried the factor to clear the black to golden tan at maturity. Some of these breeds carry the factors to produce a glossy silk coat, in some short and others long. Here then, in these Scotch and old English Terriers lay the greatest genetic bank to produce the Yorkshire as we now know him; a combination of the dog the Scottish weavers took south to the large industrial towns where, with the Yorkshiremen, they interwove the strands of the local dogs of Manchester, Halifax, Bradford and Leeds.

All that was needed at this point were fanciers ready to breed the Yorkie's points and to show his merit in the rapidly developing show rings. Through them, he would soon advance to the fore, burying the Waterside, Paisley and Clydesdale Terrier in his silken wake.

An interesting comparison. *Left,* Clydesdale Terrier, Ballochsmyle Wee Wattie, from *The 20th Century Dog,* 1904. *At right,* a registered Yorkshire Terrier (Scotland, c. 1950)—Hazy of Johnstounburn, dam of champions, owned by Mrs. Crookshank.

Plenty of factors to choose from. The Terrier, from an engraving by Sydenham Edwards, *Cynographia Brittanica,* c. 1800.

Mrs. and Mr. Jonas Foster, Bradford, England.

Mrs. Foster's Eng. Ch. Bradford Hero is the dog in rear. In front are Mrs. Troughear's Eng. Ch. Conqueror and Eng. Ch. Violet.

THE WEAVING OF THE BREED

It has been hard for many writers to accept the almost overnight production of the Yorkshire Terrier—a dog that within a few years of its introduction was producing dogs under five pounds, with clear golden tan and blue silky coats, reaching to 12 inches in length. *The American Book of the Dog*, written in 1891 by P. H. Coombs, provides some answers. Mr. Coombs, an American pioneer of the breed, had gathered the story from the last of the generation who knew the Yorkie's beginnings. In his chapter on the Yorkshire terrier in the book, he wrote:

No doubt much difficulty has been experienced in obtaining information relating to its early history; and one opinion expressed by Shaw, seems to be that substantially the history was known, but that it was kept a secret. It would be manifestly unjust to deprive the Yorkshire Terrier of the title to a pedigree running back to the progenitors of the breed.

In an interesting article of this breed, published in the *Century Magazine* in 1886 and written by Mr. James Watson of Philadelphia, is given about the first public information tending to positively identify its origin — to a certain extent at least. The writer says: "Some of our authorities have attempted to throw a great deal of mystery about the origin of the Yorkshire terrier, where none really exists. If we consider that the mill operatives (*workers*), who originated the breed by careful selection of the best long-coated small Terriers they could find, were all ignorant men, unaccustomed to imparting information for public use, we may see some reason why reliable facts have not been easily attained. These early writers show but little knowledge of the possibilities of selection. Stonehenge, for instance, in his early editions, speaks of it being impossible for a dog with a three-inch coat and seven-inch beard to be a descendant of the soft-coated Scotch Terrier, without a cross of some kind. The absurdity of this is seen when we remember that within a few years of the date of his history, Yorkshire Terriers were shown with twelve inches of coat. Then, again, he speaks of the King Charles Spaniel as being employed to give the blue and tan, a more ridiculous statement than which could not have been penned. To get a blue and tan, long, straight, silky coat, breeders were not likely to employ a black and tan dog with a wide chest, tuck-up loin, a round bullet head, large protruding eyes, and heavy Spaniel ears. The idea is too absurd to be entertained for a moment. As arrayed against all the conjectures of theorists, I have in my possession a letter from Mrs. M. A. Foster, of Bradford, England who, in writing of the dog Bradford Hero, the winner of ninety-seven first prizes, says; "The pedigree of Bradford Hero includes all the best dogs for thirty-five years back, and they were all Scotch Terriers, the name Yorkshire given them on account of their being improved so much in that region."

Following this, and about a year later, Mr. Ed. Bootman of Halifax, Eng-

Mr. Spink's "Bounce", the dog at left rear, was a grandson of Kitty and Old Crab. Woodcut from *Dogs of the British Isles*, 1872. Text below from same book.

THE YORKSHIRE BLUE-TAN SILKY COATED TERRIER.

THE last dog in the frontispiece is Mr. Spink's Bounce, a good specimen of the modern silky-haired blue-tan terrier, but not quite coming up to some of those which have been exhibited since 1865, whose coat is considerably longer, and, if possible, more silky. Excepting in colour and coat, this dog resembles the old English rough terrier, the shapes of body and head being exactly the same.

The ears are generally cropped, but if entire should be fine, thin, and moderately small. The coat should be long, very silky in texture, and completely parted down the back—the beard being often two or three inches in length, and entirely of a golden tan colour. The colour must be entirely blue on the back and down to the elbow and thigh, showing a rich lustre, and without any admixture of tan. The legs and muzzle should be a rich golden tan. Ears also tan, but darker in shade; the colour on the top of the skull becomes lighter, approaching to fawn, the two shades gradually merging into each other. Weight, 10lb. to 18lb.

Value of Points of the Yorkshire Blue-tan.

Colour—		Coat—		Ears 10	Symmetry—	
Good blue, without tan	25	Length	15		Like that of	
Good tan	25	Silkyness ...	10		Scotch terrier	15
	50		**25**	**10**		**15**

Grand total, **100.**

The silver-grey Yorkshire terrier is not a distinct breed, being merely a paler variety of the blue-tan.

land furnished an article on the origin of the breed, for publication in the *English Stockkeeper,* which that journal, "feeling the importance of all facts relating to the origin of the breed", published as follows:

"Swift's Old Crab, a cross-bred Scotch Terrier, Kershaw's Kitty, a Skye, and an Old English Terrier bitch kept by J. Whittam, then residing in Hatter's Fold, Halifax, were the progenitors of the present race of Yorkshire Terriers. These dogs were in the zenith of their fame forty years ago. The owner of Old Crab was a native of Halifax, and a joiner by trade. *(joiner — a carpenter).* He worked at Oldham for some time as a journeyman *(hired by the day),* and then removed to Manchester, where he kept a public house. Whether he got Crab at Oldham or Manchester I have not been able to ascertain. He had him when in Manchester, and from there sent him several times to Halifax on a visit to Kitty. The last would be about 1850.

"Crab was a dog of about eight or nine lbs. weight, with a good Terrier head and eye, but with a long body, resembling the Scotch Terrier. The legs and muzzle only were tanned, and the hair on the body would be about three or four inches in length. He has stood for years in a case in a room at the Westgate Hotel, a public house which his owner kept when he returned to his native town, where, I believe, the dog may be seen today.

"Kitty was a bitch different in type from Crab. She was a drop-eared Skye, with plenty of coat of a blue shade, but destitute of tan on any part of the body. Like Crab, she had no pedigree. She was originally stolen from Manchester and sent to a man named Jackson, a saddler in Huddersfield, who, when it became known that a five pound reward was offered in Manchester for her recovery, sent her to a person named Harrison, then a waiter at the White Swan Hotel, Halifax, to escape detection, and from Harrison she passed into the hand of Mr. J. Kershaw of Beshop Blaise, a public house which once stood on the Old North Bridge, Halifax. Prior to 1851 Kitty had six litters, all of which were by Crab. In these six litters she had thirty-six puppies, twenty-eight of which were dogs, and served to stock the district with rising sires. After 1851, when she passed into the possession of Mr. F. Jagger, she had forty-four puppies, making a total of eighty.

"Mr. Whittam's bitch, whose name I cannot get to know, was an Old English Terrier, with tanned head, ears and legs, and a sort of grizzle back. She was built on the lines of speed. Like the others, she had no pedigree. She was sent to the late Bernard Hartley of Allen Gate, Halifax by a friend residing in Scotland. When Mr. Hartley had got tired of her, he gave her to his coachman, Mason, who, in turn, gave her to his friend Whittam, and Whittam used her years for breeding purposes. Although this bitch came from Scotland, it is believed the parents were from this district."

The last-named writer has so fully identified the three dogs first employed to manufacture the breed, together with their names, ownership, characteristics, and other facts concerning them, that there can be no doubt as to the authenticity of the history of the origin of the breed. His history, published in *The Stockkeeper* in 1887, has never been publicly contradicted, and it is evident that there can now be no grounds for following the reasoning of writers who claim that the origin is a mystery.

We agree whole-heartedly with Mr. Coombs in his grand summation. It should still all further arguments.

Before continuing with the manufacture of the Yorkshire Terrier, let us examine the description of these three dogs. Crab with a Terrier head, three to four inch coat and a long body with tan on legs and muzzle, was most likely a Clydesdale or Waterside Terrier. Kitty, with plenty of coat of a blue shade but destitute of tan on any part of the body, was no doubt a Paisley Terrier. Whittam's nameless bitch, with her racier build and tanned head and legs and a sort of grizzle back, was likely to have been out of Old English Terriers from the Manchester area.

The threads in the loom were set and the task of weaving ready to commence. Taking the offspring of these dogs, the early breeders began spinning their bloodlines. With interest in prize winning and competition growing in numbers, the shuttles' pace increased. The Yorkshire's complete development is so woven into the developing sport of showing dogs that it is inecessary to know a little of how it began.

The first organized dog show ever held took place at Newcastle-on-Tyne in 1859. In the following 14 years, a number of shows for many breeds sprang up and, as in most things, practices crept in that emphasized the necessity of having some controlling authority.

In 1873, a group of gentlemen founded The Kennel Club in England. (The English kennel club is always called The Kennel Club.) They felt that their first priority should be the availability of recorded pedigrees. They set about compiling a Stud Book which contained the principal winners at the leading shows up to that date. It consisted of 4,027 dogs divided into forty breeds and varieties. It also contained "a code of rules for the guidance of dog shows, as well as for the manner in which field trials should be conducted." The dogs were divided into two groups, Non-Sporting and Sporting. Under Non-Sporting, the Yorkshire joined the select forty breeds as Broken-haired Scotch and Yorkshire Terriers and, since breeds were less clearly defined, some were registered as Toy Terriers (Rough and Broken-haired).

Prior to the first organized show in 1859, most of the exhibiting of dogs was haphazard. Usually the events were held in local public houses.

No one has yet been able to pin down the exact date when the showing of dogs in open competition started. Shows were mainly sponsored by publicans who, in their day, kept a dog pit, a rat pit, a boxed badger and a game bull around their establishments for the entertainment of their patrons and their dogs. Records of such dog exhibitions go back at least to 1844.

The Blue Anchor, kept by Jemmy Shaw, who was one of the first to realize the possibilities of dog exhibitions, ran an advertisement in 1849 for a show of the Toy Dog Club on May 27, 1849. The card reads:

The Toy Dog Club holds their meetings every Thursday evening at Mr. J. Shaw's, Blue Anchor Tavern, Dunhill Row, Finsbury, London. Grand show next Sunday evening May 27th, Terriers, Spaniels, and Small Toy Dogs, when nearly every fancier in London, as well as several provincials now in town, will attend with their little beauties.

It is noteworthy that both Kitty and Crab's owners were publicans.

Naming of the Yorkshire

So many of the early influential fanciers who steamed ahead to produce the Yorkshire Terrier were from Yorkshire or its close environs that they finally gave this broken-haired Scotch Terrier a new name. In 1870 Angus Sutherland of Accrington, the then reporter for *The Field*, commenting on Mozart (a son of Huddersfield Ben) taking first prize in the variety class at Westmoreland said, "they aught no longer to be called Scotch Terriers but Yorkshire Terriers for having been so improved there."

Before leaving the Yorkshire Terrier with his new designation, it is impossible not to add Dr. Gordon Staples' comment from *Ladies' Dogs As Companions*, published approximately 1876:

Scotchmen are as a rule terribly proud even if they are terribly poor. They have the misfortune to be all born gentlemen, and have an inate scorn at aught that is weakly in plant or animal, aught that can bear and brave the storms that, for seven months of the year, sweep across the land of mountain and flood. Perhaps this is the reason why they will not be accountable for the beautiful little creature, which forms the subject of this Chapter. The Yorkshire Terrier, unlike the Skye is not,

"An Imp. — hardy, bold and wild,
As best befits a mountain child."

And so Scotland disowns it. The doggie must emigrate, and take another name. It is no longer the Scotch Terrier, nor the improved Scotch — as if anything really Scotch could be improved! — but the Yorkshire pure and simple. I don't know that the little animal has lost much by the change after all. There is no more genial hospitality to be found anywhere, than you meet in Yorkshire or Northern Lancashire. The very county itself with its rolling braes, its breezy green cliffs, its wimpling burn and heather — 'mind ye o'hame'. And just hear a Yorkshireman read "Tam O'Shanter" or the "Cottar's Saturday Night." I think I've found a good home for my pretty Blue and Tan.

Huddersfield Ben, 1865–1871, founding father of the Yorkshire Terrier. This painting, the only one known to have been done of "Ben" from life, is owned by the authors.

Broken-haired Scotch Terriers. *Left,* Peto, listed as Toy Terrier—rough, broken-haired, in EKC studbook (1859–1874.) *Right,* Dr. Mark's Kate and Badger, from an 1881 book. Note similarity of head type to that of Huddersfield Ben above.

Here in his new home of genial hospitality, the broken-haired Scotch Terrier merged with the broken-haired English Terrier. Crab, Kitty and Whittam's bitch, plus the offspring of rising young sires, had woven into whole the factors to produce a fixed breed. The pattern design was laid in the next years to produce a stud dog that could found a gold and blue bloodline.

The Early Breeders

One of the early fanciers most influential in setting the style was Peter Eden of Salford, Lancashire. He was the owner of many dogs, among whom was Albert, a top winner from 1863 to 1865.

Mr. Inman and Mr. Burgess of Brighouse, Yorkshire were active in the breed from 1867 through the early 1870s. Mr. Inman's Rose was the dam of his Albert (3587) born in 1869, Benson (3591) shown 1870-1871, and of Charlie (3597) out of Mr. Burgess' Charlie (3596), shown 1867-1869. Mr. Inman's earliest registered dog was Sandy (3651). Mr. Burgess judged the breed at Manchester in 1873, giving first in over 9 lbs. to Mrs. Jonas Foster's Bruce, first in under 9 lbs. to Mrs. Foster's Ben II, and first in under 5 lbs. to her Cobden.

Mr. J. Spink helped to tailor the breed with his dogs. He owned Bounce, later sold to Mr. Ramsden. Bounce, grandsire of immortal Huddersfield Ben, of whom we'll soon talk more, was also the sire of Spot, owned by E. Cade of Huddersfield, Yorkshire, and the winner of first at Manchester in 1867. Mr. Spink also owned and registered (old) Sandy (3652), listed as under 7 lbs. (Old) Sandy was the sire of Lady, Huddersfield Ben's dam.

(Old) Sandy, bred by Mr. Walshaw of Huddersfield, was by Haigh's Teddy, one of Crab's sons out of Walshaw's Kitty. He won first prize at Leeds in 1861. In the Kennel Club's first Stud Book, there are eight Sandys in the section for Broken-haired and Yorkshire Terriers and one Sandy, owned by Mrs. Foster, in the section for Toy Terriers (Rough and Broken-haired).

Another spinner of the bloodline was Mr. Kirby of Rochdale, Lancashire. His Smart, registered as a Toy Terrier, was born in 1866.

These tailors of the breed were showing their little dogs from 1860 through 1873 in the classes for Toy Terriers under 5 lbs., Scotch Terriers, White Scotch, Fawn Scotch, Blue Scotch, two sizes in each — under 7 lbs. and over 7 lbs. There were classes for Broken-haired Scotch Terriers; Broken-haired Scotch Terriers with uncut ear, or the same classification with cut ear (i.e. cropped); Scotch Terriers under 12 lbs.; and Toy Terriers broken-haired under 5 lbs. One can readily surmise that these fanciers were keen to compete with their silken dogs.

Huddersfield Ben with his daughter Katie (Lady Giffard's "Little Kate") from Stonehenge's *Dogs of the British Isles,* 3rd edition, 1878.

Two of Mrs. Foster's notable winners. *Left,* Ch. Ted, from a woodcut by R. H. Moore. *Right,* Little Tot, winner of first prize in the Yorkshire Terrier class at 1886 Toy Dog show.

Ch. Ashton Queen and Ch. Clayton Marvel, owned by the Misses Walton and Beard, Chelsea, England. Marvel, like Ch. Ted, became prominent in American pedigrees.

Huddersfield Ben

The design was ready and if Mr. W. Eastwood's (of Huddersfield) only claim to fame was the fact that he bred Huddersfield Ben, he would need no other. The only dog of his that is ever mentioned is his old Ben, though one feels that Lady — Ben's dam — should get some notice.

Huddersfield Ben (3612), born in 1865, was purchased by Mrs. Jonas (Mary A.) Foster, Lister Hill, Bradford, Yorkshire.

Ben has been given the title "Father of Broken-haired Scotch and Yorkshire Terriers," and the pedigrees of his progeny prove his right to it. He was no flyer, but the result of the work of the manufacturers of the breed. Through his well-planned breeding he was capable of producing all the best factors wanted in the breed. Mr. S. Jessop, in his book *The Yorkshire Terrier,* first published around 1900, says of Ben: "His merits as a show dog naturally found him in great request at the stud and luckily he possessed the rare trait of transmitting his virtues to his progeny. He was a great sire, one of those animals who make the history of the breed, and whose influence is apparent generations after the progenitor has passed away."

In reading Huddersfield Ben's pedigree the easiest thing to do is to ignore his dam's side, as Lady, his dam, was also the dam of his sire, Mr. Boscovitch's dog. Thus he was the inbred offspring of a mother-son breeding.

Perhaps the most delightful way to give his pedigree is to let Dr. Gordon Staples do the job. In doing so, one must again wonder why a written record of 1876 has been so overlooked. But from *Ladies' Dogs As Companions* comes this tale from a gentleman who was — on occasion — Mrs. Foster's veterinarian:

Now, of all the Yorkshire Terriers ever I saw, I think Huddersfield Ben was the best. Many of my readers doubtless remember this most beautiful prince of dogs, although it is now some few years since he was run over on the street and killed, he being then only in his prime. But he did not die before he had made his mark. Dog shows were not then quite so numerous as they are now, but nevertheless Ben managed to win seventy-four prizes ere his grand career was shortened on that unlucky 23rd of September (1871).

"Pedigrees, few ladies I believe care to remember, so I shall not give Ben's in full, but be content with stating that he was bred by Mr. W. Eastwood, Huddersfield, and had the blood of Old Bounce in his veins, and his mother, Lady, was a daughter of Old Ben, a granddaughter of Old Sandy, and a great-granddaughter of Mr. W.J. Haigh's Teddy, and a great-great-granddaughter of Mr. J. Swift's Old Crab. I am the very worst genealogist in the world, so I cannot go back any further for fear of running on shore somewhere. Perhaps, though, Old Crab came over with the Conqueror — from Scotland you know.

So that Dr. Staples doesn't run aground, we'll fill in a few details. Mr. Boscovitch's dog (Ben's sire), whose name no one seems able to discover, was the result of Lady being bred to her grandsire Bounce, first owned by Mr. Spink, and then Mr. Ramsden. Mr. Watson in *The Book Of The Dog* describes Bounce as "Our illustration represents a very beautiful specimen of this sort, belonging to Mr. Spink of Bradford. He is the type of his class — a class deservedly popular with all admirers of rough Terriers, and in which he is famous." Going one step further, you find that Lady herself was produced by another mother-son breeding. Eastwood's Old Ben, her sire, was by Ramsden's Bounce bred to Young Dolly. Young Dolly was then bred to her sire Eastwood's Old Ben to produce Lady. One might say the material was very tightly woven. For if ever a dog was inbred, Huddersfield Ben can claim that honor. However, the results were worth the weaving of this producer of the blue and gold bloodlines.

Mrs. Jonas Foster set the fashion for the Yorkshire Terrier with the parading of her many homebred and purchased Yorkshires. She was not the only style-setter but, since she gained a great many prizes and her stud dogs were influential factors to the early American breeders, some of her development of the breed, we feel, should be included here. If you wish to learn more about these other early English fanciers, there are several English Yorkshire Terrier books that deal very sensibly with the subject.

Bradford was Mrs. Foster's choice for her kennel name and according to Mrs. Annie Swan, in her *Yorkshire Terrier Handbook*, Mrs. Foster was the first woman to judge at a Kennel Club show, Leeds in 1889. In addition to Yorkshire Terriers, she exhibited Toy Spaniels and black and tan Terriers. She showed Huddersfield Ben, winning 74 prizes with him. He produced many winning Yorkshires, among them Mr. Inman's Sandy, Hill's Sandy, Hirst's Peter, Miss Anderson's Mozart, Doctor Spark (also shown and registered as Charlie by a Mr. Stell), Mr. Mortimer's Edmond, and Lucas' Empress.

Mrs. Foster had winners sired by Huddersfield Ben in Little Kate, Bruce, Emperor, Sandy, Spring and Tyler. In addition to their winning, these dogs carried the ability to pass on their best factors.

Huddersfield Ben, after his unlucky death in 1871, like Crab, underwent the administrations of a taxidermist. Almost all of Ben's pictures are of the stuffed dog, which seems to have become the property of John Thorpe of Patriocroft, though it is doubtful if more than the glass case now survives.

Mrs. Foster had many winners and studs after Ben, one of which—Bradford Hero—had a great influence on the early American dogs. Mrs. Foster, in speaking of Hero's pedigree in 1885, said his blood "in-

Color lithograph from 1881. Mrs. Foster's "Toy Smart", at front left, was 1st prize winner at Alexandria Palace, 1879. Painting by C. Barton Barber, court artist to Queen Victoria.

Prince, owned by Mme. J. Brismere, Ostend, Belgium—1900.

Longridge Bob and Daisy, owned by Mrs. A. Vaughn-Fowler, England, c. 1900.

cluded all the best dogs for thirty-five years back, and they were all originally bred from Scotch Terriers." Bradford Hero was the grandsire of the first American bitch to gain her title.

Mrs. Foster owned Ch. Ted, a dog who was the sire or grandsire of a number of early American imports. She purchased Ted when he was four years old, at the Heckmondwike Show in 1887. Ch. Ted, bred by Mr. Fleming, weighed five pounds, and stood nine inches at his shoulder. His length, nose to set-on of tail was seventeen inches. He was said to be the shortest-backed dog in her kennel. Ted won 265 first prizes and in the year 1887, in ten months, won 22 first prizes, 6 special prizes of cups, gold medals and other prizes. He was the top dog in the breed for six years. Ted was sired by Bank's Young Royal, a grandson of Huddersfield Ben, out of Fleming's Annie, also a granddaughter of Ben's. Thus, those so-called unknown progenitors of the Yorkshire Terrier, the two bitches from Yorkshire and a Manchesterian for Lancashire had produced in Ch. Ted and the many other winners at that time, a fixed product, a purebred gold and blue silken Terrier.

One consideration in the final production of the Yorkshire is the matter of whether the Maltese was bred into the Yorkshire or vice versa.

Quoting Virginia T. Leitch in *The Maltese Dog,* we find that "Mr. Robert Mandeville was the most celebrated breeder of Maltese in the 1860s. . . . In 1864, Birmingham established a class for Maltese and Mr. Mandeville won first and second prizes at this show with two dogs, each named Fido. Both these dogs were sired by a dog named Fido owned by Mr. Tupper, one being out of Mr. Mandeville's Lilly, and one out of his Fan. . . . No records are available as to the ancestry of Mr. Mandeville's Lilly or Fan, or of Mr. Tupper's Fido, or as to where they obtained their original stock."

Now checking over old records, Mr. Mandeville showed and won 2nd at Islington in 1866 with Lilly and pups, and 3rd with Prince. In 1863, Lilly was shown winning 4th as *"other Scotch Terrier."* Prince had been registered by Mr. Mandeville as a Broken-haired Scotch and Yorkshire Terrier, his number being 3640. Lilly was beaten at the London Show of 1863, by Phin (3636), a son of (Old) Sandy out of a Huddersfield bitch. Lilly was not registered but the other four dogs in this class all were registered as Broken-haired Scotch and Yorkshire Terriers.

Mrs. Leitch also mentions as an early Maltese, Mr. T. Lee's Blondin (3593) and, again, this dog is registered in the Broken-haired Scotch and Yorkshire Terriers category. She also lists three of Mr. W. McDonald's dogs, two of whom — Flora (3611) and Janet (3615) — were registered as Broken-haired Scotch and Yorkshire Terriers. The third dog, Jessie (3994), was registered as a Toy Terrier (rough and broken-haired). We finally find that Lady Giffard and Mrs. Bligh Monck are all reported as Maltese breeders, whereas they were all Yorkshire Terrier breeders, giving them up to continue in Maltese. In fact, Mrs. Monck's famous Maltese, Mopsy, whelped in 1865, listed as being out of Mr. McDonald's bitch sired by Mr. Mandeville's Fido (Tubber's Fido ex Mandeville's Lilly), would seem to have more claim to being a Broken-haired Scotch and Yorkshire Terrier than anything else. The answer to the question of who was what is, we presume, that several of these dogs were, in fact, extremely silver Terriers carrying a strong dilution factor, which made them highly desirable to the Maltese breeders. These crossed facts are the only inclination that Maltese and Yorkshires were interbred. Herein arose the myth that the Yorkie was descended from the Maltese. Similarly, the myth that the Manchester was his ancestor probably lies in that an early Yorkshire was named Albert from Manchester.

The blue and gold silken Yorkshire caught the fancy of the Victorians. He was admired in the show ring as the best of "Fancy" Terriers. These fancy dogs with extra length of coat, of silkiness and evenness of color, brought on sales-producing extra pocket money to the men of Yorkshire. They became quite common as house pets in the Victorian way of life. In the carriage parade in Hyde Park, the Yorkie sat beribboned on a cushion at Milady's side, and was lifted in and out by a footman. The West End pet shops sold them as well as little patent leather boots, generally pale blue, which the little dogs wore to take their gentle exercise — while no doubt thinking up ways to sneak down the backstairs and kill a rat or two. However, neither the people in the pet shops, nor the purchasers and new fanciers in London, saw the progenitors from whom the Yorkie was manufactured, and, thus, his origins were forgotten and the factors used to produce him were woven into myths.

THE WHOLE
COUNTRY
IS
GOING
TO
THE
DOGS

OUT OF
OFFICE

Political cartoon, 1880, by Thomas Nast.

2

The American Pioneers

As the steam engine had provided power and work at the mills for the men of Yorkshire, so the steam engine provided and powered the ships that brought the Yorkshire Terrier across the Atlantic to the United States of America. The postwar America of 1870-1900 was a nation on the move. The first American-recorded Yorkshire Terrier was born in the last third of the 19th Century in 1872, four years prior to America's first centennial in 1876.

The Yorkshire Terrier took the prim lace-curtained Victorian society by storm. Lawn tennis became fashionable in the 1870s, and so did the Yorkshire Terrier. He was being bred and shown up and down the East Coast prior to electric lights, frigidaires, and telephones. Yorkshires were bred and shown before the Statue of Liberty came to Bedloe Island, or the monument to Washington was finished. It took nearly seven days to travel coast-to-coast, but Yorkies were as popular in San Francisco and Los Angeles as the new rage of bicycling. They flourished in the lake ports of the Great Lakes as the new steel steam-powered carriers loaded wheat at the railheads from the newly opened territories to the barges on the Erie Canal. Yorkies were being bred in St. Louis while the great steam-driven side wheelers held sway, and Chicago had several breeders before the first skyscrapers were built.

By 1900 the nation had grown to include 45 states and there were Yorkie breeders in 22 of them. They found their way to five more states by 1906.

There is no real proof of his being a frontiersman but it's possible to imagine that some little shaggy-haired, blue and tan ratting Terrier pioneered with an immigrant Yorkshire man, and there took up his duties as sod-house guardian and saloon rat-chaser. He did, we know, join at least one expedition using the new fad of photography.

The Yorkshire was originally the workingman's dog, but in the new country, the man that sold to the carriage trade in the Land-of-the-Free was certain to provide these fashionable dogs for his wealthy patrons, who so admired Victorian ways. That the Yorkie was a fashionable pet is shown by this quote from *The Practical Dogbook for Both the Professional and Amateur Fancier,* published in Philadelphia and copyrighted in 1884: "We now come to the breed that is preeminently the ladies' pet, and which by all persons ignorant of 'Doggy Lore' is constantly being confounded with the Scotch and the Skye. The Yorkshire is the handsomest of all long-haired terriers and makes a most bright, active and companionable indoor pet, and is, besides, the most fashionable dog today in this country, not excepting the Pug."

This is followed by the points of the breed and the prices for the breed which are given as: Males — $20 to $150, Females — $15 to $125; Puppies: Males — $15 to $25, Females — $10 to $20. And the Yorkshire was not just a fashionable pet, but a fashionable entrant in the breeding and showing of purebred dogs.

It has been said that the years pass and all that is left are memories, but in the case of the Yorkshire Terrier even the oldest breeder alive is too young to have memories of the start of the history of the breed in the United States. It is left for us, then, to remove the dust and search the old printed records for the early dogs and their breeders.

The first Yorkshire Terrier to have an AKC registered number was Butch (5396); the second was Daisy (5397). Both belonged to Charles Andrews, of Bloomington, Illinois. Butch, an import bred by A. Webster, England, was whelped in 1882. Daisy was whelped in 1884 and her breeder is not given. Their color is given as sky blue and tan.

The first Yorkie to actually appear in the AKC Stud Book was Belle, owned by Mrs. A. E. Godeffroy. She was first registered in the *National American Kennel Club Stud Book* in 1883. This Stud Book was taken over by the American Kennel Club in September, 1884. Both Belle and Whitman's Gypsy appear in the AKC Stud Book before Andrews' dogs, but neither had an AKC registered number.

Belle was whelped in 1877, her sire, dam, and breeder being unknown — a circumstance which seems to have been a very common occurrence with the early dogs. On the other hand, a great many of the Yorkies entered at Westminster in 1878 carried the notation that the full pedigree was available from the owner, information that is unfortunately of little use to us a century later. It does show that even at this early date these breeders knew the ancestors of their dogs.

The first bench show to be held in the United States was at Chicago on June 2, 1874. It was held by the Illinois State Sportsmen's Association. The second was held by the New York State Sportsmen's Association at Oswego, New York on June 22, 1874. The third was at Mineola, Long Island, New York, October 7, 1874 and was considered the most successful of the three. The first bench show to be held by the Westminster Kennel Club in New York City was not held until three years later in 1877.

These early shows had their own rules, and even prior to the founding of the American Kennel Club dogs won championships. The qualifications for winning a title were that a dog must win four first prizes in the Open Class, after which it was eligible to compete in the Challenge Class. When a dog had won three first prizes in the Challenge Class, he was a Champion.

The AKC was founded September 17, 1884 in Philadelphia, and this method for winning a championship was continued, the only difference being that a dog now became a Champion of Record. This simply meant that the dog's championship was recorded in the AKC and published in AKC's official magazine. All dogs having already won their titles were listed providing they were still living at that time.

Mr. Coombs, early breeder and writer, reported in *The American Book of the Dog* that his Bradford Harry "is at present (1890) the only Champion of Record in America." It is noteworthy that he did not say he "is the *first* champion in the breed". To which dog that honor goes will, we are afraid, remain an unknown fact. We do know that Mr. and Mrs. Henry Kisteman's "Hero" did win in this class, and does appear in the Certified AKC Pedigree of Joker II (AKC No. 20,793) as Ch. Hero.

Ch. Hero was imported by the Kistemans from his breeder West Lucas, Blackburn, England. Hero's sire was Peter and his dam was Flossie. In the same pedigree and same generation there also appears Ch. Dick II. That leaves us with the unanswerable question of which came first, Hero or Dick II? And what about Thomas Kaalager's "Willie", winner of the Champion class for over 5 lbs. at the New York show in 1881, or "Oscar Wilde II" owned by Miss Bessie French who won the under 5 lbs. Champion class in 1882 at New York? And then there is "Jimmie" owned by Frank Thomson who won the over 5 lbs. Champion class that same year. Kisteman's "Hero" was the winner of the over 5 lbs. Champion class in both 1883 and 1884. In 1884, the first female appears as a winner of a Champion class, this being Kisteman's "Crickie", winner of the under 5 lbs.

All the above are from the show records of the New York shows. Among the winners elsewhere, Fred Sierp's "Mash" was the winner of the Champion class at San Francisco in 1888, '89, '91 and '92.

At any rate, to keep the records straight, Mr. Coombs' Bradford Harry was the first Champion of Record becoming a champion in 1889; or, if you prefer, he was the first dog to become a champion after the establishment of the American Kennel Club. The first female Champion of Record was the imported Minnie York, owned by Dr. N. Ellis Oliver of Chicago. Minnie won her title in 1893.

That Ch. Hero and Ch. Dick II were awarded championships, there is no doubt. They won the honor under the rules then in effect for the winning of a title, and are just as rightly champions as are the many dogs of other breeds who have been recognized by breeders as champions for many years.

John Marriot, of New York City, is the oldest American breeder of whom any records are available. His "Jack" was the earliest dog of whom records can be found. Jack was born in the United States in 1872, sired by Havelock, out of Jessie.

Jack was shown in 1878 at the New York show in the over 5 lbs. class, winning second. He was already a well-known sire by this time as S. VanDyke showed two ten-months-old puppies sired by him, out of Fan, in the class for Toy Terriers under 5 lbs. at New York in 1877. There were no separate classes for the breed that year. Jack's children did not win, but Tom could be claimed for $225 and Topsey could be had for only $40.

The entry at the Westminster Kennel Club show in New York in 1878 totaled 33 Yorkshire Terriers, divided into two classes by weight. Eighteen were shown in over 5 lbs., and fifteen were entered in under 5 lbs. We cannot help but comment that as things stand in the breed at present, this class for under 5 lbs. would be a cinch to win, as only a few of present day Yorkies could make the weight limit. We can only hope that those concerned will recognize the fact that our present standard says "Must not weigh over 7 lbs." Every description in everything ever written about the breed refers to Yorkies as being one of the smallest of all Toy dogs. Ever since the breed's conception, small size has been highly prized.

All the dogs entered at this 1878 show were born before 1877, the largest portion being Centennial babies born in 1876 or in 1875. Jack was valued, or could be claimed, for one thousand dollars, so apparently Mr. Marriot thought exceedingly well of him. There was another Yorkie also valued at this amount, Grenville Kane's Lucy, shown in the class for under 5 lbs.

Jack's sire, Havelock, appears to be the first stud dog that can be traced in American pedigrees, as another of his sons, "Jeff", appears as the sire of John Enright's (San Francisco) Sally VI, who was born some twenty years later.

Aside from Jack, Mr. Marriot also showed Ben, Killy, Jerry, Tip, Charlie, Flora, Bobbie and Prince, who won first at New York in over

Bradford Peter and Eng. Ch. Bradford Ben, owned by Mrs. Jonas Foster. Ben was exported to the United States.

Ch. Bradford Harry, first Yorkie to become an American champion. Imported from England by owner P. H. Coombs, Bangor, Maine.

Lancashire Ben, imported and owned by P. H. Coombs.

5 lbs. in 1885. Mr. Marriot showed Yorkies until 1886 and was also active in Pugs, Japanese Spaniels and Toy Spaniels.

During the late 1870s and up to 1889, Henry and Lena Kisteman of New York City were the most successful and active Yorkshire Terrier exhibitors. They exhibited almost 25 Yorkies during this period, as well as Toy Spaniels, Pugs, Field Spaniels, Japanese Spaniels, and Toy Terriers. They started showing Yorkies with the New York show of 1877. They had obviously started breeding earlier, as in class 34 for Pugs they showed Katie with her three puppies. (That would take care of the problem of having nobody to stay home with them—we're not so sure about the effect on Mom and the puppies however.) At this show Lucy, born in 1875, was shown in the class for Toy Terriers (not exceeding 5 lbs.) This same bitch won second in both 1878 and 1879 as a Yorkshire Terrier. Lucy's color is given as blue in 1877. By 1879, her color had assumedly become blue and tan, as she won first prize in the class for "Yorkshire Terriers (Blue and Tan) under 5 lbs."

Four of the ten Yorkies shown by the Kistemans in 1878 were for sale and could be had for $65, $100 or $225. Daisy, who could be had for the lowest figure, was shown in over 5 lbs., whereas Prince, Terry and Lucy were all shown in under 5 lbs. The rest of their dogs shown that year — Jimmy, Charlie, Bright, Beauty, Lassie and Nellie — were shown in under 5 lbs. class. Dandy was shown in Toy Terriers under 5 lbs. and his color is given as blue, so he was probably nearer a Paisley. Nellie also won second in Cleveland in 1878 and her color is listed as silver and tan.

Ch. Hero, bred by Lucas, was the best of their dogs and first appeared in the Champion class for over 5 lbs. in 1883 — which he won. At the New York show of 1884, the Kistemans made a clean sweep in all four classes offered, winning both Championship classes and both Open classes. These were divided by weight; a division by sex does not appear until 1886.

Ch. Hero was the sire of Joseph Bell's Young Hero (purchased from the Kistemans in 1886), of Kisteman's Teddy (bred by Peter Cassidy) and of Jack III. Through this last dog, Ch. Hero's blood comes down into Yorkies being shown in the 1920s.

Our next pioneer was a gentleman whose handwriting would appear to have been most difficult to decipher. That his address was 61 Charlton Street, New York City everyone agrees, but as far as his last name goes, it is given as — Kallaher, Kaahal, Kaalager, Kaalage and Kallagher; his first name was Thomas. Since in the spelling contest Kaalager won on the number of times used, we have decided to use this version. He first showed in 1877 at the New York show with Bright and Beauty in Skye Terriers. Their color is given as blue and tan. Both dogs

48

were later shown in classes for Yorkshire Terriers, as was Bright's daughter. In this same Skye class, J.A. Brown of New York showed his Bijou — color blue and tan. Bijou was shown the next year as a Yorkshire Terrier over 5 lbs. Later, when she was sold to W.G. Demarest, she was shown as a Yorkshire Terrier under 5 lbs.

In 1878, Kaalager entered five dogs at New York winning the over 5 lbs. class with Yorkshire Charlie. In 1879, his Ben II won the special prize for Best Yorkshire Terrier, as well as first in over 5 lbs. This same year he won a H.C. (Highly Commended) with Charlie and a C. (Commended) with Charlie. As the weight was different in these classes, assumedly they were two different dogs. Apparently Charlie, or its various versions, was a popular title for a Yorkie at this time because, at this same show, Mrs. W.A. Haines, Jr. won 1st and Special Prize for "Best Toy or Pet dog exhibited by a Lady" with her Charley.

Mrs. Haines was an exhibitor in 1878 showing five dogs including Trip and Snap, who are listed as being bred by The Jolly Boys, and as having won nearly four hundred prizes before this show. Snap won the under 5 lbs. and the Special Prize for Best Yorkshire Terrier, Blue and Tan. The prize was a cup, or cash value of $50 in gold.

Both Mr. Kaalager and Mrs. Haines stopped showing Yorkies after 1880.

Mr. John Campbell of Montreal, Canada was a prominent breeder for twenty-five years. Mr. Coombs lists Mr. Campbell's principal winners, up to 1890, as Prince, Dolly, Spink, Sir Colin, and Dandy. Campbell showed his last dog in 1904.

Little of the blood of these early breeders can be traced down to today. A few, with difficulty, come down to the 1st World War but are then lost. Marriot and Kisteman's dogs' blood can be found, but tracing generation-to-generation quickly becomes a losing battle.

With Mrs. Fred Senn, of New York City, we come to a strain which *has* continued down to present time. Champions are being shown today that trace back to Mrs. Senn's dogs.

Mrs. Senn was a prominent breeder of Toy Spaniels and Japanese Spaniels as well as Yorkies. In Miss Marian Bannister's article on Toy Spaniels in Shield's *American Book of the Dog*, all the Toy Spaniels pictured were owned by Mrs. Senn. The Hon. Mrs. Lytton, in her book of *Toy Dogs and Their Ancestors* published in 1911, makes reference to her as the most prominent exhibitor of Japanese Spaniels at that time. Mrs. Senn, for the record, showed her first Yorkie in 1878 and her first Japanese Spaniel in 1879, and did not start in Toy Spaniels until 1885.

Those of you who are trying to finish your first champion can take heart from Mrs. Senn's persistence and love for the breed. It took from

Yorkies at the 11th Westminster show, 1888, from an illustration in *Harper's Weekly*.

Ch. Queen of the Fairies, first American-born Yorkie to become an AKC champion (1905.) Breeder-owner, Mrs. Ferdinand Senn, New York City.

Ashton Premier, owned by Mrs. Raymond Mallock (USA and England.) Bred by Mrs. F. Senn.

Little Swell, English import, pictured in *The Illustrated American* (Feb. 22, 1890) as a Westminster winner—in his first showing in America. The caption reported: "His owner, F. Senn, is extremely proud of his long, silky coat, blue and tan in color, which touches the ground when he stands up. Swell is indolent, however, and prefers a recumbent position."

1878 to 1905, exactly 27 years, for her to finish her first Yorkie champion. This was Ch. Queen of the Fairies, who won her title in 1905 and was a top winner for the next four years, being shown from Boston to Washington, D.C. and as far west as Milwaukee. Mrs. Senn had shown 85 Yorkies up to this point. Her main interests in the show-ring to the start of the New Century were Japanese Spaniels and Toy Spaniels. Ch. Senn Senn King, closely related to Ch. Queen of the Fairies, followed with his title in 1907.

With the birth of Mrs. Senn's Little Gem, the oldest American strain came into its own. Little Gem's birthdate is not available, but he was first shown in 1899. Little Gem sired Little Gem II, who sired Little Gem III (as well as Ch. Queen of the Fairies). Little Gem III, in turn, sired Ch. Senn Senn King, who bred to Peter Menges' Little Fairy, produced Ch. Roxy II, owned by the Menges. Mrs. Anna B. Radcliffe bred her Lady Blue to Ch. Roxy II's son Ch. Prince II, and in 1917 Ch. Boy Blue was born. Ch. Boy Blue sired Gold Mount Lady Tena out of Mrs. Radcliffe's imported Ch. Lady Tena. Gold Mount Lady Tena, when bred to Gold Mount Gay Boy in 1924, produced Ch. Gold Blaze. Mrs. Radcliffe sold Ch. Gold Blaze and Gold Mount Lady Tena to Mrs. Harold Riddock of Detroit in 1926. Mrs Riddock repeated this breeding and produced Gold Don, who was bred to May Blossom, a daughter of Ch. Gold Blaze and produced Miss June. Mrs. Riddock bred Miss June to her Canadian import, Ch. Bond's Byngo. (Mrs. Riddock had purchased this dog from Harry Draper of Toronto in 1928. Byngo was bred by Mrs. O.M. Bond of Canada.) This mating produced Mrs. Riddock's Ch. Byngo's Royal Masher, Mrs. Turnball's Ch. Byngo's Royal Tiny and Mrs. Goldie Stone's Ch. Petit Byngo Boy. The first two dogs were born in 1931 and Mrs. Stone's in 1930. The Petit blood continues down through many present day American dogs.

Mrs. Raymond Mallock bought Charlie Boy, a Harboro Swell II son, from Mrs. Senn in 1889 after his winning 2nd in "Free For All" class at New York. The name of this class always conjures up a wonderful picture of both dogs and exhibitors really fighting it out — unfortunately the class seems to have existed for only a year. Charlie Boy also won 1st in Open at the Bull Terrier show in New York the same year. We sincerely hope there were classes offered for Yorkies, for as to how they ever made Yorkies look like Bull Terriers, we've no idea. There were at least five Yorkies shown at this Bull Terrier show.

Mrs. Mallock also purchased Lady Ashton, Ashton Pearl, Ashton Marvel and Ashton Wonder from Mrs. Senn in 1899.

Harboro Swell II was the sire of Harboro Swell III who Mrs. Senn sold to John Howard Taylor of New York in 1898. Mr. Taylor purchased a number of dogs from Mrs. Senn, and was active in the breed until around 1908. His most famous dog was Ashton Premier, bred by

Mrs. Senn and purchased by Mr. Taylor in 1899. Mr. Taylor sold Premier to Mrs. Mallock in 1900, and she used this dog to illustrate the breed in her first book on Toy dogs.

Mrs. Senn sold Bessie, a daughter of Harboro Swell II, to Thomas W. Murphy in 1896. Bessie was Mr. Murphy's foundation bitch. His best known dogs were Amer. Ch. Halifax Beacon, a son of Halifax Ben, and Matchless Molly, a daughter of Halifax Marvel. Beacon was imported in 1906 from Charles Adam of Halifax, England. Mr. Murphy bred until around 1908.

Mrs. Senn's top studs included Halifax Chris, who sired Muenchinger's King's Queenie, owned by G.A. Muenchinger, Newport, Rhode Island, and Brandy, who sired Little Boy Blue, owned by Mrs. Michael Jennings, Jamaica, Long Island. Thomas W. Mead's Meade's Daisy, a daughter of Little Boy Blue, was the great granddam of Sam Baxter's Bobbie B and thus all that line, as well as all of Miss Helen Palmer's Vermont line, and some of the Arthur Mills' dogs, carried the Senn bloodline on into present day Yorkies.

Mrs. Senn's Senn Senn Kennels founded or contributed to almost all the kennels active from 1875 to 1909, and her dogs carried all the best English blood as well as all the best Amerian dogs. That her interest in the breed was deep and sincere is obvious as she was active in the breed for 31 years, and even eight years after ceasing to breed and show, she still appeared as an Active Member of the American Kennel Club.

Mrs. L.V. Hitchcock of Yonkers, New York founded her Mayfair Kennels in 1902. Her top dog was Mayfair Merry Mittens, who she sold to Mrs. Senn in 1907 when she gave up breeding and showing.

Mr. P.S. Coombs, of Bangor, Maine, was the man who first brought the breed to a position where it was a strong contender for top prizes. He was not only a breeder, but an exhibitor, a judge of the breed, a historian and authority on the breed. His article in Mr. Shield's *The American Book of the Dog* contains breeding, grooming and showing tips that are just as timely now as when they were written in 1890. Certainly the breed is indebted to him for collecting the history of the breed's beginnings.

In writing of the breed as it was in the 1870s and 1880s, Mr. Coombs says: "Unfortunately, at its first appearance at our shows, almost anything in the shape of a Terrier having a long coat, with some shade or effect of blue on the body, fawn or silver (more frequently the latter) colored head and legs, with tail docked and ears trimmed (cropped) was received and admired as a Yorkshire terrier by most everyone except the few competent judges; and the breed fashionable as it is, is still much neglected in this country for the reason that its care is not so well understood as that of many other breeds, and a good specimen soon loses its fine show condition by reason of lack of that regular and well directed care necessary to cultivate and keep the coat looking right''. It is interesting to speculate what Mr. Coombs would say of the many black dogs with little or no tan at all now being shown.

Mr. Coombs' Ch. Bradford Harry (already noted as the first AKC Yorkie Champion of Record) was first shown in 1888 and won at Boston, New York, Troy, Lynn, Buffalo and New Bedford, winning nine first prizes in succession; and, in addition, he has made the remarkable record of which few dogs of any breed can boast—that of winning every special prize for which a Yorkshire Terrier was eligible to compete at the shows where he has appeared. In one show alone he won the specials for Best Yorkshire Terrier, Best Rough-Coated Terrier — any breed, and smallest dog in the show.''

It should be noted here that classes and judges were a bit more imaginative in the early days. In 1885, at the New York show, James White won an award of Commended in Yorkshire Terriers (over 5 lbs.) with Minnie and her puppies. We assume the weight was for Minnie only. Among other special prizes given at the early New York shows was one in 1884 for "Highest Leaping Greyhound." Perhaps this could be considered as the beginning of obedience trials?

Ch. Bradford Harry was born May 16, 1885, being bred by W. Beal, Eng. Mr. Coombs gives his pedigree as: sire, Crawshaw's Bruce; dam, Beal's Lady. Bruce by Hodson's Sandy out of Patterson's Minnie; Sandy by Bateman's Sandy out of Venus; Bateman's Sandy by Spring out of Typsey; Venus by Music; Spring by Huddersfield Ben; Beal's Lady by Tyler out of Lady; Tyler by Huddersfield Ben out of Bolton's Kitty; Kitty by Bolton's Wonder.

Both the first two American Champions of Record — Ch. Bradford Harry and Ch. Toon's Royal — were closely related, going directly back to Huddersfield Ben through three of his sons, Tyler, Spring and Mozart. Harry carried Tyler and Spring and Royal carried Mozart and Spring.

Exactly how Harry came by the prefix of Bradford is not mentioned, but it is probable that Mrs. Foster of Bradford, Eng. had acquired him before he was sold to the United States. Bradford was her kennel prefix and she did buy many of the top winners for her kennel. Harry won first prizes at Newcastle and Darlington before leaving England. Mr. Coombs added to the confusion by taking Bradford as his AKC registered kennel name.

That Ch. Bradford Harry was highy thought of is evident from the fact that his offspring were to be the foundation of many of the kennels across the country.

Mr. Coombs lists as his top winners in the 1880s: Ch. Bradford Harry, Bradford Lil, Bradford Leah, and Lancashire Ben. He continued in the breed until the late 1890s, at which time he became interested in the new rage, Pomeranians, which had just come into their own. He continued active in Poms until around 1908.

Peter Cassidy started in Yorkshire Terriers with the importation of Ben in 1884. This dog carries two AKC numbers, 9175 and 30424; his registration number was reissued in 1892 because his original pedigree was incorrect. Ben was born in October, 1883 — his sire being Teddy and his dam Lil. His breeder was E. Berry, Eng. Ben was awarded an H.C. at New York City in 1885 in the over 5 lbs. class, and in 1886 won 2nd in Open. As a sire, he sired dogs for Wm. Wellman, Newark, N.J., out of Mr. Wellman's Net, who was born in 1882. Net was bred by Geo. W. Dickerman, New Milford, Pa. Mr. Wellman's kennel was called The Blue and Tan Fanciers Kennels. He was active in the breed from 1882 to 1889. Ben also sired two litters for John J. Hooley, Troy, N.Y. Both were out of Hooley's imported Starlight Daisy, who was bred by Howard Atwood and imported by Hooley in 1889. Starlight Daisy's registered color is given as blue and white, although all of her children are registered as blue and tan.

Mr. Coombs gives as Mr. Cassidy's best dogs: Ben, Prince and Jersey Lily. They were shown in the 1880s. During the early 1890s his top dog was Ben II, who he showed at New York in 1890, '91, '92 and '93. In 1891, Mr. Cassidy entered seven Yorkies at New York. During the last half of the 1890s, his dogs were shown as registered to the Huddersfield Kennels.

Ben II appears as the great-grandfather of Edwin R. Plato's Joker II. Mr. Plato, from Chicago, started breeding in 1887 and continued until around 1893. Joker II was sold to Hugh McAuley, also of Chicago. Mr. McAuley also purchased Fishpool Fanchion from John L. Lincoln, Jr., who owned the Felwyn Kennels in Chicago. Lincoln purchased Fishpool Gem in 1891 from Messrs. Symonds and Toon. Mr. Symonds imported him in 1889 and showed him extensively during 1890, winning Firsts at Boston; Rochester; Buffalo; Ottawa, (Can.); New York City; Lynn, Mass.; and Chicago.

Mr. McAuley, whose kennel name was Fishpool, was most active in the 1890s. He seems to have taken Horace Greeley's words to heart, as almost all of his breeding went West. He sold three dogs sired by Joker II to A.B. Jackson, Spokane, Washington in 1891, sold Dandy Pat to Henry B. Chase in Portland, Oregon in 1895, and sold Bradford Dot, a bitch purchased from Mr. Coombs, to E. Attridge of San Francisco.

Mr. McAuley's last top dog was the imported Telbee, a son of Halifax Marvel. Telbee's dam was a granddaughter of Ch. Ted.

Charles N. Symonds, Salem, Mass. and Mr. Toon, Sheffield, Eng. joined into partnership to sell dogs, and were active in many Terrier breeds. Assumedly, Mr. Toon picked the dogs and Mr. Symonds showed them here, selling them to prospective customers.

Mr. Symonds used two kennel names in his breeding and dealing in Yorkshire Terriers. They were Anglo-American Terriers, and the better known one of Northfield Yorkshire Kennels. Their dogs were brought over accompanied by a kennelman, or even two. This assured that the right care was given to their charges on the long sea voyage.

Symonds was a Yorkie breeder and probably did breed other Terriers. He started in 1885 and continued for around ten years. Among his imports were Prince A.I., Fishpool Gem and Ch. Minnie York. All were resold to buyers here.

Mr. Symonds won a title with Ch. Toon's Royal, showing him in both the United States and Canada. Royal was first shown in 1890, but was second to Mr. Coombs' Ch. Bradford Harry that year. However, in 1891 and 1892, Royal was 1st at New York, Baltimore, Pittsburg, Washington, D.C., Lynn, Boston, Chicago, Cleveland, Hamilton, Can. and Toronto. Royal (bred by J. Hamilton of England) was sired by Mrs. Troughear's Dreadnaught, a full brother to Eng. Ch. Conqueror.

Mr. Coombs lists as Symonds best dogs, besides those already mentioned, Harry, Daisy, Jenny, Little Sister and Floss. During the early 1890s, Symonds did very well with Venus, who won 1st prizes at twelve shows.

Dr. N. Ellis Oliver lived in Chicago and started in the breed with Rough. He won 3rd with him at Chicago in 1890. In 1891, Dr. Oliver purchased Minnie York from Symonds and Toon, finishing her championship in 1895, which made her the first female Champion of Record in the breed. Ch. Minnie York was sired by Duke of Leeds, a son of Dreadnaught out of Minnie, a daughter of Mrs. Foster's Eng. Ch. Bradford Hero. She was bred by Mr. May, Eng.

Considering traveling conditions of the early 1890s, Dr. Oliver was certainly a determined exhibitor. He won firsts with Dick York, Nellie York and Ch. Minnie York in Omaha, Nashville, Denver, and Detroit in 1892 and 1893. By 1898, Dr. Oliver was exhibiting as far away as Dallas, taking 1st with Pansy York.

Dogs of Dr. Oliver's York breeding were the foundation of Frank Mohan and Mr. Cusick's kennels, both in Chicago.

Mrs. George S. Thomas, wife of the well known judge and Terrier fancier, started in Yorkies in 1896. The Thomases lived in Magnolia, Mass. (earlier Hamilton, Mass.) and did a great deal of importing, showing the imports and reselling the dogs. In *The New Book of the Dog* (1911) by Robert Leighton, the author gives Endcliffe Muriel, Midge and Margery as her best homebreds with Endcliffe Merrit as her best import. Merrit was originally imported by J.J. Holgate and shown under his English registered name of Persimmon. Mr. Holgate imported Crown Prince as well as showing both dogs in 1900 at the New York show, winning 1st with Persimmon and Reserve with Crown Prince. Mrs. Thomas purchased both dogs, changing their names to Endcliffe (the Thomas' kennel name) Merrit and Mentor. Endcliffe Merrit (formerly Persimmon) was bred by Mr. Tinker, Eng. and sired by Eng. Ch. Merry Mascot. Mr. Leighton's description of Mascot reads: "He is five inches high at the shoulder and weighs five lbs. His head and expression (his ears being cropped) are reputed to be very Terrier-like; his eyes small and dark; body low to the ground, and perfectly level top and carriage of tail erect. Tan very deep and rich, with one of the best blue backs ever exhibited. Coat perfectly straight and of grand texture, and his action unexcelled." If the height and weight are correct as given, we would have to assume he was very long backed.

Another son of Ch. Merry Mascot's was Spark, imported in 1906 by H.J. White, Salt Lake City. The breeder was George Steale, Scot. Spark won 1st Prize at Los Angeles in 1908. Mr. Leighton was incorrect in giving the females as homebred, as they were all imports. Endcliffe Midge won her title shortly after Mrs. Senn's Ch. Queen of the Fairies in 1905 and was sold to Mrs. H. Carter. Endcliffe Muriel and Margery were sold to Mrs. Senn in 1905. In 1906, Mrs. Senn sold Muriel to Mrs. Teschemacher of St. Louis and Margery to a Mrs. Grant.

Mrs. Thomas imported Mascotte (later Endcliffe Mascot) in 1900, reselling him to Mr. Phalen. Mascot sired Masterpiece Shonsey, a top stud dog in the early 1900s. Shonsey was owned by the Masterpiece Kennels of Mrs. and Miss L. Siegert, Chicago. Both Mrs. H.W. Kirkland, of Chicago, and Mrs. F.S. Frederick, Chicago, used Shonsey extenively in their breeding.

Mrs. Frederick started her kennel in 1900 with Rannie, a bitch bred by Mrs. Senn; Rannie was a daughter of Mrs. Senn's Brandy. Mrs. Frederick bred for ten years. Mr. Julius L. Brown of Atlanta, Ga. owned another child of Shonsey, a bitch named Juno. Mr. Brown was active in the early 1900s.

Mrs. Thomas sold Endcliffe Martin and Master to M.F. Doherty, Massachusetts, in 1902. Doherty remained in the breed for only three years, selling both dogs to Mrs. Geo. H. Jacques in 1905.

Mrs. Jacques lived in Quincy, Mass. and first showed in 1904 with Kaiser and his daughter, Miss Kitty. Kaiser was sired by Endcliffe Master out of Queenie, a bitch of Mrs. Senn's breeding. Mrs. Jacques also owned Little Chris and Senn Senn Queen, one of the last dogs bred by Mrs. Senn and purchased by Mrs. Jacques in 1908.

Mrs. Thomas, like Mr. Coombs, became very active in Pomeranians in the early 1900s, and after 1905 there are no further records of the Thomases breeding Yorkshires.

Mrs. Raymond Mallock, whose maiden name was Lillian C. Moeran, was considered an authority on the breed as well as on other Toy dogs, especially Toy Spaniels and Pekingese, for which she gave up breeding Yorkies. She was the author of several books on the breed including *Toy Dogs,* published in 1907 by Dogdom Publishing company, and *The Up-to-Date Pekingese and all other Toy Dogs,* published by herself.

In *Toy Dogs,* Mrs. Mallock illustrates the breed with Ashton Premier. In the *Up-to-Date Pekingese* (etc.), he is listed as Ashton-More Premier. The reason for this was that while living in the United States, prior to her marriage, Mrs. Mallock used the kennel name "Ashton", but on moving to England she had to change the kennel name to "Ashton-More" as Ashton was already being used by Mesdames Sheard and Walton.

Mrs. Mallock owned and showed dogs in England, America and Ireland. The dogs traveled back and forth, but Mrs. Mallock did not win a title with any of the Yorkies.

Ashton dogs were the foundation of the Childema Kennels in 1904. Childema was located in Worcester, Mass. and was owned by Ernest J. Gwilliam.

Mrs. H.H. (Flo) Teschemacher was the most active breeder in the St. Louis area from 1891 to 1910. She imported several English dogs and bought a number of top American-bred winners. With the exception of Endcliffe Muriel, all her dogs were shown either in St. Louis or Kansas City, Mo. Muriel was shown by Mrs. Teschemacher at New York, Washington, Pittsburg and St. Louis in 1906.

Of Mrs. Teschemacher's dogs, Boy is the dog who can be traced down to present time. Boy was originally shown as Rosedale Teddy, and why she chose to register him just Boy rather than the fancier name gives room for all sorts of ideas. Boy was the grandsire of Gaby Keller, owned by Mrs. Beck, San Francisco. Gaby was the great-granddam of Boots, bred by Mrs. Beck, and acquired by Mrs. Goldie Stone in the 1930s. Through Mrs. Stone's dogs the line continued into a number of kennels of the late 1930s, coming on down to present time.

In 1895, L. Cullen of St. Louis bought his first dog, Actor, from James Foster who bred from 1882 to the late '90s and was located in Providence, R.I. All Cullen's other dogs were imports, the first ones being Chelsea King and Chelsea Prince. He purchased Endcliffe Maud and Model from Mrs. Thomas who had imported them. Mr. Cullen, in 1898, imported Eng. Ch. Bradford Ben and Bradford Sultan from Mrs. M.A. Foster. Bradford Ben was one of Mrs. Foster's top winners and was pictured in several books as an example of the breed. Bradford Ben and Sultan were only shown once in the United States, placing 1st and 3rd at Pittsburgh the same year they arrived. Mr. Cullen was active in the breed until 1902.

Mrs. W.C. Bishop of Detroit also imported a dog from Mrs. Foster, his name being Bradford Rejected. Rejected was imported in 1895 and was a double grandson of Foster's Ch. Ted. Rejected he was apparently not, as he won firsts at New York, Detroit, Chicago and Pittsburgh.

Bradford Rejected was the sire of, or grandsire (in some cases, both), of all the dogs owned by Mrs. Beulah G. Seebach, Peru, Indiana. All of Mrs. Seebach's dogs were named for people. Hence she had such dogs as Ben Paderewski, Marie Seebach, Fan Davenport and Teddy Roosevelt, among many others, during the five years that she bred.

Fred W. Sierp, San Francisco, was the pioneer breeder on the West Coast. His first dog, Mash, was born in 1883. Mr. Sierp lists himself as the breeder but, strangely enough, gives the sire and dam as unknown. We can only assume that the answer to this amazing feat lies in that he wasn't sure of what breed the parents were so he forgot, didn't know the actual sire (although to list himself the breeder, he surely must have known who the dam was) or, perhaps, he just never named the sire and dam. Whatever — Mash was good enough to still be winning the Champion class at the age of nine years in 1892 at San Francisco. He was the sire of D.H. Everett's Mash J. and Mrs. Grace's Sis, both born in 1892.

Mrs. E.B. Grace of San Francisco started breeding in 1893 when she bought Sis from Mr. Sierp. She showed in both San Francisco and Los Angeles. Besides from Mr. Sierp, she bought Sally VII from John Enright of San Francisco. Sally VII was a great-grand-daughter of Marriot's Jack thru her sire Prince. Sally VII's dam was Sally VI who was out of Sally V., who was out of Sally IV, so we would assume it is safe to say there was a Sally III, II and just plain Sally.

In 1896 Mrs. Grace entered Sally VII at San Francisco, but the listing of awards in this show catalogue say "Dead" beside her name. We're not sure whether that was the judge's opinion, or an actual fact.

Mrs. Grace won an "equal first prize" at this show for Best Yorkshire with Frank. His equal was Joker II owned by E. Attridge, and bred by Plato. The prize at this show for best Yorkie was "one-half dozen bottles of Claret", as well as a gold medal. The claret, I expect, was easily divided but the gold medal would be a problem. Mrs. Grace

Mr. and Mrs. J. Hardman, English breeders of the early 1900s.

Ch. Yankee Kitty, weight 1¾ lbs., claimed at time (early 1900s) to be smallest Yorkie of record. Owner, Mrs. W. A. Beck, California.

won some prizes that are certainly different from those offered these days. Among hers were one box of candy, one parasol, one dog brush, one-half dozen dog soap and, finally, a bicycle racing suit.

Mrs. Grace continued breeding until 1900, her last top dog being Duke of York, an import purchased from Sam Williams of Haverford, Pa., bred by Mrs. White, Edinburgh, Scotland.

During the 1890s, San Francisco also was the home of W.R. Kay, Mrs. C.H. Bloomer, Mrs. C.H. Morrel and Mr. W.P. Feeny, all breeders. Mr. Feeny later moved to San Mateo in 1904, winning a championship with Ch. Weenie in 1908.

In 1893, a Yorkshire Terrier — Topsey — was registered to Edward Darcourt of Diaz, Mexico — first of the breed in that country.

3

The New Century Breeders

IN the golden interlude between 1900 and the First World War, the comfortable time bridging the end of "the good old days" and the arrival of Modern Times, there were some 65 major breeders of Yorkshire Terriers in America.

Yorkies were being bred all across the country. Railroads crisscrossing the nation were utilized in the exchange of bloodlines. The new transportation, the Tin Lizzie, made it easier to travel to purchase new stock, or to exhibit at the ever-increasing number of dog shows.

In 1905, two years after the Wright brothers had flown the first flying machine, the first American-bred Yorkshire gained her title. Who in that day would have believed that there would come a time when the "silly contraptions" would be flying dogs to shows toward their championships?

The Early Decades

Newtonville, Massachusetts was the site of the Hunslet Kennels of Mrs. Emanuel Battersby. This kennel was founded in 1907 with the imported bitches Lady Mona and Hunslet Zena. Zena became an American champion in 1909. She was bred by Mrs. Swinburn, Leeds, England and was linebred on Mrs. Foster's dogs. She carried Ch. Ted on her sire's side and Bradford Rejected, Mrs. Bishop's 1895 import, on her dam's side. It was from Zena that Mrs. Battersby took her kennel name. Lady Mona was bred by W. Swainston, Leeds, England.

In 1913 Mrs. Battersby imported Little Shannon Jr., winning his title in 1915. Shannon was bred to Leay's Bridget, whose sire Blue Shannon was a half-brother to Little Shannon Jr. Their daughter Hunslet Countess, bred to her half-brother Athaclee Lord Robert, produced Hunslet Lady Ramsey. From Hunslet Lady Ramsey, Mrs. Battersby produced Ch. Rochdale Queenie and Playmate. The sire of these two was Ch. Conran Toy, a dog imported by Mrs. Battersby in 1920. Toy was a full brother to Conran Pride, a top English stud, who was prominent in the English bloodlines of Invincia and Supreme during the 1920s.

Ch. Rochdale Queenie and Playmate were the foundation bitches of the Rochdale Kennels of Mr. and Mrs. John Shipp, Providence, R.I. Queenie, through her daughter Olinda Queen, was the great-granddam of Mrs. Stone's Ch. Petit Byngo and Mrs. Riddock's Ch. Byngo's Royal Masher.

Although dogs of Mrs. Battersby's breeding continued to play an active part in the top kennels all through the 1930s and 1940s, Mrs. Battersby actually ceased breeding in 1925 after the death of her husband, who died of injuries suffered in an automobile accident.

Mrs. Michael Jennings of Jamaica, Long Island bred for only eight years, but her breeding was the connecting link between Mrs. Senn's line and several kennels that flourished in the 1920s. Her Little Boy Blue, purchased from Mrs. Senn in 1906, sired by Senn's Brandy II, was the sire of Mead's Daisy, the foundation bitch of the Mead's Kennels owned by Mr. and Mrs. Thomas Mead of Ridgewood, New Jersey. Mead's Daisy, in turn, was the granddam of Bide-a-wee, who was the bitch Sam Baxter used to found his kennel when he started in the late '20s.

Mrs. Jenning's dogs usually carried the letter J after the dog's name. She finished one champion, that being Ch. Beauty J in 1913.

Mr. and Mrs. Peter Menges of New York City purchased a bitch from Mrs. Jenning in 1912, a daughter of Little Boy Blue named Molly J. Their foundation bitch was Little Fairy who they bought from Mrs. Senn. Little Fairy was bred to Frank McCarthy's Frank, a dog of Mrs. Senn's line. Mr. McCarthy bred Yorkies from 1886 to 1912 in New York City. The breeding of Fairy and Frank produced the Menges' first champion, Ch. Roxy II who won his title in 1913.

Roxy was a top stud dog and bred to Toodles, a daughter of Senn Senn Nipper, produced the first litter-mate champions in the breed, Ch. Billy and Ch. Prince II.

With the advent of World War I, the Menges ceased breeding. They sold Ch. Prince II to Mr. and Mrs. James Dwyer, Philadelphia, Pa. in 1914. Ch. Prince II sired Ch. Boy Blue II who was the foundation stud of Anna Radcliffe's Gold Mount line, as well as Lady Peg Wuffington, the bitch on which Anna William Dreer founded her line of Hassit dogs in 1925. Mr. and Mrs. Dwyer were very active in the breed until 1927.

Mr. and Mrs. George Peabody of Newton, Mass. were one of the most ardent supporters of the breed during the early 1900s. They started the Douro Kennels in 1904 with the importation of Masterpiece, a Halifax Marvel grandson, bred by G.H. Wilkinson, England.

The Peabodys showed until the start of World War I. During this period they imported many top dogs, including Am. Ch. Douro Chief, a son of Armley Fritz bred by Lawrence Bains, Leeds, Eng. Chief was the top winning dog in the United States during 1909. Armley Nicco was imported by them in 1907, winning his title in 1909. Nicco was sired by Armley Toff and traced to Halifax Marvel. He sired two champions — Mr. F.L. Parnham's Ch. Nemo, and the Thomas Lomasney's Ch. Sporting Lady.

Douro Kennels produced Champions Douro Violet, Douro Prince, Douro Saucy Bob and Douro Wee Dolly. The Peabodys' dogs were the foundation of a number of kennels, the most important being those of the above mentioned Lomasneys of Boston, who bred from 1908 until 1916 using the kennel name of Norway. The Lomasneys also won a title on Little Dot, a daughter of their top stud dog Newsboy, a son of Ch. Armley Nicco.

F.L. Parnham, who founded his kennel on the Douro dogs, showed and bred from 1909 to 1917. He was also a judge of the breed. Besides Ch. Nemo, he won a title with Little Bright in 1914. Little Bright's sire was Tony Boy, owned by Delia Smart, who bred from 1904 to 1936 in Cambridge, Mass.

Mr. Peabody was a delegate to the AKC for the first Yorkshire Terrier Club, which was The Yorkshire Terrier Club of America, started around 1912. This club, according to AKC records, held its first licensed speciality in New York on February 12, 1918. Unfortunately, no record remains of the winner at this show. This club, although not an AKC member club, held the status of Associate Subscriber, and continued in existence until about 1920.

Mrs. Anna Bell purchased Champions Douro Saucy Bob and Douro Wee Dolly in 1914 from the Peabodys. These two dogs and the import Billy Boy were the foundation of her Madero Kennels in Bairdstown, California. Billy Boy won his championship in 1917. He was a son of Little Bully, who was by Eng. Ch. Westbrook Fred, and his breeder was Thomas Hughes of England. Mrs. Bell sold Lill, a granddaughter of Ch. Douro Saucy Bob, to Mrs. Beck in 1924. Mrs. Bell ceased breeding in 1925.

Mrs. M.W. Baldwin founded the Fairie Kennels in Sioux City, Iowa in 1906 with the import Pride of Elland, a granddaughter of Halifax Marvel. Mrs. Baldwin maintained the breed in this area until 1920. She was the breeder of K.C. Judy, owned by Gilbert E. Morton, Kansas City, Missouri, was was a breeder for a few years. Judy was the top winner in the Midwest in 1915. Mrs. W.A. Beck bought Canfield Jingles from Mrs. Baldwin in 1919, just shortly before Mrs. Baldwin retired from breeding.

Mr. William Cummings of Newark, N.J. was the owner of the Delmar Kennels, a kennel that was active in the breed for only four years, but which was to have a long reaching effect. Delmar Kennels bred from 1913 to 1917. During this time Mr. Cummings finished two dogs, the homebred Ch. Delmar Beauty, and the import Ch. Teddy Boy. Teddy Boy was a grandson of Armley Fritz and was bred by Mrs. Brockbank, Eng.

In 1917, Mr. Cummings sold a male named Haslingden's Jack Oh Boy, a son of Ch. Teddy Boy out of Masie, to John H. Kenyon of Toronto. Masie was bred by A.J. McGookin, Newark, N.J., a breeder from 1909 to 1915. McGookin's dogs were based on a combination of the early American bloodlines — Mrs. Senn and J.C. Daly of So. Boston, Mass. Daly was a breeder from 1886 to 1913 and his dogs were mostly of Mrs. Senn's breeding. These were crossed with the blood of the imported Ch. Halifax Beacon. Mr. Kenyon showed Jack Oh Boy to his Canadian title before selling him to Mr. and Mrs. Harry Smith, Can. in 1922. The Smiths continued breeding until 1949 carrying on the kennel name of Haslingden which they had taken over from Mr. Kenyon. Jack Oh Boy was the great grandsire of Ch. Bond's Byngo. A pattern was set with this dog that was to carry on during the 1920s and '30s, that of breeding back and forth across the border. Without this pattern Yorkies would have been in serious trouble during the late '20s and early '30s.

Canada was the home, or original home, of such stud dogs as American and Canadian Chs. Haslingden Dandy Dindy and Bond's Byngo, and Canadian Chs. Haslingden Mons, Mickey, Rags, and Lord Byng, Royal Prince, and the English imports Can. Chs. Jetsam, Little Monitor, Little Briton, Monsieur, Eng. and Can. Ch. Cave Canem and the three Pellon imports, Chs. Star of Pellon, Pellon Earlsmead Bobby and Wee Pellon Eclipse.

Mrs. Thomas W. Murphy of New York City became active in the breed in 1896 with Bessie, a bitch bred by Mrs. Senn. In 1906 she imported Halifax Beacon bred by C. Adam, Halifax, Eng. sired by Halifax Ben, a son of Halifax Marvel. Beacon's dam traced to Eng. Ch. Merry Mascot. Beacon became a champion in 1908. Mrs. Murphy also owned other dogs of Halifax Marvel's blood such as a daughter — Matchless Molly — and Halifax Baden, a half-brother to Beacon. Mrs. Murphy gave up breeding in 1908.

Mrs. H.S. Lanahan of Indianapolis, Indiana was a breeder from 1902 to 1907. In 1907 she imported Firmstone's Eng. Ch. Grand Duke. Al-

"PELLON WEE SIR DANDY."

F. GREENWOOD. INGROW.

AT STUD, the Premier Sire and latest Crystal Palace Championship winner

PELLON WEE SIR DANDY

K.C.S.B. 173180   Weight 3¼lbs.

Huddersfield Marvel				Hanson's Tiney			
Pickwick		Rose		Lord Byron		Trixey	
Ch. Clayton Marvel Little Dorrit		Lumb's Royal Armstrong's Lady		Ch. Hunslet Ted Fly		Pickwick Rose	
Royal Harry Violet	Ch Ben Peggy	Jarratt's Marwood Lumb's Rose	Huddersfield Ben II. Townsend's Nellie	Ch. Ben Violet	Aphor Polly	Ch Clayton Marvel Dorrit	Lumb's Royal Lady

Pellon Wee Sir Dandy has proved himself on the show bench and as a sire to be easily the best Toy Yorkshire Stud Dog living to-day. He is a winner of over 200 firsts, Cups, Medals, and Diplomas at our best shows, under specialist judges. As a sire he stands alone, having sired classic winners far too numerous to mention, including **Champion Lively Boy**, Cruft's Championship winner, 1917; **Lady Dandy**, Blackpool winner; **Little Dandy**, Australian winner; and the coming sire, **Wee Pellon Dandy**, L.K.A. winner, 1916. **P.W.S.D.** is a Toy to whom the tiniest bitch can be mated with safety. He is very prolific, and a certain stockgetter. As a breeder of achievement, and a judge of experience, I can with confidence recommend Sir Dandy to all breeders wishing to breed exhibition stock. **Blood will tell.**

Stud card of the early 1900s.

"Damaris", "The Grand Duke" and "Idol", bred by Mrs. C. E. Firmstone, England. Eng. Ch. The Grand Duke was imported to U.S. by Mrs. H. S. Lanahan.

Eng. Ch. Armley Boy, winner of 8 Challenge Certificates (1911–13.) Owner, J. Wood, England.

Eng. Ch. Ashton Duke, owned by the Misses Walton and Beard, England.

Eng. Ch. Merry Mascot, owned by Tom Hooten, England.

though she showed him that year, she never registered him nor bred from him. In 1907 she also showed three bitches, Juno, Dolly and Maude, but there is no record of Mrs. Lanahan past that year.

Julia H. McGoldbrick of Los Angeles started showing Yorkies in 1914. She purchased Eastney Little Midge from Mrs. Carlin, N.Y.C. Mrs. Carlin owned Eastney Kennels, but she was only active in the breed from 1912 to 1914, her main interest being Poms. Little Midge became a champion in 1915. Mrs. McGoldbrick purchased Pellon Wee Sonny from Mrs. Maude Dickerson of Pasadena, Calif. in 1915. Mrs. Dickerson had imported him from T. Pollard, Eng. Sonny was by Pellon Wee Dandy out of Halifax Minnie.

Another California exhibitor of this period was Mrs. D. Neustadter of Los Angeles. She purchased Ch. Weenie from Mr. Feeny in 1908, and also The Major from Mrs. W.W. Strettheimer of San Mateo. The Major became a champion in 1909.

The Columbine Kennels of E. Proctor were located in Denver, Colorado from 1905 to 1909. Proctor's top Yorkie was Columbine Cinderella. Mrs. Edward Spencer of Long Island, N.Y. won a championship with Ch. Sweet Face in 1915. Mrs. J.A. Whelpley of Jersey City bred from 1901 thru 1907. All her dogs carried the letter W after their name. Mrs. E.F. Thurman was an exhibitor from Ft. Smith, Arkansas. Her top dog was Taggs, bred by Mrs. Teschemacher, and shown in 1915. James Milroy's kennel was located in E. Milton, Mass. and he bred from 1911 to 1914. He was the breeder of Bell Boy and Ring Boy, both owned by the Lomasneys. Mrs. J. and Martha Englehart owned the Englehart Pet Dog Kennels in Cincinnati, Ohio. Although they were primarily interested in Pugs, they did breed and show Yorkies in the Cincinnati area from 1899 to 1908. H.A. Dalrymple, Port Allegheny, Pa. owned the Dalmore Kennels, and was active in Yorkies from 1907 to 1909. During this time he imported a bitch named Dalmore Wee Girlie, who he sold to the all-breed judge Otto Gross. Mr. Gross finished Wee Girlie to her title in 1909. Mrs. Thomas Scranton, Philadelphia, bred and showed from 1908 to 1915. Her kennel name was Scranton.

Mrs. August Kohlmeyer bred for twenty years in Chicago. Starting in 1895 and continuing until 1915, she produced a number of top winners and showed a total of 33 dogs while active in the show ring. Her best dog was Prince Kohl who traced to Ch. Bradford Harry and Dr. Oliver's Dick York. Prince Kohl was born in 1906 and was a top winner during 1907 to 1909, as well as being Mrs. Kohlmeyer's best stud dog. Her other top winners were Duke, who won the breed at the Chicago Pet Dog Club in 1901 in an entry of sixteen Yorkies, and was shown until 1907, and Tiny Kohl, who won the breed at the all-breed Chicago show in 1913 and 1914. Her foundation bitch was Tudsie, a daughter of Coomb's Ch. Bradford Harry and Bradford Dot. Tudsie was the dam of Prince Kohl.

Mrs. W.A. Beck of Watsonville, California must be considered one of the breed's major breeders. Her span of breeding started in 1907 and continued until 1938. Her dogs contained the blood of every top dog starting with Coomb's Ch. Bradford Harry, continuing through to Mrs. Riddock's Ch. Bond's Byngo, Nicholas Sharkey's Ch. Rodger and the John Shipps' Ch. Robinhood.

Her first dogs, Cyndrella and Lord Skyudle were acquired from Mrs. Teschemacher of St. Louis. They carried the blood of Ch. Bradford Harry and Lincoln's Fishpool Gem.

During her extensive career, Mrs. Beck finished at least three dogs. The first one was Ch. Clayton Wee Marvel, a dog that had been imported by Mrs. Maud Thorpe in 1914, and purchased by Mrs. Beck in 1917. Wee Marvel was bred by J. Nasworth, England. Mrs. Thorpe of Sheepshead Bay, Long Island, N.Y. was a breeder from 1907 to 1917. Mrs. Thorpe also imported and finished Ch. Clayton Prince Eric who was a top winner in 1910 and 1911, and Ch. Clayton Wee Girl.

Mrs. Beck's second champion was O'Boy who finished in 1925. O'Boy was a homebred son of Ch. Clayton Wee Marvel.

In 1914, Billie Beck was born. She was a daughter of Mrs. Bell's Ch. Douro Saucy Bob out of Abby, a granddaughter of Mrs. Teschemacher's Boy. Billie was the dam of English Tommy, one of Thomas Mead's foundation studs. Tommy was bred to Mrs. Beck's Pollyanna II, a Ch. Clayton Wee Marvel daughter producing SoLong Letty who was a top brood bitch for Mrs. Beck. Letty's best known offspring was Boots. Boots was by Pellon Sir Dan, a dog bred by Mrs. Nutting. Dan was a son of Mrs. Nutting's imported Merry Nibs, whose sire was Pellon Sir Dandy. Boots has always been referred to as the Pellon-bred bitch, which she obviously was not as, in truth, her great-grandfather on her sire's side was the only true Pellon in her pedigree. This is unfortunately the sort of confusion that always happens when kennel names are borrowed.

Mrs. Beck sold Boots to Mrs. Goldie Stone in 1933. Boots was bred to Ch. Petite Byngo Boy producing Petite Bo-Peep. Bo-Peep was sold to Mrs. Henry Black and appears in many of the pedigrees of dogs from the 1930s including those of Mrs. Black, Sam Baxter, Helen Palmer and the Arthur Mills.

In 1926, Mrs. Beck sold Billy Beckwith and Peggy Beckwith to Mr. Henry Beckwith of San Rafael, California, and they became the foundation of the Beckwith line. Billy was a grandson of English Tommy and Peggy a daughter of Ch. Clayton Wee Marvel. Mr. Beckwith imported Pellon Young Bugler from Mr. J.H. Greenwood, Eng. in 1928. He later added Walkley Countess, imported from Canada, bred by Harry Draper, a grandson of Ch. Cave Canem and Ch. Lord Byng. Mr. Beckwith showed his last dog in 1935.

In 1928 Mrs. Beck sold Donald D to Mrs. Fred (Indie) Rice of Los Angeles. Donald was by Newstyle out of Naughty Sue, two dogs Mrs. Beck had purchased from Nicholas Sharkey. In 1933, Mrs. Rice bought Kitty Kitty from Mrs. Beck.

Mrs. Beck's dogs provided the foundation for many kennels; besides those mentioned, they were prominent in the dogs of Cora Donaldson, Mrs. Denver Harmon, Blanche Dunbar, Miss Bessie Carmicheal, Mrs. L.E. Copeland, A.W. Canfield and Wm. Morenini. Mrs. Beck did have a kennel name, that of Niquoia, but it was never used on any of the Yorkies. She retired in 1938.

Two major breeders started breeding on the East Coast just prior to the First World War. Their dogs provided the base for many breeders who came into the breed later.

Mrs. Herbert (Anna) Radcliffe of Philadelphia started in 1914 and continued until 1926. She first showed at Atlantic City, New Jersey with her imported Liverpool Lad, a half-brother of Anna Bell's Ch. Billy Boy. Both were sired by Little Bully and traced directly to Mrs. Foster's Ch. Ted.

Her most famous brood bitch was Lady Blue, a granddaughter of Chelsea King, who had been imported by L. Cullen of St. Louis in 1896, and later transferred to Mrs. Teschemacher. Chelsea King was a great-grandson of Huddersfield Ben's son Bismark. Lady Blue represented a direct line from Huddersfield Ben to Mrs. Stone's Ch. Petite Byngo Boy.

Lady Blue, bred to the Dwyer's Ch. Prince II, produced Ch. Boy Blue. Bred to Liverpool Lad, she produced Gold Mount Gay Boy, a dog who was to play a major part in Mrs. Riddock's Olinda line.

Left, Eng. Ch. Sprig of Blossom, winner of 16 CCs. Owned by Mr. and Mrs. R. Marshall. *Right,* English import, Am. Ch. Little Babs, Best of Breed at Westminster 1921. Owner, Anna Radcliffe, Philadelphia.

Mrs. Radcliffe imported and won titles on Ch. Young Messenger and Ch. Little Babs. Babs was the winner of the breed at Westminister in 1921. At this show, Babs is listed in the catalog as being available for $200, and Ch. Boy Blue was priced at $500. After this win she apparently was no longer for sale, as in the catalog for Westchester, 1921, she no longer carries a price tag.

Mrs. Radcliffe imported Little Gent and Dandy King, two grandsons of Eng. Ch. Gold Mount from Mr. R. Marshall, Eng. in 1921. It was from Ch. Gold Mount that she took her kennel name.

In 1924 Mrs. Riddock of Detroit purchased Olinda Dottie from Mrs. Radcliffe. Dottie was by Gold Mount Gay Boy, and became Mrs. Riddock's foundation bitch for her Olinda line.

Mrs. Radcliffe finished at least four champions and was the breeder of Mrs. Riddock's Ch. Gold Blaze. In 1926 Mrs. Radcliffe sold all her remaining stock to Mrs. Riddock and retired.

The other major breeders on the East Coast were Mr. and Mrs. William C. Thompson, who established their Gatenby Kennels in 1913 and continued their interest in the breed until 1942, a period of 29 years.

Mrs. Thompson was the president of the second Yorkshire Terrier club. This club was called the Yorkshire Terrier Association of America and flourished for about five years, starting around 1919 and fading away around 1923 or 1924. The Association offered many prizes at shows across the United States. The top trophy was one given annually to the member scoring the greatest number of wins from January 1st to December 31st.

The Thompsons' first homebred Champion was Ch. Gatenby's Little Billy, a son of two imports — Gatenby's Prince, bred by F. Pratt, Eng., and his dam Gatenby's Hanley Bella, bred by J. Johnson, Eng. In 1914, the Thompsons imported Gatenby's Saint Wilfred's King, bred by Miss Leeming. In 1914, King was the second highest winning Yorkie in the U.S., being beaten out in wins by the Peabodys' Ch. Douro Prince. However, the next year they changed places. King became a champion in 1916, and was the Thompsons' most famous winner.

Their top stud dog was Ch. Gatenby's Armley Little Dick, a son of Armley Resistance, imported in 1916 from Richard Squires of Leeds, Eng. Dick, whelped in 1914, was never shown in England, but in the United States he was a top winner, helping to maintain the winning record of the Gatenby dogs. The Thompsons finished six dogs to their titles. The Gatenby dogs were in their zenith from 1912 until about 1924, after which the Thompsons did little showing, but continued breeding. All their dogs were based on Armley and Pellon lines, the males carrying the Armley line and the bitches the Pellon lines of Ch. Pellon Conqueror and Ch. Pellon Earlsmead Bobby.

70

Jeanne Grimsby

From Armistice to Armistice (1920 to 1946)

In the two decades from 1900 to 1920, 45 Yorkshires were finished to championship. But stoppage of imports during World War I, and the diversion of breeders into war-time activities, reduced the number of active Yorkshire Terrier breeders at end of the War to eight American and two Canadian kennels. However, they began to put their blood-lines back together, laying a foundation for the next generation.

The Rochdale Kennel of Mr. and Mrs. John Shipp was one of the most prominent during the 1920s and '30s. Started in 1920, it was active

Ch. Rochdale Queenie, BOB at Westminster 1925. Bred by Mrs. Emanuel Battersby and owned by Mr. and Mrs. John Shipp.

Am. & Can. Ch. Bond's Byngo, top winner 1929–1931. Owner, Mrs. Henry T. Riddock.

Ch. Rochdale Queen of the Toys, owned by Mr. and Mrs. Shipp.

until 1937. The kennel was located in Providence, Rhode Island and later in Edgewood, Rhode Island.

Their first dog was Hunslet Lady Ramsey, a bitch purchased from Mrs. E. Battersby, and their first champion was Rochdale Queenie who won her title in 1923. Queenie was the breed winner at the Westminister Kennel Club show in 1925.

The Shipps took over all of Mrs. Battersby's remaining Hunslet dogs in 1924, and in 1925 they acquired most of the stock of the Athaclee Kennel. The Athaclee Kennel was owned by Mrs. John McHugh, Southville, Massachusetts, an active breeder from 1918 to 1925.

The outstanding Ch. Robinhood had been imported by the Shipps in 1925. Robinhood was a son of Eng. Ch. Boy Blue, a winner of eleven Challenge Certificates in England, and a daughter of Haworth Bessie. He was bred by Mr. H. Lemmon of England and traced to Armley and Ovenden Breeding.

In 1927 the Shipps sold to Mrs. Riddock, of Detroit, a bitch named Olinda Queen. Queen was purchased back in 1929 by the Shipps in whelp to Gold Don. Ch. Rochdale Goldie came from this litter. In 1930 Olinda Queen was bred to André Patterson's Ch. Haslingden Dandy Dinty, producing Ch. Rochdale Queen of the Toys. This bitch was a top winner for the Shipps, placing in a number of Toy Groups, including 3rd in the group at the Westminister show of 1935.

Olinda Queen's third champion child, Ch. Rochdale Honey, was born in 1932 and was a full brother to Queen of the Toys. Honey placed in several Groups. Olinda Queen was also the dam of Mrs. Riddock's May Blossom, who was born in 1927, registered in 1929, and transferred to Mrs. Goldie Stone of Columbus, Ohio in January of 1931. May Blossom was by Mrs. Riddock's Ch. Gold Blaze. Without question, Olinda Queen had the greatest effect on the breed of all the Shipps' dogs.

André Patterson, of Buffalo, New York, started breeding in 1920 and based his line primarily on the Canadian dogs. He retired in 1937. Patterson's kennel name was Dandy and his first two dogs were Dandy Nish and Dandy Patsy. They were both bred by Mrs. J.W. Weldon of Galt, Ont. Mrs. Weldon started exhibiting and breeding in 1913 using the kennel name of Round Bay for a few years before changing it to Galt. The Galt line appears behind many Canadian dogs, and Mrs. Weldon was the breeder of Can. Ch. Royal Prince and Edna of Galt, who was a daughter of Can. Ch. Star of Pellon. Ch. Star of Pellon was, as far as we can ascertain, the first Yorkshire Terrier to win Best in Show in Canada, which he did at the Canadian National Show held in Toronto in 1916. Mrs. Weldon also sold Monitor's Cricket, a daughter of Edna of Galt to Mr. Patterson.

Mr. Patterson's Armley Star, bred in Canada by Mrs. Kehrer, was sired by the imported Eng. and Can. Ch. Cave Canem. Patterson's most famous winner and stud dog was Am. and Can. Ch. Haslingden Dandy Dinty, who was bred by Harry Smith of Canada and was sired by Can. Ch. Little Briton out of Haslingden Jewel. Dandy Dinty won Best of Breed and 3rd in the Toy Group in 1934 at Westminister, as well as BOB at this show in 1930 and 1931. Dandy Dinty was the sire of five champions and of Sam Baxter's top dog, Bobbie B.

In 1933, Mr. Patterson purchased from Mrs. Bond of Canada, a full brother of Ch. Bond's Byngo, named Earl Byng, who won the breed and placed fourth in the Toy Group that same year at Westminister.

Patterson purchased Dandy Hero from Thomas Watmough of Williamsville, New York. Hero was sired by Ch. Haslingden Dandy Dinty out of Lady Gray who was a half-sister to Dinty, both being sired by Ch. Little Briton. Watmough's line was bred on Canadian blood using primarily Ch. Star of Pellon and Haslingden dogs. Mr. Watmough bred dogs that were owned by Sam Baxter, Helen Palmer, Robert W. Englert and Medor Kennels, and he was an active breeder for twenty years from 1921 to 1941.

Charles McCloud of Cleveland bred from 1927 till 1938. He bred Jolly Boy who was one of Mrs. Beck's top stud dogs and was prominent in many West Coast lines. Jolly Boy combined the blood of Rochdale, Henry Shannon's line and Mrs. Riddock's Ch. Bond's Byngo.

Mrs. Harold Riddock of Detroit was probably one of the breed's greatest enthusiasts, a breeder who upheld the breed and carried on at a time when the breed's popularity was at its lowest ebb. She joined the breed in 1924 when she purchased Anna Radcliffe's remaining Gold Mount stock and retired from breeding in 1948. Her dogs formed the foundation of many kennels including Mrs. Stone's Petite Kennels, Mrs. O.L. Billing's Monitor Kennels, Nicholas Sharkey's Naughty Kennels, the Kennels of Charles McCloud, Henrietta Stabler, and Mrs. W.A. Beck, Harry Smith's Haslingden Kennels, Mrs. Henry Black's Cantie Kennels, and the Arthur Mill's Millbarry Kennels.

Mrs. Riddock used the kennel name of Olinda, but for some reason it was used mainly on the bitches, rarely on the males. Her first champion was Ch. Gold Blaze (Gold Mount Gay Boy ex Gold Mount Lady Tena) who she purchased from Mrs. Anna Radcliffe. Ch. Gold Blaze was bred to Olinda Queen, a daughter of Ch. Robinhood and Ch. Rochdale Queenie. This breeding produced May Blossom. Mrs. Riddock bred May Blossom several times before selling her to Mrs. Goldie Stone in January of 1931. Among her children was the bitch, Miss June, who was sired by Gold Don, a full brother to Ch. Gold Blaze. Miss June was the dam of three champions.

Can. and Am. Ch. Bond's Byngo, bred by Mrs. O.M. Bond of Canada, was purchased by Mrs. Riddock in 1928 from Harry Draper, owner of the Walkley Kennels of Holland Landing, Toronto, Ont. Mr. Draper was an outstanding Canadian breeder, a man who loved the breed and helped many breeders with advice on care and breeding when they were beginners. He had attended his first Yorkie specialty in 1890, and his knowledge of the breed's history was very deep. Mr. Draper was of great help to us and we will always be thankful to have known him so well. Mr. Draper came to Canada in 1913 and bred from 1923 to 1954, maintaining his interest until his death. His last best known dog was Can. Ch. Petite Lord Byngo of Walkley, bred by Goldie Stone and purchased by Mr. Draper in 1949.

Mrs. Riddock's Ch. Bond's Byngo was a combination of English and Canadian blood tracing back to American bloodlines. His sire, Can. Ch. Lord Byng, traced to J.H. Kenyon's English import Can. Ch. Monsieur. Byngo's dam, Cave Girl, was sired by Eng. and Am. Ch. Cave Canem. Cave Canem's full sister was Eng. Ch. Lilyhill Mademoiselle. Cave Girl's dam, Fluff, bred by Mrs. K. Ried of Toronto, was a daughter of Can. Ch. Haslingden Jack Oh Boy. Ch. Bond's Byngo's full brother was André Patterson's top winner, Earl Byng.

Mrs. Riddock kept one male from the breeding of Miss June and Ch. Bond's Byngo, Can. & Am. Ch. Byngo's Royal Masher, who won his AKC title in 1934. She showed him during 1933 to 1936, winning at least ten Group placings, including 2nd in the Toy Group at the Chicago International K.C. in 1935. Mrs. L. Turnball of Pleasant Ridge, Michigan purchased Ch. Byngo's Royal Tiny, another Yorkshire from the breeding of Miss June and Ch. Bond's Byngo, winning at least three group placings with her. Mrs. Goldie Stone purchased the future Ch. Petite Byngo Boy from Mrs. Riddock at six weeks of age. Byngo was from Miss June's first litter, the other two champions were from a later litter. Mrs. Riddock finished six champions of which four were homebreds.

Mrs. Orrae L. Billing of Norwich, N.Y. was a very active exhibitor in the late 1920s using the kennel name, Monitor, which she took from the famous Canadian dog, Can. Ch. Little Monitor. In 1927, Mrs. Billing purchased Ch. Gold Blaze from Mrs. Riddock along with several bitches. Mrs. Billing's greatest winner was Monitor's BlueBelle, a daughter of Little Monitor's Double and Pride of Tyndall. BlueBelle was bred by George Kemshead of Canada.

Mrs. Henry Black lived in Columbus, Ohio and began breeding in 1934 with two dogs, Cantie Spider, a male bred by Mrs. Riddock, and a bitch, Petite Bo-Peep, bred by Mrs. Stone. Spider was by Ch. Byngo's

Royal Masher. Bo-Peep was a daughter of Ch. Petite Byngo Boy out of Boots, the bitch bred by Mrs. Beck. Bo-Peep's best known children were the Arthur Mills' Millbarry Sylvia and Esther Lantis' Goldie Sunflower. Mrs. Lantis was a breeder in Wichita, Kansas from 1937 to around 1949. Her dogs were primarily based on Mrs. Stone's Petite line and dogs of the Henry Shannon's line.

Mrs. Black's last top winner was Kiltie's Sporran who she imported from England after World War II in 1948. Sporran was sired by Midge's Pal, a full brother to Mr. Bains' Fairy Prince and half brother to Eng. Ch. Tufty of Johnstounburn. Sporran was bred by H. Ferier of England.

Nicholas Sharkey was English by birth but his kennel was located at Haworth, New Jersey. He maintained residences in both countries so that it's hard to call his dogs either American-bred or imports. His best known dog, Ch. Rodger, was bred by him in England and Mr. Sharkey brought him with him to the United States, winning his title here. Nimble Step, who he sold to Mrs. Beck, shows the following on its registration: "Owner — N. Sharkey, U.S.A. and Eng. Breeder-Owner." Mrs. Beck bought five other dogs from Mr. Sharkey including Naughty Snippy, a bitch bred by Mrs. Riddock, and Seelum, a stud dog that appears in many West Coast pedigrees during the late 1930s. Mr. Sharkey bred from 1925 to 1935, a period of ten years.

Sam Baxter, who had been Andrew Carnegie's coachman until he retired, purchased his first Yorkie for two dollars and fifty cents. It was a little dog he saw perched beside the driver of an ash and dust cart. We have been told that Mr. Baxter was a rotund, jolly little man who took up breeding after retiring. He had a heart ailment and since his apartment was on the third floor of a walk-up building, he preferred to have visitors knock on the vestibule door. He would then lower the latch key on a string so that the visitor could open the door and let themselves in to climb the stairs to visit the Bobbie B dogs.

Mr. Baxter's first show dog was Gatenby's Bobs who he purchased in 1925 from the William C. Thompson's Gatenby Kennels in New York City. Bobs was eight years old and was an import bred by Mr. Hewitt out of Armley Little Bobs. Mr. Baxter's first big winner was Bobbie B who was bred by Thomas Watmough, and it was from this dog that Mr. Baxter took his kennel name. Bobbie B was a child of Can. and Am. Ch. Haslingden Dandy Dinty out of Lady Gray, a daughter of H. Smith's Can. Ch. Little Briton. Bobbie B was a full brother to Andre Patterson's Dandy Hero.

Of Mr. Baxter's dogs, the best known one was Bobbie B III, who was born in 1934 by Bobbie B II out of Beebe. Bobbie B III was Best of

Can. Ch. Lord Byng, bred and owned by Harry Draper, Canada. Sire of Ch. Bond's Byngo.

Canadian Yorkshires owned by Susan Pike, Victoria. Dog on left bred by Harry Draper.

Ch. Byngo's Royal Masher, bred and owned by Mrs. H. T. Riddock.

Breed and 3rd in the Toy Group at the Westminister shows in both 1936 and 1937. Mr. Baxter, although gaining a number of points on various dogs, never actually won a title on any dog. However, his dogs produced top breeding stock for many kennels, especially on the East Coast.

Mr. Baxter was elected President of the third Breed Club in 1937. Like the present day club, it was known as the Yorkshire Terrier Club of America. It faded out with the onset of World War II. Its vice-presidents were Mrs. Edward Spencer of New York City for the East Coast and Lily Harris of Los Angeles for the West Coast. Mr. Baxter gave up breeding in 1940.

Henry Shannon and his wife commenced breeding Yorkshires in 1927 in Fox River Grove, Ill. Their dogs were originally from England as were the Shannons themselves. They imported dogs from Clenshaw's Harringay Kennels, Mr. Scolley's Mendham Kennels, and Mrs. Lingwood's Cherry Orchard Kennels. Unfortunately, the Shannons did not use a kennel name and in tracing their dogs it is necessary to resort to the AKC stud books, old catalogs and pedigrees as well as show records. During the time that they bred and showed, they used no kennel name on some of their dogs, used Harringay or Mendham prefix on others, and left to the owners the job of naming still many others.

Their best known dog was a bitch, Madame Be You, who was sold to Goldie Stone in 1930. Madame was the first Yorkie to produce five champions. She was a daughter of the Shannon's imports, Harringay Quality Boy and Miss Why Be You. Mrs. Thomas Moroney of Barrington, Illinois owned an older sister to Madame who was named Lady Ears Up.

The Shannons based their line on English breeding of Armley and Pellon lines. It is interesting to note that bloodlines descending from these two lines have consistently produced the top winners, and are still doing so today. Both lines descend directly from line breeding on Mrs. Foster's Ch. Ted. The Shannons relied heavily on the Harringay dogs, importing many of the same blood that produced the immortal Eng. Ch. Harringay Remarkable. Their foundation bitches were two littermates named Miss Why Be You and Little O.I., and a half-sister to these two called Mattie. All three were sired by the Clenshaw's foundation stud dog, Blue Coat Boy. The Shannons' stud dog was Harringay Quality Boy, a son of Harringay Young Laddie out of Rose, a daughter of Durrand Gaffer.

Of all that we have researched, the Shannon dogs bore some of the strangest titles. Besides those already mentioned, they had dogs named The Doormat, The Killer, Buddha, The Limit, I'm Alone and The Menace.

Monitor's Bluebell, a 1928 winner, bred by George Kemshead, Canada, and owned by Mrs. O. L. Billing, Norwich, N. Y.

Can. Ch. Little Jetsom, English import winner of 3 BIS and 19 Groups in Canada in early '30s. Owner, Col. John Rose, Canada.

Eng. Ch. Harringay Remarkable, pictured in 1935 at 3 years, 8 months. Winner of 9 CCs and 10 times Best Toy in Show. Breeder-owner, E. H. Clenshaw.

Ch. Petit Magnificent Prince, first American-bred Yorkshire to win an all-breeds Best in Show (1954.) Pictured in 1953 at 3 years of age, 3 pounds in weight. Bred and owned by Mrs. Goldie Stone.

Ch. Petite Byngo Boy, sire of 5 champions. Owned by Goldie V. Stone.

The Shannons showed only at local shows and, although they were quite successful at these, other breeders did far better in the ring with dogs of their breeding. The Shannons bred from 1927 until their tragic deaths in 1946. As per their wishes, the dogs that survived were rescued by Mrs. Myrtle Durgin and Mrs. Ethel Ferguson.

Mr. and Mrs. George Roberts founded their Harrogate Kennels, located in Chicago, in 1931, when they purchased Harrogate Ann from the Shannons. Ann's daughters, Harrogate Blue Bell and Harrogate Lady Bug, both placed in Toy Groups during 1933. Mr. Roberts died in 1942 and Mrs. Roberts gave up breeding at that time.

Mrs. Russell Crosthwaite of Chicago based her breeding on the Shannons' line. In 1933 she purchased Pudgy, a daughter of Harringay Quality Boy, breeding her to Shannons' Nickey Brown. This produced a bitch who became Ch. Acushla, a top winner who placed in a number of Toy Groups during 1934 to 1937. The last dog owned by Mrs. Crosthwaite was Petite Precious Friendship, purchased from Goldie Stone in 1942.

Mrs. Mazie Wagner, of the famous Mazelaine Boxer Kennels, has been an ardent lover of Yorkies for many years and has bred and owned quite a number over the years. Her Harringay High Tracy, bred by Mr. Shannon, placed in a number of Toy Groups during 1941. Our own Ch. Mazelaine's Gold Gambit was bred by Mrs. Wagner in 1961. Mrs. Wagner also owned Pellon Lady Azure, a bitch bred by Mrs. Goldie Stone in 1939.

Mary P. Lawerence of Hollywood, N.Y. used the kennel name of Lawlock and bred from 1937 to 1942. Her top winner was Lawlock's Little Tottie. Tottie, bred by the Shannons out of Mendham Jackie Boy and Mendham Her, placed in five Toy Groups during 1938. The late Mrs. Marjorie Siebern, owner of the Seyberne line, purchased her first Yorkie from Mrs. Lawerence in 1941.

The start of the Petite Kennels of Mrs. Goldie Stone in Columbus, Ohio was the point at which the breed began its climb to its present popularity. Of the early breeders, the fame of the Petite Kennels has been the most lasting.

Mrs. Stone's dogs brought recognition to the breed in the show ring. Her combining of the older American and Canadian blood with the breeding of the Shannons' English imports produced the greatest number of top winners and champions ever produced by one kennel up to this time. The Petite Kennels produced seventeen champions, of which twelve were shown to their titles by Mrs. Stone.

Mrs. Stone's interest in the breed dated from 1908 when she saw a Yorkshire Terrier for the first time. Mrs. Stone and her husband, Charlie, were in vaudeville with a tight wire and balancing act. On the

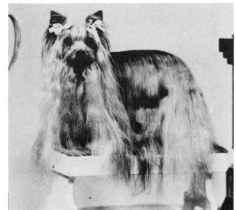

A quartet of Group winners of the 1930s, all from the Petite Kennels of Goldie V. Stone. *Top left,* Ch. Petit Wee Wee. *Top right,* Ch. Petite Baby Jill. *Lower left,* Ch. Petit Lord Dandy II. *Lower right,* Ch. Petite Tiny Trinket. Wee Wee, Jill, and Trinket were all sired by Ch. Petit Byngo Boy. Lord Dandy II was a son of Trinket.

bill with them at the time was an act in which "Mike", a 5 pound Yorkie, was teamed with a 200 pound woman in a versatile song and dance routine. After falling in love with "Mike", Mrs. Stone determined that, upon retirement, she would take up breeding Yorkshire Terriers.

In 1931, some eighteen years later, Mrs. Stone purchased from Mrs. Riddock a six-week-old puppy who was destined to become the founding father of the Petite Kennels. This puppy grew up to become Ch. Petite Byngo Boy, a top winner of the early 1930s and a sire of five champions. His champion children included Ch. Petite Queen of the Fancy, Ch. Petite Baby Jill, and Ch. Petit Wee Wee.

Ch. Petit Wee Wee was the holder of the record for the top winning Yorkshire in the United States until 1951. He won the Toy Group at the Morris and Essex Show in 1937 and was the winner of 20 Bests of Breed, 14 Toy Groups and 5 Group Placings during his show career which lasted from 1935 to 1937.

In 1929 Mrs. Stone bought a puppy named Sweetheart from the Henry Shannons and the following year she bought Madame Be You. Mrs. Stone bred Petite Lady Brillance to Patterson's Ch. Haslingden Dandy Dinty and this breeding produced Ch. Petite Lady Brillance II. Petite Kennels home-bred Petit Baby Dumpling produced three champions including Mrs. Stone's great last winner, Ch. Petit Magnificent Prince. Prince became the first American-bred, homebred, to win an all-breed Best in Show, which he did on October 31, 1954 at Delaware, Ohio. Prince was the winner of three Toy Groups and was the last dog exhibited by Mrs. Stone, although she still retains her interest in the breed.

Mrs. Fred (Indie) Rice saw her first Yorkshire Terrier in about 1897 while in San Francisco. In 1899, having heard of an English family that was breeding, she purchased her first Yorkshire Terrier puppy. It was from this start that Mrs. Rice always claimed her adventure of showing and breeding began. Mrs. Rice showed her last Yorkie in 1966 at the age of eighty-nine years.

The first Yorkie to be registered by Mrs. Rice was Donald D, bred by Mrs. Beck and born in 1926. This dog was followed by a bitch named Kitty-Kitty, also of Mrs. Beck's breeding. During the late 1930s and early 1940s she purchased a number of Brunhaven dogs from Mrs. Ethel Brun of San Francisco. The Brunhaven line was based on the kennels of the Henry Shannons and dogs from Mrs. Thomas J. Moroney of Barrington, Illinois. Mrs. Brun used Master Quality extensively in her breeding program. Ethel Brun was active in the breed from 1934 to 1949.

The first champion finished by Mrs. Rice was Ch. Bee's Super Boy, who was bred by Mrs. Leota Whytock, West Hollywood, Calif. Mrs. Rice used "Bee" as a kennel name. Mrs. Whytock and her daughter, the movie actress Mary Carlisle, were both breeders just prior to World War II. Mrs. Whytock owned Am. Ch. June Rose, a daughter of Col. John Rose's Can. Ch. Little Jetsom. (Col. Rose owned the Rose line and bred in Canada. Can. Ch. Little Jetsom was the top winner in Canada, winning nineteen Toy Groups and three Best in Shows during the early 1930s.)

Mrs. Whytock was also the owner of Am. Ch. Raemon of Soham, who she imported from Lady Edith Windham Dawson, owner of the Soham Kennels in England. The Soham Kennels were later moved to Ireland at the start of the Second World War. Raemon was bred by J. Wilkes, Eng., and was the winner of at least two Toy Groups in the United States. Mary Carlisle owned Ch. Fritty, having purchased him in 1939 from Mary and Arthur Mills, who had imported him in 1938.

Mrs. Rice was the breeder of Pearl Johnson Kincarte's Ch. Hifalutin C.D. who was the sire of five champions and the top stud dog in the breed during the early 1950s. Other dogs bred by Mrs. Rice were Kay Finch's Ch. Pixie Prince of Crown Crest, and Mrs. Charles Anderson's Ch. Chandy's Dawn of Peace. Mrs. Rice's top winner was Ch. Gwen-Mar Bitty Britches, bred by the Krakeurs. Bitty was the winner of two Toy Groups and seven Group Placings during 1948 and 1949. Little Wee Won, bred and owned by Mrs. Rice, won Best in Match at the second sanction match of the Yorkshire Terrier Club of America held in 1953 under judge Mrs. Denver Harmon, owner of the Denjo Kennels of Huntington Park, Calif.

Mrs. Harmon first started breeding in 1937 and continued as a breeder until 1948. She bred Feathers of Castlethorpe, the foundation bitch of the Castlethorpe Kennels, owned by Blanche Dunbar. Feathers was sired by Seelum, a dog owned by Mrs. Beck. Mrs. Lily A. Harris started her Belvedere line with Tippet of Belvedere, a little sister to Feathers. Mrs. Harmon won a title with Ch. Brownstone Blue Heather around 1948. Heather was bred by Mrs. Bessie Carmichael, owner of the Brownstone Kennels, situated in San Francisco. Mrs. Harmon also owned dogs bred by Cora Donaldson, a breeder from Glendale, California from 1933 to 1947, who based her line on Mrs. Riddock's and Mrs. Beck's. Mrs. Donaldson owned Gold Craze, a son of Ch. Gold Blaze. Among dogs bred by Cora Donaldson was Kay Finch's Star Dust of Crown Crest.

Charles Rutherford of San Rafael, California registered his first Yorkshire in 1924 and continued breeding until 1943. His dogs were based primarily, on dogs of Mrs. Beck's line which he purchased from Henry Beckwith. His kennel name was Ruthe-mar and he won a title with Ch. Ruthe-mar Princess Pat in 1938.

Yorkies have always had great appeal for the glamorous. *Above,* photo of movie star Betty Bruce is inscribed with thanks to Arthur Mills "for my beautiful 'Bessie'." *Below,* Mary Carlisle—star of early Bing Crosby musicals—pictured in 1939 with Ch. Raemon of Soham (in her lap) and Ch. Fritty—both Toy Group winners.

Above: Lineup of Yorkies bred by Miss Helen Palmer of Pittsfield, Vermont. *At left:* Dandy v. Enzian, bred in Germany, imported and owned by Miss Palmer.

Nicky, wh. 1940, bred by Milbarry Kennels, and Poquito, wh. 1937, bred by Sam Baxter. Both owned by Mrs. Ira Warner.

Mrs. L.E. Copeland of San Francisco purchased Lothian Lollipop from Mr. Rutherford in 1933. Mrs. Copeland started her breeding program in 1929 when she purchased Bobolink from Mrs. Beck. In 1932, Mrs. Copeland imported Sonny Boy of Sutler from Mrs. Lingwood's Cherry Orchard Kennels in England. Sonny Boy became a top stud and appears in many pedigrees of dogs from the late 1930s. In 1939 Mrs. Copeland transferred all the dogs to her daughter Irma, who continued breeding until the beginning of the 1950s. Irma Copeland bred the beautiful Ch. Frittlaria in 1942. He was a son of Ch. Fritty. Mrs. Copeland also owned Sweetheart Rose, a daughter of Ch. Raemon of Soham. Probably Miss Copeland's best known dog during the 1940s was Ch. Winsom Blue Binky, who was a top winner in the breed.

The Dongan Hills Kennels, owned by Mrs. Sarah Hazelet Averell of Staten Island, New York were active for twelve years from 1934 to 1946. Mrs. Averell's dogs were based on stock purchased from Sam Baxter and Helen Palmer.

Edna Apetz started her Wee Sweetie Kennels in Hollishead, New York in 1935 with the purchase of Pellon Wee Sweetie from Mrs. S.L. Martin, who had imported him from Mrs. A. Collins of England. Wee Sweetie's sire was Pellon Wedgewood Blue Select, a dog advertised by the Pellon Kennels as being "four pounds in weight, with outstanding color and ideally suited for all Pellon bitches." Mrs Apetz took her kennel name from this dog and occasionally used the Pellon name on dogs she bred which, as always, has led to confusion in ascertaining a dog's true bloodline. Her top stud was Little Man What Now, a son of the imported Prince Bobo of Soham. Mrs. Apetz bred until 1949.

Helen Palmer started her Vermont Kennels (located at Pittsfield, Vermont) when she returned from Germany with her sister Grace in about 1922. Miss Palmer brought two of her Yorkshires with her; both were bred in Germany based on English ancestry. These two dogs, Dandy V. Enzian, the male, and Maja V. York, were based on the Armley line and were the foundation of the Vermont line. Miss Palmer bred to Mr. Baxter and the Arthur Mills' stud dogs. She also purchased several bitches from Goldie Stone including Petite Busy Body, a half sister to Ch. Petit Magnificent Prince. Miss Palmer bred one champion, a male named Ch. Minute Man of Tewar Mawr, owned by Mrs. Davis of Indianapolis. Minute Man was by Flipper of Vermont and Dinny of Vermont; both were children of Bobbie B III. Miss Palmer continued active in the breed until 1960 when she passed away at the age of eighty-five.

Ch. Millbarry Sho-Sho winning Best in Show at the Progressive Toy Dog show, 1943, under judge Anton Rost, with breeder Mary Mills handling. Sho-Sho won the Toy Group at Westminster in 1944.

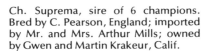

Ch. Miss Wynsum, Best Toy at Westminster 1938. Winner of 8 Toy Groups. Bred by Mrs. E. G. Cornish, England, and owned by Mary and Arthur Mills.

Ch. Suprema, sire of 6 champions. Bred by C. Pearson, England; imported by Mr. and Mrs. Arthur Mills; owned by Gwen and Martin Krakeur, Calif.

Mrs. Blanche Dunbar of Los Angeles started the Castlethorpe line in 1937 with the purchase of Seelum from Mrs. Beck, and several dogs from Mrs. Harmon which included Feathers of Castlethorpe, Martha Washington and Blue Bloomers. The last two dogs were litter sisters bred by Cora Donaldson and were bred on Mrs. Riddock's Olinda line. Mrs. Dunbar was the breeder of at least three champions—Ch. Bee's Dandy owned by Lew Collins; Ch. Spency of Castlethorpe and Ch. Claire's Wee Doll owned by the Charles Andersons. Mrs. Dunbar continued actively breeding until 1961, her last top dog being Rob Roy of Castlethorpe.

Mrs. Lily A. Harris of Yorba Linda, California purchased her first Yorkhire from Mrs. Denver Harmon in 1937. Tippet of Belvedere traced to the Olinda line on her dam's side. Her second foundation bitch, Petite of Belvedere, came from Taylor E. Walker of Barboursville, West Virginia. Mr. Taylor bred for three years, basing his dogs on Mrs. Stone's Petite line. In 1940 Mrs. Harris purchased Millbarry First Lady, a daughter of Ch. Suprema, from the Mills. First Lady became Mrs. Harris' first champion.

With the close of the Second World War, Mrs. Harris imported the beautiful stud dog Totis Cairnleigh Old Gold, bred by H. Harrison and exported by his owner, Wm. Hayes.

Mary and Arthur Mills started the Millbarry Kennel of Yorkshire Terriers in 1936. The kennel was first situated in Roseland, New Jersey, then moved to Devon, Pennsylvania, and later located in Radnor, Pennsylvania. Their original foundation dogs were from Mrs. Black of Columbus, Ohio. Cantie Spider and Cantie Jewel O'Dinty were two of these first dogs, and were the parents of Derry, born in April of 1937 and sold to Barbara Wolferman. Miss Wolferman was later to become a partner with Ann Seranne in the Mayfair Kennel.

In 1938, after a vacation in England, the Mills returned with three Yorkshires that were destined to play a major part in the history of the breed. These three dogs were to become the Am. Chs. Fritty, Miss Wynsum and Suprema. Ch. Miss Wynsum won her title in 1939 after having become the first Yorkshire to win the Toy Group at Westminister, which she did in 1938. This description was given of her: "Missy created a sensation when Mary Mills and she arrived in the Toy Group ring at Westminister with a small velvet covered box on which Missy was posed in order to show her exquisite length and color of coat." Miss Wynsum was bred by Mrs. E.G. Cornish of England and was by Sunny Boy out of Bronte Connie. During her show career she was the winner of eight Toy Groups.

Ch. Suprema was bred by C. Pearson of England, sired by Eng. Ch.

Supreme out of Little Bess. Suprema won two Toy Groups and several Group Placings and was a top stud siring six champions. These included the Mills' beautiful Ch. Millbarry Sho-Sho and Kay Finch's outstanding winner, Ch. Pretty Please. Ch. Suprema became the property of Gwen and Martin Krakeur in 1942, as did Suprema's son, Ch. Millbarry's Sho-Sho, in 1945. The Krakeurs were the owners of the Gwen-Mar Kennels in N. Hollywood, California, breeding from 1940 to 1947. The Gwen-Mar dogs were handled by Violet Boucher, a professional handler. (Miss Boucher judged the first sanction match of the Y.T.C.A. in 1952.) Millbarry Sho-Sho was the second Yorkshire to win the Toy Group at Westminister, which he did in 1944 while still owned by the Mills. After he became the property of the Krakeurs he continued winning during 1945 and 1946, amassing a record of twelve Toy Groups. Suprema sired a number of champions including Mrs. Finch's lovely Ch. Tidbit, who was a top winner in the early 1950s.

Ch. Fritty was bred by W. Butterworth and was sired by Broadlane Binkie out of Blue Bubbles. In 1939, Fritty was sold to the movie star Mary Carlisle and, after Miss Carlisle's marriage and subsequent move to South America, he became the property of Mrs. Rice. In all, Ch. Fritty won ten Toy Groups and many Group Placings. In 1954, Ch. Fritty was voted the club mascot of the present Y.T.C.A. and was used as the model for the club's official pin. Among his children were Mrs. Harris' Ch. Frittlaria and Mrs. Ethel Smith's Ch. Blue Knight, who was the winner of one Toy Group and several other Group Placings during 1941. Mrs. Smith lived in Philadelphia, and also owned two champion children of Ch. Suprema's. They were Ch. Millbarry's Blue Heather and Ch. Millbarry's Blue Minister. In 1941, Mrs. Smith puchased Ch. Olinda Pearl, but the start of the War brought her breeding to a close.

In 1950 the Mills imported their last top winner, the beautiful Ch. Gay Princess of Cayton, bred by E. Marshall, England. Her sire was Masterful Midget and her dam was Little Miss Thisteldown. "Jenny", as she was known, was the winner of several Toy Groups, but her career was cut short when she died from an overdose of anesthetic while undergoing minor surgery.

Ch. Millbarry Allegro was the granddam of Ch. Shareen Tee-See (owned and bred by Margaret Spilling), a top winner during 1969 and the early 1970s. The Mills continued exhibiting and breeding until about 1956. Mary Mills judged the Sweepstakes of the Yorkshire Terrier Club of America in 1969 at the Speciality held in New York City.

In all, the Millbarry Kennels owned or bred twelve champions.

Mrs. Goldie Stone in 1941 with Ch. Petit Sweet Boy and Ch. Petit Wee Gaffer.

A quartet of notable mid-century breeders:

Mrs. Fred Rice with handful of Best Brace winners.

Mrs. Paul L. Durgin with Ch. Durgin's Mickey, Ch. Durgin's Pilot and Ch. Durgin's Pansy.

Mrs. Stanley E. Ferguson with Can. & Am. Ch. Soham Bobbie, Ch. Tenderisle Fatimah.

Eng. Ch. Lord Ronald of Soham, foundation of the Soham "R" line.

Eng. Ch. Chilawee of Soham, foundation of the Soham "C" line.

Eng. Ch. Brian Boru of Soham, top stud dog and winner of the late 1930s.

Dewbarian Jerrie, sire of a number of American imports.

Yorkshire Terriers owned by Lady Edith Windham-Dawson's Soham Kennels (Ireland) in the late 1930s.

4

In Our Time

THE PERIOD from World War II to the present has seen the Yorkshire Terrier become "popular". The breed has risen from 96th place to 18th in popularity of AKC-registered breeds (19,233 registered in 1974), and is currently leading *all breeds* in the number being exported from England.

But Yorkshire fanciers should not make this an occasion to ring bells or wave flags. Rather, it should be a concern for them. Quality, not quantity, is what makes for furtherance of a breed.

The newer breeders owe an immeasurable debt to those who preserved the Yorkshire Terrier through the pestilence and difficulties of breeding and raising puppies under wartime conditions. To the men and women of Great Britain, who held the greatness of their breeding stock through the dark war years, go the thanks of present breeders. For with their faith that "There'll always be an England, and England shall be free as long as there's a cottage small beside a garden wall", they kept the continuation of the great southern lines in production. The northern lines were preserved by sending some to Scotland to the protection of the vastness of the Highlands.

In Ireland, where Lady Edith Windham-Dawson had removed to her estate near Dublin, the awful disaster of hardpad and the dreadful scourge of rat poison laid inroads into the magnificently bred and prepotent Yorkies that had come with her to safety in that country. The unbelieveable overcoming of this disaster was an inspiring example of true dedication. The bloodlines that existed in Ireland were combined with her remaining dogs to raise the breed to an elevation of dogs beautiful to look at, well balanced, and of such strength that they passed on their fundamental overall quality.

Left, Ch. Durgin's Pilot and Ch. Durgin's Pansy winning Best Brace in Show. *Right, closeup* of Ch. Durgin's Pilot. Owner, Mrs. Paul L. Durgin, St. Paul, Minn.

A Crown Crest trio. *Top left,* Ch. Forever Amber of Crown Crest, a 1946 champion granddaughter of Ch. Suprema, bred by Kay Finch and owned by Indie Rice. *Top right,* Ch. Pretty Please, bred and owned by Mrs. Finch. *Lower left,* Ch. Tidbit, bred by Ruby Bixler and owned by Mrs. Finch.

In America, too, the pre-war breeders kept their fine true breeding bloodlines going. Despite gas and meat rationing, they got dogs from the Atlantic Coast to the Pacific Coast, and up and down the far-flung prairies. The thin line of blue and gold, silky, glossy, proud little Yorkies joined the jubilation of V-J Day and their owners encouraged new breeders to join the line and swell the ranks.

Mrs. Paul L. Durgin started her kennel in St. Paul in 1940. Her first champion, Ch. Durgin's Mickey, was born that same year and was the son of Petit Lord Byngo's Double and Durgin's Gill Girl. Lord Byngo was from Mrs. Stone's breeding as was Gill Girl. Both were purchased by Mrs. Durgin from Mrs. C.M. Hill of Minneapolis, who bred from 1935 to 1944, breeding with stock from the Petit Kennels.

Ch. Durgin's Mickey was a top winner from 1942 through 1948 with wins that included 2 Toy Groups and 21 Group placings. He was Best of Breed at Westminster in 1945. Mickey sired four Champions including Cuban & Am. Ch. Durgin's Pilot, winner of 3 Toy Groups and a number of Group placings in the United States during 1950 and '51. Pilot sired four Champions including three Toy Group winners.

Other Group winners bred or owned by Mrs. Durgin were: Mrs. Townsend's Ch. Durgin's Lady Dorothy, Mrs. Trudgian's Ch. Durgin's Sensation, R. Quick's Ch. Bob's Beau Brummel, Mr. Lane's Ch. Durgin's Clear Crystal Gem, and her own Chs. Durgin's Jim Dandy and Durgin's Princess Lillibit.

Ch. Durgin's Pilot and his sister, Ch. Durgin's Pansy, won several awards for Best Brace in Show, their first such award being at the St. Paul show in 1949.

After World War II, Mrs. Durgin imported a number of dogs from Ireland, especially from Ross Buckley's Pretoria Kennels, whose line was based primarily on the Lotons' Clu-mor line.

In all, Mrs. Durgin has bred or owned 21 champions, and her dogs have sired or produced 30 more champions. Her imported Pretoria Allspice sired four champions.

Kay Finch is a well-known artist and sculptress, as well as a top breeder of Afghan Hounds and Yorkshire Terriers. Her Crown Crest Kennels in Corona Del Mar, Calif. began breeding Yorkies in 1941 when Yorkshire Puddin' and Peggee of Belvedere were purchased from Lily Harris' Belvedere Kennel. Peggee was a daughter of Lum of Dorn and Ch. Millbarry First Lady.

The Dorn line was bred by Jasper Daniels of Surrey, B.C., Canada. His Ch. Blue Boy of Dorn was a Group winner in the United States in 1940. Glamour Boy of Dorn sired Ethel Schrader's Ch. Oakcrest Request. Ethel (Leonard) Schrader was the owner of the Two Gate Kennels in Palo Alto, Calif. and owned Ch. Wee Willie of Crown Crest, who placed in several Groups in 1953.

In 1942, Mrs. Finch bred Peggee to her grandsire, Ch. Suprema, producing Chs. Petit Point and Pretty Please. The latter won 22 Bests of Breed and was never defeated in her sex.

With the advent of World War II, little breeding or exhibiting was done, but in 1948 Ch. Petit Point's son, Ch. Pixie Prince of Crown Crest, was born, sired by Charlotte's Sensation, a dog of Goldie Stone's Petit line. Prince was a top winner for Crown Crest, accounting for a Toy Group and 4 Group placings during 1950 and 1951.

In 1950, Mrs. Finch purchased Ch. Tidbit from his breeder, Mrs. J.O. Bixler, owner of the Acama Kennels, in North Hollywood, Calif. Mrs. Bixler started breeding in 1945, and has bred five champions. Her Ch. Acama Quite-a-Bit sired five champions. Ch. Tidbit was a son of the Krakeurs' Ch. Millbarry Sho-Sho and Millbarry Miss Prim, a daugher of Ch. Suprema. Tidbit finished his title at Westminster in 1951. At this show there were only 15 Yorkies entered but interestingly enough, although few in number, eight of these dogs were, or became, Toy Group winners.

Tidbit sired Nell and Kirill Fietinghoff's Ch. Tid-le-wink, as well as three other champions, all bred by Mrs. Bixler. In the ring Tidbit won a Toy Group and several Group placings in 1951.

Mrs. Finch has owned, or bred, nine Yorkshire Terrier champions. Her enthusiasm was the guiding hand in the formation of the present YTCA, and she was the club's first president serving from 1951 through 1954.

Mrs. Stanley E. Ferguson of Lake Geneva, Wisconsin registered her first Yorkshire in 1941 and, during the late 1940s and 1950s, her imports had a great effect on the breed.

Her first Yorkshires were purchased from Henry Shannon of Fox Grove, Ill. In 1945 Mrs. Ferguson purchased Minikin Dazzle, a son of Ch. Durgin's Mickey, from Myrtle Durgin. Dazzle came down on the train with Mrs. Durgin and was transferred in the train depot as Mrs. Durgin was on her way to the Westminster show in New York City. Dazzle sired Ch. Minikin Baby Blue, the first homebred champion for Mrs. Ferguson's Minikin Kennels. Baby Blue won her title in 1947.

In 1947 Mrs. Ferguson started importing top dogs from England and Ireland. Many of these dogs have set great show records and have, through their breeding records, left a lasting mark on the breed. Probably the most famous of these imports was the immortal Ch. Star Twilight of Clu-mor, who was imported from Ireland with his litter sister Ch. Clu-mor Nina in 1951. Star Twilight was sold to the authors' Wildweir Kennels in 1952 and went on to set the breed's show record in

Three of the outstanding Yorkies imported by Mrs. Stanley E. Ferguson's Mininkin Kennels. *Top left,* Ch. Holly of Achmonie, 1951 Group winner, owned by Mrs. Ferguson. *Top right,* Holly's littermate—Ch. Noella of Achmonie, top winning bitch of the mid-50s, owned by Mary E. Schaller, Calif. *Lower right,* Ch. Clu-Mor Nina, litter sister of Ch. Star Twilight of Clu-Mor and herself winner of 5 Toy Groups, owned by Mrs. Ferguson.

Obedience trained Yorkies owned by Pearl Kincarte Johnson, Calif.

Left, Haslingden Miss Bridget with her sons, Ch. Petit Wee Billy Boy Lao and Ch. Me Too Mommy. *At right,* Ch. Petit Wee Billy Boy. All owned by Ruby Erickson.

Ceramic designed and made by Kay Finch.

Left, Ch. Fantasy of Crown Crest, Group winner of the early 1950s, bred by Kay Finch and owned by Bette and Bud Trudgian. *Right,* Ch. Abon Hassan's Lady Iris, Canadian-bred, owned by Mr. and Mrs. Trudgian.

wins. Ch. Clu-mor Nina was the winner of 5 Toy Groups and a number of Group placings.

Ch. Victorian of Soham (Ch. Soham Victor ex Anna Mia of Soham), imported in 1947 from Lady Edith Windham's Soham Kennels in Ireland, was one of the finest Yorkshires we have seen.

In all, 40 Yorkshires were imported by Mrs. Ferguson. They included such top dogs as: Ch. Reiltin of Adelaide, bred by Mrs. Hunt, Ireland, and sire of 2 champions; Ch. Soham Dorothy, bred by the Misses Loton, winner of 1 Toy Group; Ch. Holly of Achmonie, bred by Mrs. McDonald, England, a Group winner in 1951; Ch. Noella of Achmonie (a sister to Holly, purchased from Minikin by Mary Schaller)—top winning bitch in the breed in 1954 and '55 with 11 Toy Groups. Holly and Noella's litter sister, Carol, also became an American champion. Ch. Flook of Achmonie, purchased by the authors in 1954, finished his title in three shows and sired Mrs. Nancy Donovan's Ch. Wildweir War Bonnet, a Group placer.

In 1955, Mrs. Ferguson imported five puppies from Lady Edith Windham. They were by Eng. & Irish Ch. Twinkle Star of Clu-mor out of Regene of Soham. Two became champions—Ch. Twinkle Toes of Soham, owned by Dora Galloway's Dunlookin Kennels in Glasford, Ill. and Ch. Blue Velvet of Soham, a Best in Show winner owned by our Wildweir Kennels.

Other top imports were Ch. Soham Pearl, purchased from Mrs. Ferguson by the Albion Kennels of Mr. and Mrs. E.J. Hornung; Eng. & Am. Ch. Blue Dolly and Ch. Buranthea's Petite Jewel, both owned by Wildweir; Ch. Rosencavalier of Soham, owned by Maxine Rigenberger, Rockford, Ill.; Ch. Siegelinde of Soham, Ch. Tenderisle Fatimah and Irish & Am. Ch. Bambino, all owned by Minikin.

Ch. Soham Bobbie (Rupert of Soham ex Ailis of Adelaide) bred by Mona Conlan of the Adelaide Kennels in Ireland, was the top winning Yorkshire in the United States in 1958. He was imported and owned by Mrs. Ferguson in 1956 and won 7 Toy Groups and sired a Champion.

Although Mrs. Ferguson has not been an active exhibitor since the late 1950s, she still maintains an interest in the breed.

Mrs. Pearl (Kincarte) Johnson founded her P.J. line in 1942 with dogs from Mabel Burneau Webb. Mrs. Webb owned the Burneau Yorkies in Santa Cruz, Calif. and bred from 1938 to 1948. The Burneau line was based on dogs of Mrs. W.A. Beck's breeding and on Nicholas Sharkey's Naughty line.

Mrs. Johnson's kennel was located in Del Rosa, Calif. Her best known dog was Ch. Hifalutin C.D., who was sired by Charlotte's Sensation, a dog of Goldie Stone's breeding bred by Charlotte V. Mauer, out of Gwen-Mar's Lady Allure. Hifalutin was a top stud dog produc-

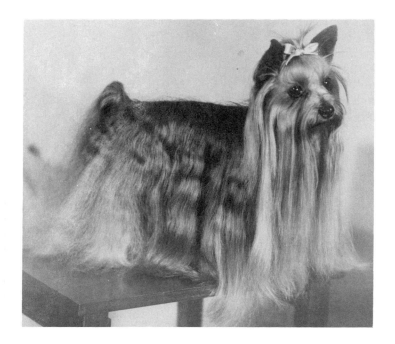

Above:
Ch. Little Sir Model, first Yorkshire Terrier to win Best in Show all-breeds in U.S. Breeder, Mrs. Allen (England). Owner, Wildweir Kennels.

At right:
Ch. Star Twilight of Clu-Mor, foremost winning Yorkshire Terrier of all time (26 BIS and 81 Toy Groups.) Pictured scoring BIS under judge Louis Murr. Bred by Maud and Florence Loton (Ireland) and owned by Wildweir Kennels.

ing five champions including Ch. P.J.'s Little Sweet William, a top winner during the early 1950s.

Mrs. LeMoyne Eastwood founded the Le Yorkies in 1942 when she purchased Bonny Blue Connie from Irma Copeland. Connie traced to the Shanon line and to the Ruth-Mar dogs of Charles Rutherford. Connie's Ch. Sugar n' Spice of Le was a top winning bitch of the 1950s.

Ruby Erickson started breeding Yorkies in Santa Rosa, California in 1945. Her first bitch was "Tootie," formally known as Haslingden Miss Bridget, who was bred by Mary Smith after her husband, Harry, had passed away. Miss Bridget was born in 1944, sired by Can. Ch. Haslingden Rags ex Haslingden Miss Winnie.

Miss Bridget was the dam of the first Yorkshire to win both a title in conformation and all her Obedience titles — Ch. Miss California of '48, C.D., C.D.X., U.D. — who unfortunately died in 1953 at the age of four years from distemper.

Miss California's sire, Mrs. Erickson's Ch. Petit Wee Billy Boy, sired three champions and was defeated only once as a champion, by his own son—Ch. Me Too Mommy. Ch. Billy Boy was born in 1944, bred by Mrs. Stone out of Petite Wee Tammy ex Ch. Petite Baby Snooks. He weighed 4½ lbs., was 8 inches at the shoulder, and his topknot was 16½ inches long, his mustaches 14½ inches, his beard 12½ inches and his sidecoat, 17½ inches long. These measurements were taken prior to his coat being trimmed for a show as it would, at this length, be too long for him to gait properly. Billy Boy's third champion child was Ch. Petit Wee Billy Boy Lao, Ch. Me Too Mommy's litter brother.

Mrs. Erickson also owned Ch. Petite Souvenir, bred by Betty Hagan, and Petit Sunny Boy, a litter brother to Can. Ch. Lord Byng of Walkley who was bred by Mrs. Stone.

Although Mrs. Erickson has not bred or exhibited for some years, she still maintains her interest in the breed.

In 1946, while visiting Crown Crest in search of an Afghan Hound, Bette and the late Theron Trudgian met their first Yorkie. Several months later, Fantasy of Crown Crest (Ch. Rose's Thom Thumb ex Peggee of Belvedere) joined the Trudg-Inn Kennels in Denver. Fantasy became a champion rapidly and went on to become the top winning bitch in the breed from 1950 through 1953, with wins that included a Toy Group and 4 Group placings.

In 1951 the Trudgians imported from Canada Am. Ch. Abon Hassan's Lady Iris. Iris was bred by Ron Thompson, owner of the Abon Hassan Kennels in Vancouver, B.C. Mr. Thompson's Yorkies include

Can. & Am. Ch. Kathleen Pride, top Canadian Yorkie in 1962, and Ch. Abon Hassan's Magic Star, the top Yorkie in Canada in 1960. He was the breeder of Ch. Abon Hassan Mister Jones, who was a Canadian Group winner in 1952 and the foundation stud of Ken Morgan's Tim-Clu line in Canada.

From 1955 to 1958 the Trudgians' Ch. Abon Hassan's Lady Iris won a total of 12 Toy Groups and many Group placings. She was by Ron Thompson's imported Can. Ch. Martywyn's Superior ex Lady Iris of Walkley, a bitch bred by Harry Draper of Canada.

The Trudgians won Toy Groups with Ch. Durgin's Little Sensation, and with their imported Ch. Sir Michael of Astolat, who was bred by Mrs. Charlton-Haw of England. In all, the Trudgians owned or bred 13 champions.

Mrs. Trudgian served as president of the YTCA in 1968.

Mrs. Stella Sally Myers of San Gabriel, California began showing and breeding in 1947. She was well-known for the high scoring work of her Yorkies, eight of whom won Obedience titles; five of these were also champions. Her first Ch. and C.D. winner was Ch. Myer's Baby Doll C.D. (Ch. Petit Wee Gaffer ex Rose's Miss Canada), bred by Mrs. Stone. Baby Doll was the dam of two champions including Ch. Myer's Sioux City Sue C.D., C.D.X. and of Myer's Blue Bunny II. Blue Bunny II was BOS and Best Puppy in Match at the 1st YTCA Sanction Match in 1952 in Los Angeles. Sue bred to Ch. Hifalutin produced Ch. Myer's Little Peanut C.D., who won his championship going Winners Dog at the first YTCA Specialty in 1954. Mrs Myers gave up breeding in the early 1960s following the death of her husband.

Mrs. Aileen (Rusco) Martello's Iney's Kennels are located in Lancaster, Calif. Mrs. Martello has been, for many years, the columnist for the breed in *Dog World* magazine and is the author of *The Yorkshire Terrier,* published in 1971 by Exposition Press, Inc. She served as President of the YTCA in 1964, 1965 and 1966.

Mrs. Martello began her breeding in 1948 when Olinda Deane (Olinda Chief ex Olinda Maud), bred by Mrs. Riddock and purchased in 1946, whelped the first Iney's litter. Four titles have been won by dogs carrying the Iney prefix.

Mrs. Mildred Townsend of Prairie Village, Kansas started the Clonmel Yorkies in 1950. Her best known dogs were Ch. Durgin's Lady Dorothy and Ch. Durgin's Dandy Mite. Lady Dorothy won 3 Toy Groups as well as a number of Group placings during 1951 and '52. Dandy Mite was seriously injured in an auto accident, but after extensive care he recovered to finish his title.

Ch. Blue Velvet of Soham, BIS winner. Bred by Lady Windham-Dawson (Ireland) and owned by Wildweir Kennels.

Eng. & Am. Ch. Buranthea's Doutelle, winner of 4 BIS. Bred by Marie Burfield (England) and owned by Wildweir Kennels.

Am. & Ir. Ch. Proud Girl of Clu-Mor, first Yorkie bitch to win an all-breed BIS. Bred by Maud Loton (Ireland) and owned by Wildweir Kennels.

Ch. Trixie of Kansas (Eng. Ch. Blue Symon ex Bright Sunshine), imported in 1956, was bred by Mrs. W. Wilkerson, Eng. Trixie was a Group winner in 1957, and won BOS at the 1958 YTCA Specialty.

Mrs. Townsend served as President of the YTCA in 1955, '56 and '57.

Which brings us to the Wildweir Kennels of Glenview, Illinois, owned by the authors. While aiming to include everything pertinent, we have tried to keep our accounting in accord with that of our stories of other kennels. We hope we have been successful in this balance.

The Wildweir line has been developed primarily on a base of the crossing of the Harringay, Clu-Mor and Soham lines, all of which trace to the Pellon dogs who were based on Ch. Ted, through his sons Ch. Bradford Ben, Halifax Marvel and Royal Ted. In addition, dogs tracing to Eng. Chs. Lilyhill Supreme and Delite of Invincia through Ch. Mr. Pim of Johnstounburn and Ch. Vemair Principal Boy (half brothers sired by Parkview Prince) and dogs tracing to Eng. Ch. Tinker of Glendinan through Paddy of Glendinan and Don Progress have been bred in, but always with care that half of the pedigree contained the blood of the first three lines mentioned. The Invincia and Glendinan lines traced to Armley, which goes to Ch. Ted through Halifax Marvel, Hunslet Ted and Halifax Ben, Ch. Aston Duke's full brother.

Ch. Little Sir Model, our first top winner, was imported in 1950. He was bred by Mrs. M. Smart and was by Eng. Ch. Ben's Blue Pride, who was the first Yorkie to win his English title after World War II. Pride was a son of Mr. B.A. Williamson's Blue Flash and traced to Pellon Golden David. Jill, Pride's dam, was sired by Ch. Harringay Remarkable, a son of Ch. Mendam Prince. Ch. Harringay Remarkable was the sire of Am. Ch. Alexandrie of Soham, owned by Mrs. Charles F. Dowe of Chestnut Hill, Mass. Alexandrie won 2 Toy Groups and 18 Group placings from 1939 to 1943. Remarkable was also sire of Promise of Harringay, the hero of the "Tapiola" stories.

Ch. Little Sir Model's dam, Allenby Queen, was a granddaughter of Ch. Harringay Remarkable. We purchased Model from Ben Williamson, who also owned Ch. Ben's Blue Pride. Mr. Williamson never owned a female; as a matter of fact, he wouldn't even have one in the house, but bred all the visiting bitches in a small rose arbor. He had a great eye for a dog and always picked a top one from the litters resulting from his stud dogs.

Model sired the Group winner Ch. Pride of Leyton, who was owned by Catherine Miller's Kasam Kennels in N. Olmsted, Ohio. Bred to Iola (Suhr) Dowd's Gayway's Tim's Mite, Model sired two top producing bitches, Mrs. Dowd's Patoot's Abigail, and our first top producing brood bitch, Cover Girl, dam of five champions. These included Ch.

Ch. Wildweir Fair N' Square, winner of 3 BIS and sire of 17 champions. Bred and owned by Wildweir Kennels.

Am. & Ir. Ch. Continuation of Gleno, winner of 5 BIS. Bred by Eugene Weir (Ireland) and owned by Wildweir Kennels.

Ch. Wildweir Moon Rose, winner of 3 BIS. Bred and owned by Wildweir Kennels.

Ch. Wildweir Contrail, a Continuation daughter, winner of 3 BIS. Bred and owned by Wildweir Kennels.

Ch. Wildweir Pomp N' Circumstance, all-time top sire of the breed with 95 champions. Homebred of Wildweir Kennels.

Left: Ch. All-Star of Wildweir, first American-bred to win the Yorkshire Terrier Club of America Specialty (1959.) Bred and owned by Wildweir Kennels. Below: Ch. Royal Picador, Group and Specialty winner. Bred by Mrs. Beatrice Kelly (Ireland) and owned by Wildweir Kennels.

Wildweir Shining Star and Ch. Star Dusk of Wildweir (BOW at the 1958 YTCA Specialty at Chicago).

Model was the first Yorkshire Terrier to be credited with winning an all-breed Best in Show. In all, he won 4 Bests in Show, 31 Toy Groups, 24 Group placings and 63 Bests of Breed.

Ch. Golden Fame was also imported from Mr. Williamson, his sire being his Blue Coat Danny. Fame's breeder was Mrs. D. Shave. Danny's sire was a grandson of Martywyn Kennels' Little Blue Boy and of Monarch of Harringay. His dam, Maureen Gay Girl, was a daughter of Eng. Ch. Ben's Blue Pride. Golden Fame won the 1st Sanction Match of the YTCA in 1952 at Los Angeles, as well as 2 Group placings. His best known offspring was Eng. Ch. Blue Symon, who was bred by Miss Armstrong and owned by Mrs. John. Golden Fame, through his children Ch. Blue Symon, Bea's Finale and Wildweir Periwinkle, is found in the background of more American Best in Show winners than any other dog. These include: Windamere Kennels' Ch. Progress of Progresso; Mayfair Kennels' Ch. Gaytonglen Teddy of Mayfair, and Ch. Mayfair's Barban Loup de Mer; the Lanards' Ch. Mayfair Barban Yam n' Yelly; Shareen Kennels' Ch. Shareen Mr. Tee See; the Mansfields' Ch. Heart G's Spunky Sparky; Frances Cohen's Ch. Wildweir Sandwich Man; the Merrill Cohens' Ch. Wildweir Prim n' Proper; the Richard Sakals' Ch. Camelot's Little Pixie; Betty Conaty's Ch. Wenscoe's Why-not of Shaumar and Victor Recondo and Jerry Vine's Ch. Trivar's Princess Jervic.

Our Eng. & Am. Ch. Sorreldene Honeyson of the Vale was bred by Mrs. E. Sharp, and imported from Mrs. G.M. Bradley of the Sorreldene Kennels in England. He was a full brother to Blue Coat Danny, being by Harringay Little Dandy ex Pretty Paulette.

Honeyson was the grandsire of our Ch. Sorreldene Orange Boy (Sorreldene Toffee Apple ex Gaytime). Orange Boy was bred by Mrs. E. Boam and purchased from Sorreldene Kennels. He was WD at the 1956 Specialty and won a Toy Group and 4 Group placings. He sired three champions and was the grandsire of Ch. Wildweir Falderol, a Pomp n' Circumstance daughter, who was WB at the 1964 Specialty. Orange Boy's litter brother, our Ch. Sorreldene Tangerine, was a Group placer.

Sorreldene Toffee Apple, who was a grandson of Australian Ch. Blue Lad of the Vale, a Ch. Ben's Blue Pride son, also sired our Ch. Gloamin Christmas Cracker. Cracker was bred by Mrs. N. Wilkinson, owner of the Gloamin Kennels in England. His dam, Gay Susan of Gloamin, was a daughter of Eng. Ch. Stirkean's Chota Sahib. Cracker won 3 Bests in Show, 11 Toy Groups and was Best of Breed at the 1960 Specialty.

Ch. Sorreldene Saffron (Wee Dinks ex Pension) was bred by Mrs.

Boam and imported by us from Mrs. Bradley. Saffron was the dam of a champion, and of Melba Green's Wildweir Queen of the Stars, who won 2 Toy Groups, the first Yorkshire to do so in Alaska.

Eng. & Am. Ch. Blue Dolly, bred by A.H. Coates, England, was the first bitch to win a Toy Group for Wildweir. She was by Eng. Ch. Ben's Blue Pride ex Little Marionette. She was the winner of a Toy Group and 3 Group placings. Eng. & Am. Ch. Martywyn's Wee Mischief, bred by F. Hall, was also imported from Mr. Coates and won a Toy Group and 4 Group placings.

Ch. Star Twilight of Clu-mor was purchased from Ethel Ferguson in 1951. His sire was Eng. & Ir. Ch. Twinkle Star of Clu-mor, a great-grandson of Master Pellon of Clu-mor, out of My Pretty Maid, a litter sister to Ir. Ch. Wee Benjamin. Pretty Maid was a daughter of Ch. Little Willie Winkie and a granddaughter of Harringay Wee Lassie.

Star Twilight set, and holds, the record for the breed, having won 26 Bests in Show, 81 Toy Groups, 22 Group placings and 104 Bests of Breed. He was Best of Breed at four YTCA Specialties, winning in 1954, '55, '56 and (from the Veterans class) in 1958. He won the Toy Group at Westminster in 1954 and 1955, placing 2nd in the Group in 1956. He sired 15 champions including two Toy Group winners, Ch. Wildweir Shining Star and Wildweir Queen of the Stars. His son Ch. Wildweir Lickety Split sired three champions, and was the sire of Wildweir Dilly Dally, dam of four champions including Kay Radcliffe's Am., Mex., Bda. & Can. Ch. Wildweir Ten O'Clock Scholar, sire of 20 champions.

Other Star Twilight children include: Ch. Twinkle Star of Wildweir, who was BOW at the 1959 Specialty at Santa Monica; My Pretty Maid of Wildweir, dam of two champions including BIS winner, Ch. Wildweir Sandwich Man; Ch. Star Dusk of Wildweir, WD at the 1958 Specialty. Wildweir Forever Amber, dam of Ch. Wildweir Ticket to the Moon, who was WB and BOS at the 1961 Specialty. Ticket's four champion children included Betty Hall's Ch. Wildweir Ribbon of Moonlight and our Ch. Wildweir Brass Hat, sire of nine champions. Ticket's litter sister was Wildweir Time and Tide, the dam of nine champions including the Merrill Cohen's BIS winner Ch. Wildweir Prim n' Proper and Ch. Wildweir Admiral of the Blue, who was BOW at the 1968 YTCA Specialty.

Ch. Prince Moon of Clu-mor (Irish Ch. Clu-mor Wayward Roy ex-Vivacious Suzette), bred by the Misses Loton, Ireland, was the sire of Ticket, Time and Tide, and of Ch. Wildweir Moonrose, who was the winner of 3 BIS, 26 toy Groups, and the 1964 and 1965 YTCA Specialties. Moonrose was the dam of Nancy Donovan's Group winner, Ch. Wildweir Belle of the Ball. Moonrose's dam was our imported Ch. Rose Petal of Clu-mor, a Group placer, as was Ch. Prince Moon.

Ch. Patoot's Maryetta, bred and owned by Iola Suhr Dowd, Calif.

Ch. Ru Gene's King Corkyson, Group and Specialty winner, owned by Ruth and Gene Fields, Calif.

Ch. Little Sir Chuck of Ramon, bred and owned by Stella and Swede Davis, Calif.

Ch. Valleyend Wistful, owned by Flora Dunn.

Ch. Green's Chipsal Blu Twink, bred by Melba Green and owned by Muriel Krieg, Calif.

Ch. Fran-Dell's Yes Sir, bred and owned by Francis E. Davis, Calif.

Am & Cuban Ch. Drax Little Craftsman, only Yorkie known to have won a Toy Group in Cuba. Breeder-owner, Mrs. Felix Drake, Florida.

Ch. Pearl of Soham, Ch. Timothy Puff of Albion (as a puppy) and Ch. Little Tim of Nottingham, all owned by Alice Hornung, Calif.

Ch. Wildweir Cock of the Walk, a Star Twilight son, produced five champions, the two best known being Ch. All-Star of Wildweir, the first American-bred Yorkshire to win a YTCA Specialty (1959 at Santa Monica, Calif.) and Ch. Wildweir Pomp n' Circumstance, sire of 95 champions.

Ch. Blue Velvet of Soham, imported by Mrs. E. Ferguson in 1954, was purchased by us as a 4-month-old puppy. He was a half-brother to Star Twilight, being by the same sire, Eng. Ir. Ch. Twinkle Star of Clu-mor ex Regine of Soham. He was bred by Lady Edith Windham Dawson of the Soham Kennels in Ireland. Regine was a daughter of Ir. Ch. Prince Igor of Soham and a granddaughter of Eng. Ch. Soham Victor. Blue Velvet won 1 BIS, 17 Toy Groups, 30 Group placings and 50 Bests of Breed, and was sire of a champion. His granddaughter, the Berry's Wildweir Forget-Me-Not, is the dam of 4 champions including our Ch. Doodletown Counterpoint, winner of 9 Toy Groups. Blue Velvet's daughter, our Wildweir Whimsey, produced 3 champions: Ch. Wildweir Fare thee Well, Ch. Wildweir Face Card (a Ch. Wildweir Fair n' Square daughter who was BOB in 1968, and BOS in 1969 at YTCA Specialties, and winner of 2 Group placings), and Ch. Wildweir Contrail, a daughter of Irish & Am. Ch. Continuation of Gleno. Contrail won 3 BIS, 13 Toy Groups, 26 Group placings, 47 BOBs and was Best of Breed at the 1973 Specialty of the YTC of Greater St. Louis, as well as BOS at the 1973 YTCA Specialty at New York.

Ch. Starial of Clu-mor (Irish Ch. Clu-mor Wayward Roy ex Vivacious Suzette), bred by Maud and Florence Loton, was imported in 1958. Suzette was also the dam of our imported Ch. The Duchess of Clu-mor, who was Winners and Best of Opposite Sex at the 1959 YTCA Specialty. Starial placed in 3 Groups and sired 3 champions. Ch. Rose Petal of Clu-mor, a Starial daughter, was sired and whelped in Ireland, and joined her sire at Wildweir in 1960. She was Winners and Best of Opposite Sex at the 1960 YTCA Specialty and placed in 2 Toy Groups. She was the dam of three champions, each of which was a Best in Show winner. They were Ch. Wildweir Moonrose, Ch. Wildweir Fair n' Square, and Columbian Ch. Wildweir Paper Dragon, winner of 2 BIS in that country.

Am. & Irish Ch. Proud Girl of Clu-mor was imported by us in 1963 from her owner Eugene Weir, of the Gleno Kennels in N. Ireland. She was bred by the Misses Loton and is by Herbert of Clu-mor out of Clu-mor Queen of Hearts, a full sister of Ch. Star Twilight. With her win of Best in Show in 1963, she became the first female Yorkshire to win this award. In all, she won 22 Toy Groups, 19 Group placings and 49 Bests of Breed.

Eng. & Am. Ch. Buranthea's Doutelle was imported in 1959 from his breeder, Mrs. Marie Burfield, of the Buranthea Yorkshires in England.

111

Doutelle was sired by Eng. & Irish Ch. Mr. Pim of Johnstounburn and his dam was Buranthea's York Sensation, a granddaughter of Ch. Ben's Blue Pride, and a great-granddaughter of Irish Ch. Clu-mor Wild Boy and Clu-mor Peggy. Mr. Pim traced to Ch. Tinker of Glendinan, Ch. Delite of Invincia and Ch. Lilyhill Supreme. Doutelle was a Best in Show winner in England, and in the United States his record was 4 Bests in Show, 24 Toy Groups, 37 Group placings, 71 Bests of Breed, and he won the 1961 and 1962 YTCA Specialties. He was the sire of the Fietinghoffs' Ch. Wildweir Coat of Arms, sire of ten champions and our Wildweir Fairytale, dam of three champions. In all, Doutelle sired ten champions.

Ch. Yorkford Chocolate Boy, imported in 1962 from his breeder Mrs. Daphne Rossiter, England, was sired by Doutelle's litter brother Buranthea's Aristocrat Pim of Johnstounburn; his dam was Gold Dinky of Arcady. Chocolate won 1 Best in Show, 3 Toy Groups, 15 Group placings, 21 Bests of Breed, and was Best of Winners at the 1962 YTCA Specialty. He sired two champions and his daughter, Mrs. Neuguth's Wildweir Hot Fudge, produced four champions.

Ch. Royal Picador and Ch. Lovely Milanda were imported in 1965 from their breeder, Mrs. Beatrice Kelly of Ireland. Their sire was Palermo, an Irish Ch. Toy-pride Topoleno son and a grandson of Ch. Mr. Pim of Johnstounburn. Their dam Vanity Fair, a daughter of Irish Ch. Mr. Bootsie, was a granddaughter of Herbert of Clu-mor. Picador won 14 Toy Groups, 16 Group placings, 34 Bests of Breed and the 1967 YTCA Specialty. He was the sire of two champions including the Merrill Cohens' homebred Specialty winner, Ch. Wildweir Briefcase. Milanda was the dam of two champions.

Irish & Am. Ch. Continuation of Gleno was imported in 1968 from his breeder Eugene Weir, Ireland. Continuation was sired by Eng., Irish & Jap. Ch. Wedgewood's Starmist, a grandson of Ch. Clu-mor Wayward Roy and Herbert of Clu-mor. His dam, Joybelle of Gleno, was also a grandchild of Ch. Clu-mor Wayward Roy. He won a number of BIS in Ireland, as well as winning Best of Breed at Yorkshire Terrier Specialties in Ireland and North Ireland. In the United States, he won 5 BIS, 28 Toy Groups, 37 Group placings and 74 BOB. He was BOW and BOB at the 1969 YTCA Specialty, and again BOB at the 1970 Specialty. Continuation sired the Best in Show winner, Ch. Wildweir Contrail.

Other Wildweir Group winners have been Irish & Am. Ch. Wedgewood's Frivolity (Wedgewood Thady ex Wedgewood Imperial Lady), winner of 4 Toy Groups, bred by Katherine Morris, Ireland; Ch. Coulgorm Gay Lady (Tinkers Cuss ex Coulgorm Baby Bunty), winner of 2 Toy Groups, bred by Mr. A. Hughes, Eng.; Ch. Lyndoney Kindrum Valentine (Bonnie Wee Willie ex Lyndoney Annabelle), winner of a

112

Ch. Tid-le-Wink, bred and owned by Nell and Kirill Fietinghoff, Calif.

Ch. Kirnel's Yum Yum, bred and owned by Nell and Kirill Fietinghoff.

Ch. Wildweir Coat of Arms, sire of 10 champions. Bred by Wildweir Kennels, and owned by Mr. and Mrs. Fietinghoff.

Kelpie's Belziehill Dondi, sire of 16 champions. Bred and owned by Mrs. George E. Hornbrook, Ithaca, N.Y.

Eng. Can. & Am. Ch. Progress of Progresso, Best in Show winner and sire of 14 champions. Bred by Mrs. Connie Hutchins (England) and owned by Br. Priser and J. Nickerson, Windamere Kennels, Muncie, Ind.

Ch. Pequa Mustang, Best in Show winner. Bred by Myrtle Young, and owned by her in partnership with Joe Glaser.

Toy group, bred by Alan Burrell and imported from her owner, Mrs. D. Johnson.

Kelsbro Blue Tan Jenny Wren (Kelsbro Quicksilver ex Kelsbro Wee Bunty), bred by Mrs. Platt and imported from Mrs. H. Cross, Eng., was WB and BOS at the first YTCA Specialty in 1954.

Of all the dogs owned or bred by Wildweir, the one that has had the most influence on the breed in the United States, without question, has been Ch. Star Twilight's double-grandson, Ch. Wildweir Pomp n' Circumstance. "Pompey" was born in 1959, a son of Ch. Wildweir Cock of the Walk and Capri Venus (a Star Twilight daughter and a granddaughter of Eng. Ch. Ben's Blue Pride). Pompey won his final points by winning Best of Winners at the 1960 YTCA Specialty at Chicago when 11 months old. His first champion was Ch. Wildweir Pomp n' Pageantry, whose dam, Starlite of Soham, was a litter sister to Ch. Blue Velvet of Soham. In all, Pompey sired 95 champions and twice tied for honor as the Top Stud Dog, all breeds—in 1965 and 1966.

His offspring include 3 BIS winners, and 13 Toy Group winners. Six of his sons have produced 10 or more champions. Am., Can., & Mex. Ch. Wildweir Keepsake has sired 28 champions; Am., Can., Mex. & Bda. Ch. Wildweir Ten O'Clock Scholar has sired 20 champions.

Ch. Wildweir Fair n' Square, a Pompey son, has sired 16 champions and won 3 Bests in Show, 25 Toy Groups, 37 Group placings, 69 Bests of Breed and was Best of Breed at the 1967 and 1968 YTCA Specialties. His champion children include the Specialty winner, Ch. Wildweir Facecard; Ch. Wildweir Fair Victor, who won the Sweepstakes and BOW at the 1970 Specialty; Mrs. Ruth Cooper's Ch. Cottleston Culprit, winner of the 1967 YTCA. Sweepstakes at Chicago, and Carol Fencl's Am., Can. & Bda. Ch. Kajo's Wendy on the Go, winner of BOS at the 1970 Specialty.

In all, Wildweir has bred or owned 169 champions.

The Patoot Kennels had their start in St. Paul, Minnesota in 1950, but were later moved to El Monte, Calif. They are owned by Iola (Suhr) Dowd. The first Yorkie owned by Mrs. Dowd was Oakcrest Tiny Trinket, bred by Agnes Wilkie and Ken Rickman, owners of the Oakcrest line in Victoria, B.C. Canada. The Oakcrest line was active in Canada in the 1940s and early 1950s. The top dog of this kennel was Can. & Am. Ch. Oakcrest's Queen Blue, a Group winner in the United States in 1953. The Oakcrest line traced to the Haslingden bloodline.

Mrs. Dowd owned Irish & Am. Ch. Peter of Nordlaw, imported from Ireland in 1953 from Irene O'Neil's Nordlaw Kennels. Peter was by Little Comet of Clu-mor ex Little Defiance and he was the winner of a Toy Group in 1955. He sired two champions, one of whom was Patoot Kennel's top winner, Ch. Patoot's Maryetta. She was the winner of 4 Toy Groups, 18 Group placings and 35 Best of Breeds. Her litter brother, Patoot's Jonathon, was owned by Mr. and Mrs. Allen Davis, and sired 7 champions for Ramon Kennels.

Mrs. Dowd's first champion was Ch. Little Sir Echo of Yorktown, who won his title in 1952. Sir Echo was by Can. Ch. Yorktown Blue Moon out of Rose's Miss Vancouver. He was bred by Violet Dalton, owner of the Yorktown Kennels in Clarkton, Ont. Yorktown was established in the late 1930s and her dogs traced to the Canadian lines of Galtonian, Walkley and to J.H. Kenyon's English import Can. Ch. Monsieur. Yorktown's top dogs were Can. Ch. Yorktown Prince Romeo, Can. Ch. Yorktown Blue Moon and Mrs. R. Bedford's Am. & Can. Ch. Yorktown Little Blue Prince. (Mrs. Bedford lived in Union, N.J.) Prince placed in several Groups in 1946 and was a Group winner in 1948.

Both Ch. Kelsbro Half Sovereign and Ch. Kelsbro Blue Tippet, who were imported from Mrs. H. Cross, England, won Toy Groups. Mrs. Dowd was the breeder of Mrs. Bender's Patoot's Winsome Willie, who was a Group winner in 1959.

The Ramon Kennels of Stella and Allen Davis, Jr. were started in 1950 in Palm Springs, Calif. They were the owners or breeders of 11 champions.

Crown Crest Tinker Toy, purchased from Kay Finch, was the sire of Ch. Chelsea of Ramon, who was sold to Anita and Paul Grove. Chelsea was the sire of the Davis' Ch. Sheba of Ramon, dam of the top winners Ch. Little Sir Chuck of Ramon, Ch. Little Sir Hermie of Ramon, and Ch. Little Sir Hughie of Ramon. All three were sired by Patoot's Jonathon, who Mr. and Mrs. Davis purchased from Mrs. Dowd in 1957.

Ch. Little Sir Chuck nearly died from a snake bite in 1962, but in 1963 he won the Toy Group at Las Vegas. He was the winner of the 1966 YTCA Specialty at Beverly Hills, Calif., 3 Toy Groups, 8 Group placings and 18 Bests of Breed. Sir Hermie was Best of Opposite Sex at the 1963 YTCA Specialty at Long Beach, Calif. and won 3 Group placings. Sir Hughie sired Louise Jeremy's Ch. Jeremy's Little Mr. Dynamite, and he is the grandsire of Arlene Appell's Am. & Can. Ch. Yot Club Jiminey Cricket, (Yot Club's Tiny Limey ex Yot Club's Sweet Pie) bred by Ken McGuire. Jiminey was the winner of 9 Toy Groups and a number of Group placings during 1970, '71 and '72.

In 1955 Star Prince of Wildweir was purchased. A son of Ch. Star Twilight of Clu-mor ex Eng. & Am. Ch. Jessica of Westridge, Star Prince was the sire of two champions. His daughters, Starbright's Little Lady and Starbright's Gem of Tabitha, were the foundation broods of Carmen Greenamyer's Starbright Kennels in Running Springs, Cal-

Am. & Can. Ch. Caprice of Pagham and his two daughters, Ch. Pequa Minute Maid and Ch. Pequa Summer Smoke. Owner, Myrtle Young.

Am. & Can. Ch. Clarkwyn Jubilee Eagle, Toy Group and Canadian Specialty winner. Bred by Ila Clark, and owned by Ruth Jenkins, Issaquah, Wash.

Am. & Can. Ch. Toy Clown of Rusklyn, winner of 10 Toy Groups. Bred by L. W. Tong (England) and owned by Ila Clark, Wash.

Am. & Can. Ch. Yorkfold Jackanapes, Group winner. Bred by Mrs. D. Rossiter (England) and owned by Lynne Devan, Michigan.

Ch. Windamere Beau Jangles, bred by B. Priser and J. Nickerson, and owned by Mr. Nickerson.

Ch. Lamsgrove Pinnochio winning Best in Show at Manitowoc, Wis. under judge Edward Klein. Handler, Norm Patton. Owner, Pearl Trojan.

if. Mrs. Greenamyer owns Ch. Starbright Son of Keepsake and Can. Ch. Starbright Jack in the Box and is the breeder of Mrs. Goldman's Ch. Starfire Gold Bangle.

Patoot Jonathon's daughter, Ch. Lily of Ramon, was owned by Mr. and Mrs. George Hermel, owners of the Nomar Yorkies in Palm Springs, Calif. Lily won 2 Toy Groups and several Group placings. Her last Group was won at 9 years of age, and for her final appearance she wore a diamond solitaire in place of the usual bow.

Ruth and Gene Field's Rugene Kennels were started in 1951 when they obtained Field's King Corky and Myer's Blue Bunny. Since then, 13 champions have been bred or owned by Rugene.

Their first homebred show dog was Field's Silver Tinker Belle (Ch. Myer's Little Peanut ex Myer's Blue Bunny). Tinker Bell's son was their first Champion; he was by Ch. Rugene's Toy Tiger, a son of Ramon Kennels' Patoot's Jonathon. Toy Tiger bred to Rachel Gowing's Ch. Lady Godiva of Wildweir sired two champions for the Don Deigo Kennels.

Ch. Rugene's King Corky, a son of Patoot's Jonathon out of Rugene's Princess Ramona, was the top winning dog on the West Coast from 1966 to 1969. He was the winner of 2 Toy Groups and 11 Group placings. King Corky sired 7 champions.

His son, Ch. Rugene's King Corkyson out of Peggy O'Neil of Albion, was bred by Patricia L. Sonderman. Corkyson has been a top winner and was the No. 2 Yorkie in the breed in 1969. He has won 5 Toy Groups, 17 Group placings, 32 Best of Breeds and was the winner of the 1969 YTCA Specialty. To date, he has sired two champions, including the Field's 1973 Group placer Ch. Rugene's Mr. Lucky II.

Two of King Corky's daughters have won Winners' Bitch at YTCA Specialties; in 1964, Ch. Rugene's Black Eyed Susan won at Long Beach, California and, in 1969, Ch. Rugene's Zig-Field's Girl won at New York City.

Mrs. Fields served as club president in 1961, '62 and '63.

Mrs. Muriel Kreig has been a breeder since 1952. Her Goldenblue Kennel is located in Anaheim, Calif. She started in Obedience with Ginger Lei who was bred by Stella Myers out of Pride of Oakstone and Oakcrest My Sapphire. Ginger won her C.D in 3 straight shows and was highest scoring dog in the Obedience classes at the first YTCA Specialty at Beverly-Riviera Kennel Club. Ginger, with her homebred daughter Ch. Kathy Dorn, won Best Brace in Show at the 1957 Beverly-Riviera show. Kathy was sired by Patoot Kennels' Ch. Kelsbro Half Sovereign.

In 1962, Mrs. Kreig's Green's Chipsal BluTwink (later Champion) won Best of Breed from the Puppy Class at the YTCA Specialty in San Francisco. Twink was only eight months old and is the youngest Specialty winner. He was bred by Melba Green out of her imported Yorkfold Chipmunk. Twink's dam was Green's Pioneer Girl of Alaska, the first Yorkie to be born in Alaska.

Mrs. Kreig served as President of the YTCA in 1958.

Mrs. Felix Drake's Drax Kennels are located in Hialeah, Florida and were started in 1952. Drax is the home of the only Yorkie we know of to win a Toy Group in Cuba, Am. & Cuban Ch. Drax Little Craftsman (in 1962). Craftsman's sire traced to Ch. Little Jetsom, Can. Ch. Petit Swanky Boy and Shannon's dogs. His dam was the daughter of Ch. Peter of Nordlaw. Craftsman sired two champions; Mrs. Drake has owned or bred six champions.

Mrs. Charles Anderson of Cupestino, Calif. was the owner of Ch. Mr. E.J. of Belvedere, bred by Lily Harris. E.J. was a Group winner in 1952 and won several Group placings.

Frances E. Davis' Fran-Dell Kennels were started in 1953 when Mrs. Davis purchased a puppy from Mrs. Myers. The puppy grew up to become Ch. Myers' Prince Mike C.D. The Fran-Dell Kennels were located in El Monte, Calif.

Mrs. Maxine Mitchell owned the Lavenir Kennels in Los Angeles. Her Ch. Fran-Dell's Yes Sir won 12 Best of Breeds and 4 Group placings.

The Marlee Kennels of Mary and Lee Schaller were started in LaMesa, Calif. in 1953 with Crown Crest Jim Dandy, a son of Ch. Tidbit. They purchased Ch. Noella of Achmonie in 1953 and won 11 Toy Groups, 17 Group placings and 32 Bests of Breed.

Mrs. Madeline Hoffman of New York City in 1953 imported (from Madame Chardon, owner of the Assam Yorkshires in Paris) Fr., Belg., Lux., & Am. Ch. W'Monarch of Assam (V' Mr. Pepys of Assam ex Gold Bud of Assam). Monarch was Best in Match at the third YTCA Sanction Match in 1953 and was a Group winner in 1954.

Ch. Valleyend Wistful (Hugh of Pagham ex Valleyend Petula), owned and imported by Flora Dunn of Scotia, N.Y. from Miss L.M. Phillip's Valleyend Kennel in England, was the winner of 1 Toy Group and 3 Group placings during 1955 and 1956. Mrs. Dunn also imported Ch. Valleyend Will O' The Wisp, who was sold to Margaret Pond and placed in several Groups in 1957.

120

Ch. Yorkfold Gold Choice, bred by Mrs. D. Rossiter (England) and owned by Lynne Devan, Michigan.

Littermates, Am. Ch. Devanvale Jasmine and Am. & Jap. Ch. Devanvale Sonny Jack, bred by Lynne Devan, Mich.

Ch. Trivar's Gold Digger, a repeat Best in Show winner. Gold Digger, a daughter of Ch. Trivar's Tycoon, was bred and is owned by Johnny A. Robinson, Jr. and Morris Howard, Trivar Yorkshires, Maryland.

Am. & Can. Ch. Trivar's Tycoon, winner of 31 Toy Groups and a Canadian BIS, and the sire of 16 champions including BIS winner Ch. Trivar's Gold Digger. Bred and owned by Johnny A. Robinson, Jr. and Morris Howard.

Ch. Heskethane Honeybun, bred and owned by Beryl Hesketh, N. Y.

Sallie Stewart started the Marjorie Lane line in 1953 in Baltimore, Md. with the purchase of Soham Andrea (Dargle Bruce ex Dargle Annalissa of Soham) from Mrs. Ferguson who imported Andrea from the Dargle Kennels of Miss Bellew in Ireland. Andrea was a top producer, being the dam of five champions.

Ch. Marjorie Lane Futfut (Amer. Ch. Midnight Gold of Yadnum ex Soham Andrea) sired Ch. Futsong of Cygnet Reach who was owned by J. Vincent Smith and Charles Worth of the Capricorn Kennels in Maryland. Futsong, a daughter of Mrs. F.D. Rambo's Ch. Spring Song of Cynget Reach, was BOS at the 1962 YTCA Specialty.

Alice Hornung started in the breed in 1956. Her Albion Kennel was located in San Diego, Calif. Ch. Little Tim of Nottingham was the top winner for this kennel, winning in 1957–1959 a total of 8 Toy Groups, and 28 Group placings. His breeder was Vera B. Clarke, owner of the Nottingham Kennels in San Diego, Calif. Tim's sire was Nemrak Kennel's Ch. Fancy's Sky King, a grandson of Ch. Holly of Achmonie. King was owned by the Jack Kingerys, owners of the Nemrak Kennels in San Diego, Calif. King sired three champions and Little Tim sired five, including Kirnel Kennels' Ch. Kirnel's Yum Yum and the Hornungs' Ch. Timothy Puff of Albion, who was out of the Hornungs' foundation bitch Nell Gwyn of Wildweir (Ch. Sorreldene Orange Boy ex Moyaway Molly), the dam of two champions.

The Kirnel Kennels of Nell and Kirill Fietinghoff in Downey, Calif. started in 1953. Ch. Kirnel's Yum Yum was the first bitch to win a YTCA Specialty in 1963 at Beverly Hills. Yum Yum, a daughter of the Hornung's Ch. Little Tim of Nottingham, won 7 Toy Groups, 15 Group placings and 37 Bests of Breed. Like her dam Lady Candy Barr, Yum Yum produced three champions, all sired by the Fietinghoffs' Ch. Wildweir Coat of Arms (Eng. & Am. Ch. Buranthea's Doutelle ex Ch. Sorreldene Two Shoes). Coat of Arms, bred by Wildweir Kennels, sired 10 champions.

The first top stud dog owned by the Fietinghoffs was Ch. Tid-le-Wink (Ch. Tidbit ex Crown Crest Rose), a homebred who sired 8 champions, and won a Toy Group and a Group placing.

Ch. Wildweir Dinner Jacket (Ch. Wildweir Stuffed Shirt ex Wildweir Time Marches On) has sired 11 champions including Ch. Kirnel's Buckaroo, winner of the 1973 YTCA Specialty, and 7 Group placings. Jacket's son, Ch. Baby Bandit of Kirnel has sired three champions.

Mrs. Fietinghoff was president of the YTCA in 1959 and '60.

Frank and Marjorie Kitson of Oakland, California owned Chs. Wee Nina of Bridle and Nicholas of Bridle, bred by and imported from Mrs.

Margaret Riley of Eng. Mrs. Kitson co-owned with Mabel Ennis, owner of the Enrose Kennel in San Leandro, Calif., the top winning bitch Ch. Lady Roberts of Marfrakit. Lady Roberts was Winners Bitch and BOS at the 1956 YTCA Specialty, and again BOS at the 1957 Specialty. Lady Roberts was the dam of one champion.

Louise Jeremy founded the Jeremy Yorkshires in Artesia, Calif. in 1956. Seven titles have been won by Jeremy dogs.

At the 1961 YTCA Specialty held at Santa Monica, Calif., Ch. Jeremy's Buster Brown (Acama Dandy Bit ex Ch. Little Betsy of Nottingham) was Best of Winners. In 1960 Mrs. Jeremy purchased Betsy and bred her to the Allen Davis' Ch. Little Sir Hughie of Ramon. This produced Betsy's third champion offspring, Ch. Jeremy's Little Mr. Dynamite, who has sired two Group-winning champions: Ch. Jeremy's Kid Kelly of Mr., owned by Mr. and Mrs. William Jordan, and Ch. Jeremy's Mr. Impressario, owned by Mrs. Peggy Hamilton.

Mr. and Mrs. George Houston's Judlu Kennels were begun in 1956 in Bayside, Long Island, N.Y. and were active until Mrs. Houston's death in 1972. Ch. Beechrise Trudy of the Vale (Blue Nibs ex Amber of Beckanbee), bred by Mrs. H. Griffith's Beechrise Kennels in England, was a Group winner in 1956. Trudy was the dam of five champions including Ch. Judlu's Milady Macwee, a Group placer in 1957. Macwee was sired by the Houston's import Ch. Jolliboy of the Vale (Williwee of the Vale ex John's Fancy), bred by G. Wheeler, and purchased from Marjorie Nunn's Vale Kennels in England. Jolliboy sired eight champions. The Houstons owned or bred 11 champions.

The Pequa Kennels of Mrs. Myrtle Young were started in 1957 in North Arlington, N.J. and moved to Ontario, California, in 1966, where it is now located. Pequa's first champions were litter sisters, Ch. Tully Tincel and Ch. Tully Trinket, Irish imports bred by Mrs. M.K. McFadden out of Rubert of Soham and Prosperous Judy. Tincel was the dam of two champions.

Twenty-one championships have been won by dogs owned or bred by Mrs. Young. Her top stud dog was the import Ch. Caprice of Pagham (Pagham Sehow Special ex Pagham Girlie of Westridge), bred by Miss P. Marter, England. Caprice was the sire of 12 champions. His top winning child, Ch. Pequa Mustang, who Mrs. Young co-owned with Joe Glaser during his show career, was the winner of a Best in Show, 4 Toy Groups and 7 Group placements, and sired 2 champions including Ch. Pequa Amigo. Amigo, who has placed in several Groups, is the foundation dog of Phyllis Silberman's Philgold Kennels in Duluth, Ga. Caprice also sired Mrs. Young's Group winner, Ch. Pequa

Ch. Wildweir Prim N' Proper, 1970 Best in Show winner with 16 Group Firsts. Owned by Helen and Merrill Cohen, Baltimore.

Ch. Carnaby Rock N' Roll, current all-breed and Specialty Best in Show winner. Bred, owned and handled by Terence Childs and Joseph R. Champagne, Woodbury, Conn.

Ch. Sweet Talking Witch, bred and owned by Vic and Lorraine Berry, Calif.

Ch. Wildweir War Bonnet, owned by Nancy Donovan, Michigan.

Ch. Wildweir Super Girl, bred and owned by Helen and Merrill Cohen.

Ch. Wildweir Briefcase, 1971 Specialty winner, bred and owned by Helen and Merrill Cohen.

Geronimo Tu, and Lawrence Wright's Bonnie Sun of Innisfree, Winners Bitch at the 1962 Specialty at Washington, D.C.

Mrs. Young imported Eng. & Am. Ch. Don Carlos of Progresso (Eng. Ch. Martywyn's Wee Teddy ex Shirloin Sally). Don Carlos had sired three English champions before leaving England. In the United States, Don Carlos sired five champions, among them Mrs. Young's Group winner, Ch. Pequa de Lovely.

Mildred Hornbrook's Danby Belziehill Kennels in Ithaca, N.Y. started in 1958 when she registered Belziehill Lindy Loo and her two offspring, Margie and Kelpie's Belziehill Dondi. Lindy Loo was imported in whelp to Lilyhill Gem of Hintonwood from Thomas Morrison's Belziehill Kennels in Lanarks, Scotland.

Dondi was the sire of 16 champions—14 American and 2 Canadian. His first champions were born in 1961 from a breeding with his dam, Lindy Loo. This breeding produced Ch. Taydor Belziehill Tassel, owned by Doris Meigs, Ithaca, N.Y. and the Group winner, Ch. Gaybrook Steiff Toy, owned by Grace Getz, Lake City, Pa. Toy sired two champions including the late William Sloan's Ch. Gaybrook Mister Bix, who was Best of Winners at the 1964 YTCA Specialty in St. Paul, Minn. Mr. Sloan served as President of the YTCA in 1972 and until his death in 1973.

Steiff Toy was the first Group winner produced by Mrs. Hornbrook's kennels, which has since bred two others, both owned by Mayfair-Barban kennels. They are Chs. Danby Belziehill Amanada and Danby Belziehill Raindrop.

Dondi was the sire of Mary L. Blackburn's homebred top winner, Am. & Can. Ch. Cedarlane Rum n' Coke, a son of Renrel's Riot of Cedarlane. Rum n' Coke was a Best in Show winner in his native Canada and the top winning Yorkie there in 1965 and 1966.

Daisy of Liberty Hill (Belziehill Petit Adorable ex Jill of Liberty Hill), bred by W. Provan of Scotland, is the dam of 9 champions, all sired by Dondi. Her daughter, by Dondi, Danby's Belziehill Abigail, is already the dam of six Champions and her granddaughter, Danby Belziehill Anya, owned by Mayfair, produced 9 Champions. Two of Abigail's children have won Best in Sweepstakes: Ch. Danby Belziehill Olde Blue and Judy Light's Danby Belziehill Debra, who won the Sweepstakes at the 1972 Specialty of the YTC of Greater St. Louis.

In all, Mrs. Hornbrook has bred 22 champions.

Since its inception in 1958, the Windamere Kennel has consistently shown top winning Yorkshires. Windamere is located in Muncie, Indiana and was started by Bud Priser and Jim Nickerson. Mr. Priser died in 1971 at age of only 45, but Mr. Nickerson has carried on.

Windamere has owned or bred 40 champions. These include Best in Show winner, Eng., Am., & Can. Ch. Progress of Progresso, who was imported from his breeder Mrs. Connie Hutchins in 1962. Progress was sired by Eng. & Am. Ch. Don Carlos of Progresso, who was imported by Myrtle Young of the Pequa Kennel. Progress' dam was Eng. Ch. Coulgorm Chloe, who was a top winner in England.

Ch. Progress won 1 Best in Show in the United States, 2 BIS in England and 1 BIS in Canada. He won a total of 53 Bests of Breed, 11 Toy Groups and 34 Group placings and sired 14 champions.

The first champion finished by Windamere was Ch. Holly Hill's Kewpie Doll (Petit Byngo Boy's Spirit ex Modic's Little Bell) in 1958. Kewpie Doll was bred by Helen Modic, owner of the Holly Hills Kennel in Cleveland. Mrs. Modic's top dog was the import Eng. Ch. Markus of Pagham (Emperor of Yadnum ex Precious of Pagham), bred by Miss P. Marter. Markus was a Group winner in 1959.

Ten dogs owned or bred by Windamere have won Toy Groups; these include the homebreds Ch. Windamere Velvet Doll, her son Ch. Windamere Beau Jangles, and Ch. Windamere Dina.

The top stud dog of Windamere is the imported Ch. Mr. Kipps of Grenbar (Beamshaw Lad ex Grenbar Kandy Kisses). Mr. Kipps was bred by Mr. and Mrs. S. Bartholomew of the Grenbar Kennel in England. He is the sire of 20 champions and was a Group winner. His half brother, Ch. Grenbar Tippacanoe, was also a Group winner.

Mr. Kipps sired Ch. Windamere Gay Valentine, whose dam was Minikin Lovely Lady Bridget. Valentine's half brother is Ch. Windamere Lil' Blue Ben (Ch. Mr. Kipps of Grenbar ex Ch. Windamere Toy Princess). Both Ben and Valentine are owned by Dr. and Mrs. Wiley Jenkins of New Orleans, La. and both are Group winners.

Ch. Windamere Minnipoo, owned by Mrs. June Fisher (formerly of Kailua, Hawaii, but now living in Annandale, Virginia) is the dam of Ch. Minnipoo's Blue Tiffany, the first Yorkshire born and bred in Hawaii to win a championship. Tiffany won her title with all majors and two Toy Groups.

The Clarkwyn Kennels, owned by Mrs. John Clark, located in Seattle, Washington, have owned or bred 18 champions since starting in 1958. Mrs. Clark's first Yorkie, Clarkwyn Miss Debutante, who is the foundation bitch of this kennel, came from Clonmel Kennels.

In 1960 Mrs. Clark purchased Am. Can. Ch. Toy Clown of Rusklyn who became her top winning and top producing Yorkie. He won 10 Toy Groups, 21 Group placings and sired 5 champions. Bred by L.W. Tong in England, he was sired by Sorreldene Master Cutler, out of Rusklyn Dinkie Duffles and traced to Winpal and Atherleigh lines. He was the winner of the dog C.C. at Cruft's dog show in 1960.

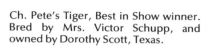

Ch. Wildweir Sandwich Man, 1970 Best in Show winner. Bred by Wildweir Kennels, and owned by Frances Cohen, Maryland.

Ch. Pete's Tiger, Best in Show winner. Bred by Mrs. Victor Schupp, and owned by Dorothy Scott, Texas.

Ch. Raybrook Rear Admiral. Breeder-owners, Ray Ryan and Ken Thompson.

Ch. Raybrook Paladin, son of Ch. Raybrook Rear Admiral. Bred and owned by Ray Ryan and Ken Thompson.

Am. Can. & Berm. Ch. Ka-Jo's Wendy on the Go, bred and owned by Carol Fencl, Illinois.

Three of Mrs. Clark's champions were sired by Ch. Wildweir Pomp n'Circumstance. His daughter, Ch. Clarkwyn Dreamy Doll, produced two champions. Clarkwyn Lancelot Dreamy Doll's son by Ch. Wildweir Poppycock, sired two champions, one of which was Am. Can. Ch. Heart G's Spunky Sparky.

Sparky, owned by Mr. and Mrs. Charles Mansfield of Portland, Oregon, was bred by Marjorie Gunnell, owner of the Heart G's Kennel. Sparky's wins in the States include Best in Show, 5 Toy Groups and 17 Group placings. In Canada, he has won 2 Best in Shows, 12 Toy Groups, and 11 Group placings. He was Best of Breed at the 1972 YTCA Speciality in San Francisco, and is sire of a champion.

Mrs. Clark's Ch. Clarkwyn Fanciful Sue is the dam of four champions, and her Ch. Clarkwyn Gina Marie is a Group winner and was Best Brace in Show at Renton, Wash. with Ch. Clarkwyn Dreamy Doll.

Delores Lewis and Maurine Middleton began Spring Holly Yorkshires in 1959 in St. Louis, Mo. and have won titles with 11 Yorkshires. Both Mrs. Lewis and Mrs. Middleton have been very active in the foundation of the YTC of Greater St. Louis.

They are the breeders of Marjorie Bunse's Ch. Majara Meduff of Spring Holly, BOS at the 1968 YTCA Specialty at St. Louis. Ch. Spring Holly Hanky Panky (Ch. Wildwier Pomp n' Circumstance ex Spring Holly Blue Shamrock) has sired three champions.

Mrs. Jane W. Johnson owned the Pop-n-Jay line in Texas. Mrs. Johnson started breeding in 1959 and is the owner of Ch. Pop-n-Jay's Fly By Night, winner of 2 Toy Groups, and of Ch. Pop-n-Jay I'm A Little Indian Too, who placed in several Groups. The Pop-n-Jay dogs trace to Mrs. Dowd's Ch. Peter of Nordlaw and Wildweir Kennels.

Mrs. Ruth Edwards of Houston, Texas owns the Jo-Ed Kennels. Mrs. Edwards began her line in 1960 with dogs from Pop-n-Jay. Her English import, Ch. Christopher of Valleyend—who was bred by Miss Philips—is a top producer, having sired five champions including Ch. Jo-ed's Tantalizing Twiggy, who won a Group in 1973.

The Devanvale Kennels, owned by Lynne Devan in West Bloomfield, Michigan, were established in 1959. Twenty champions were bred or owned by Devanvale. Both Danby-Belziehill and Mayfair-Barban have top producers and top winners that are sired by stud dogs from this kennel.

Ch. Yorkfold Jackanapes, sired by Yorkfold Grand Pim (a grandson of Ch. Mr. Pim of Johnstounburn) and out of Cindylou of Redhill (a granddaughter of Pagham Sehow Special), bred by J. D. Baldwin, England, was Devanvale's top winner. He was a Group winner in 1964 and won a number of Group placements. He sired five champions and was the sire of Mrs. Hornbrook's top producing bitch, Danby-Belziehill Anya.

Jackanapes' son, Am. Ch. Devanvale Jackson, bred to Devanvale Marvel Queen (Ch. Wildweir Pomp n' Circumstance ex Ch. Yorkfold Little Pixie of Theale) sired: Ch. Devanvale Jasmine, Winners Bitch at the 1967 YTCA Specialty; Mayfair-Barban Kennels' Ch. Devanvale Jennifer, the granddam of their Ch. Mayfair Barban Loup de Mer; Am. Can. Ch. Devanvale Sonny Jack, the sire of Mayfair-Barban Kennels' Ch. Devanvale Jack in the Box and of Chs. Mayfair Upsa-Daisy, Mayfair Unbelievable and Mayfair U-Betcha. Ch. Yorkfold Little Pixie of Theale (Yorkfold Grand Pim ex Burghwallis Buttons) was imported by Mrs. Devan and produced one champion.

Ch. Yorkfold Gold Choice, Jackanapes litter sister, produced five champions, all sired by Ch. Wildweir Pomp n' Circumstance. Of these, Mrs. Devan's Ch. Devanvale Sunshine was a Group winner; her Ch. Devanvale Shropshire Lad sired three champions.

The Heskethane Yorkshires of Beryl Hesketh have been bred in three countries. The kennel was started in England, then moved to Venezuela when her husband was transferred there. In 1960, Hesketane Kennels moved to the United States. They have bred or owned 38 champions.

Ch. Bermyth Lad of Heskethane (Ch. St. Aubrey Tzumiao's Lil' Apollo ex Bermyth Jara of Grandeur), bred by Bertha Smith's Bermyth Kennels in New York, was shown to his title by Mrs. Hesketh, and was sold to Mr. and Mrs. James R. Genteel, owners of the Jarna Kennels in Staten Island, New York. Lad has sired nine champions; his sire, Apollo, sired six champions.

Ch. Amanda of Heskethane (Ch. St. Aubrey Tzumiao's Lil' Apollo ex Tango of Tolestar) is the dam of six champions and is Heskethane's top brood bitch.

Am. & Jap. Ch. Heskethane Hot Tempo (Ch. Wildweir Pomp n' Circumstance ex Stirkean Lulu) was bred by Mrs. Hesketh and owned by Anne Goldman prior to his sale to Japan. His son Heskethane Blue Tempo owned by Mrs. Hesketh, has sired three champions. Another son, Heskethane Jazzbo, owned by Terrence Childs and Joe Champagne's Carnaby Kennels in Woodbury, Conn., has sired four champions. Jazzbo's son, Ch. Carnaby Trad Jazz, has placed in Toy Groups and is the sire of four champions. Ch. Carnaby Rock n' Roll, Jazzbo's son, is a Best in Show and Group winner.

Trivar Kennels, established in 1960 and located at Potomac, Maryland, are owned by Johnny Robinson and Morris Howard.

Am. & Mex. Ch. Camelot's Little Pixie, America's top winning Yorkie in 1970. Winner of 3 all-breed BIS. Breeder-owners: Lee and Richard Sakal, Calif.

Ch. Shareen Mr. Tee See, Best in Show winner. Breeder-owner, Margaret Spilling Inman, Florida.

Ch. Windamere Gay Valentine, Group winner, owned by Dr. and Mrs. Wiley Jenkins, La.

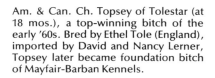

Am. & Can. Ch. Topsey of Tolestar (at 18 mos.), a top-winning bitch of the early '60s. Bred by Ethel Tole (England), imported by David and Nancy Lerner, Topsey later became foundation bitch of Mayfair-Barban Kennels.

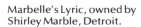

Ch. Whitecross Kate Tee, owned by Hazel Thrasher, Kansas City, Mo.

Marbelle's Lyric, owned by Shirley Marble, Detroit.

Ch. Bambi Lass, purchased in 1960, is their foundation bitch and traces to Pequa Kennels' Ch. Willow of Pagham. Her daughter, Trivar's Contessa, has produced six champions including the kennels' top winner, Ch. Trivar's Tycoon. Contessa's sire is Trivar's Big Ben and she traces to Eng. Ch. Stirkean Chota Sahib.

Ch. Trivar's Tycoon (Ch. Trivar's BonVivant ex Trivar's Contessa) has won 31 Toy Groups, 35 Group placings and 85 Bests of Breed. He is a Best in Show winner in Canada. He was Best of Breed at the 1972 YTC of Greater St. Louis Specialty, and was Best of Winners at the 1968 YTCA Specialty. Tycoon has sired 16 champions to date.

Tycoon is the sire of the Robert Pricer's Group-placing bitch, Ch. Marie Two of Jo-Ra-Ka, whose dam is the Group winner, Ch. Marie of Glengonner (Glamour Boy of Glengonner ex Sorreldene Nectarine), bred by D.A. Peck of the Glengonner Kennels in Scotland. Jo-Ra-ka is located in Virginia Beach, Virginia.

Tycoon's daughter, Ch. Trivar's Golddigger, whose dam is May Queen of Asfolat, has won 2 BIS, 10 Groups and 18 Group placings.

Ch. Trivar's Bon Vivant (Ch. Dandy Duke of Mayfair ex Trivar's Lady Letita) died at an early age, but sired 5 champions prior to his death. He was the sire of the Best in Show winner, Ch. Trivar's Princess Jervic, owned by Victor Recondo and Jerry Vine of Puerto Rico.

Ch. Fashion Wise of Astolat (Sir Jason of Astolat ex Lady Fliptop of Astolat), bred by Mrs. C. Carlton-Haw of the Astolat Kennels, Eng., was Trivar's first Group winner in 1963.

Trivar has bred or owned 34 Champions.

David and Nancy Lerner's Renrel Kennels were located in Port Chester, N.Y. from 1957 to 1963 and they owned two top winners.

Am. & Can. Ch. The Vale Tiny Mite (Williwee of the Vale ex Patricia of the Vale), bred by Marjorie Nunn of England, was imported by Dana Miller of New York, and purchased by the Lerners in 1957. Tiny Mite won 7 Toy Groups and 18 Group placings in the United States and Canada and sired two champions.

The Lerners' second top winner was a bitch who was better known as belonging to Mayfair Kennels—Am. & Can. Ch. Topsey of Tolestar (Totis Treasure ex Michaela of Tolestar), bred by Ethel Tole of the Tolestar Kennels in England. Topsey was imported with her littermates at ten weeks of age in 1958. She won her American title at 11 months and her Canadian title at 13 months. Topsey, while owned by the Lerners won 21 Toy Groups and 24 Group placings in the United States and Canada. She was the top winning bitch in the U.S. in 1960 and '61. Topsey produced one Canadian Champion prior to her sale to Miss Seranne in 1962. She became foundation bitch of the Mayfair-Barban bloodline.

The Mayfair-Barban Kennels, one of the prime contenders for top winning show honors in the United States, is owned by Ann Seranne and Barbara Wolferman. It is located in Newton, New Jersey.

Miss Seranne started the kennel in 1960, with Miss Wolferman joining her in 1966. Miss Wolferman had registered her first Yorkshire in 1953, a puppy purchased from the Arthur Mills' Millbarry Kennels. Mayfair was originally located in New York City, but moved to New Jersey where it is now high on a hill overlooking the Pocono Mountains. Mayfair was the original name of the kennel, but the dogs are now named with the Mayfair-Barban prefix.

Miss Seranne's first champion, finishing in 1960, was Ch. Renrel Wee Puddn' of Yorkshire (Am. & Can. Ch. The Vale Tiny Mite ex Ebonwood Honey), bred by David and Nancy Lerner. In 1962, Miss Seranne purchased Am. & Can. Ch. Topsey of Tolestar (Totis Treasure ex Michaela of Tolestar) from the Lerners. Topsey had been a top winner while owned by the Renrel Kennels, and was to be a top producer for Mayfair. In her first litter at Mayfair, she produced their first homebred top winner—Ch. Dandy Diamond of Mayfair, and Ch. Dondy Duke of Mayfair—the sire of two champions owned by Ann Summa.

Diamond and Duke were sired by Mildred Hornbrook's Kelpie's Belziehill Dondi, a top producing stud dog. Dondi's paternal granddam was Candy of Hintonwood, a full sister to Michaela of Tolestar (Topsey's dam) and to Wildweir's Sorreldene Salome. All three bitches were by Eng. Ch. Blue Symon ex Honey-Queen.

Dandy Diamond was born in 1964 and won 14 Group placings, 39 Bests of Breed and placed in the Top Ten Yorkies in 1966.

His son, Am. Can. Ch. Mayfair's Oddfella was the kennels' next top winner. Oddfella's dam, Mayfair Goody Two Shoes, traces to Ch. Blue Symon through her dam Tilda of Tolestar. Tilda was also the dam of Ch. Wee Geordie of Heskethane. Oddfella won 12 Toy Groups, 35 Group placings and 76 Bests of Breed. His Groups included winning the 1968 Progressive Dog Club show for Toy breeds.

Am. & Can. Ch. Gaytonglen Teddy of Mayfair was purchased as a puppy from Doris Craig of Richmond, Va. Teddy is a son of Ch. Progress of Progresso and his dam, Gaytonglen's Golden Tammie, is a granddaughter of Progress through her sire, Tenbliss Coat of Arms. Tenbliss was the kennel name belonging to Mrs. Betty Wooten of Memphis, Tenn.

Teddy arrived at his new home in 1967 at the age of twelve weeks of age and won his title in 1969. He is the winner of 4 Bests in Show, 26 Toy Groups, 55 Group placings, 115 Bests of Breed and won the 1970 and '73 YTCA Specialties in New York City. He has sired 22 champions including Philip Lanard's Ch. Mayfair Barban Yam n' Yelly,

Above: Am. & Can. Ch. Gaytonglen Teddy of Mayfair, winner of 4 Bests in Show and 26 Toy Groups, and sire of 22 champions. Bred by Doris Craig. Owned by Ann Seranne and Barbara Wolferman, Mayfair-Barban Kennels, New Jersey. Handled by Wendell J. Sammet.

Right: Ch. Mayfair Barban Loup de Mer, at this printing already winner of 3 BIS and 33 Groups. "Loup", a grandson of Ch. Gaytonglen Teddy of Mayfair, was bred by his owners, Ann Seranne and Barbara Wolferman, and is handled by Wendell J. Sammet.

Ch. Gold Sherie of Bridle, bred by Margaret Riley (England) and owned by Barbara Clark, Tex.

Am & Berm. Ch. Darn Toot'n of Gayelyn, owned by Mel Davis, New York City.

Ch. Spring Song of Cygnet Reach, owned by Chuck Worth and Vincent Smith, Maryland.

Ch. Drax Fleurette, bred by Mrs. F. Drake, owned by Doris Craig, Virginia.

Ch. Gaytonglen Tom Thum, bred and owned by Doris Craig.

winner of 1 BIS, 3 Toy Groups and 3 Group placings. Yam n' Yelly was Winners Bitch, Best of Winners, and Best of Opposite Sex at the 1972 YTCA Specialty at New York City. Teddy is the grandsire of Mayfair's Best in Show winner, Ch. Mayfair Barban Loup de Mer (Ch. Devanvale Jack in the Box ex Ch. Mayfair Barban Lady Finger.) Jack in the Box is a grandson of Lynne Devan's Ch. Yorkfold Jackanapes and a great-grandson of Ch. Wildweir Pomp n' Circumstance. Lady Finger is a daughter of Ch. Gaytonglen Teddy of Mayfair ex Mayfair's Poor Pitiful Pearl, a daughter of Ch. Dandy Diamond of Mayfair, and a great-granddaughter of Ch. Yorkfold Jackanapes and Ch. Wildweir Pomp n' Circumstance. Loup de Mer is the winner to date of 3 Bests in Show, 33 Toy Groups and 42 Group placings. He was Best of Winners at the 1973 YTCA Specialty in New York City.

Other Group winners owned or bred by Mayfair-Barban are: Ch. Danby's Belziehill Amanada, Ch. Danby Belziehill Raindrop, Ch. Mayfair Barban X-Tract, Ch. Mayfair Barban Mocha Mousse, Ch. Mayfair Barban Kasha and Ch. Mayfair Barban Upsa-Daisy (Best of Opposite Sex at the 1969 and 1970 YTCA Specialties at New York City.) Daisy is the dam of Ch. Mayfair Barban Mocha Mousse, who has sired 7 Champions including two Group winners, X-Tract and Raindrop. She is by Am. & Jap. Ch. Devanvale Sonny Jack, a son of Jackanapes and a grandson of Ch. Wildweir Pomp n' Circumstance. Her dam, Danby's Belziehill Anya, was bred by Mrs. Hornbrook and was sired by Ch. Yorkfold Jackanapes out of Danby's Belziehill Tangue. Anya is the top producing bitch owned by Mayfair, having produced 9 Champions.

Ch. Danby's Belziehill Amanada (Kelpie's Belziehill Dondi ex Daisy of Liberty Hill) was Mayfair's first Toy Group winner in 1967. She was Winners Bitch at the 1967 YTCA Specialty held with the Westchester Kennel Club show. Bred to Ch. Gaytonglen Teddy of Mayfair, she produced Ch. Mayfair Barban Ala Mode, Best of Winners at the 1970 YTCA Specialty in New York.

Mayfair-Barban has owned or bred 45 Champions.

The Yorksmith Kennel of Betty J. Smith is in Blairstown, N.J. The line has been founded on Mayfair-Barban breeding and 11 championships have been won by Yorkshires owned or bred by Yorksmith. At the 1969 YTCA Specialty in New York City, Ch. Yorksmith Blue Bonnet (Ch. Mr. Kipps of Grenbar ex Ch. Danby's Belziehill Pangue) won the Sweepstakes. At the 1970 Specialty, Ch. Yorksmith Fosdick of Mayfair (Ch. Mayfair's Oddfella ex Ch. Mayfair's Ohme-Ohmy) was Winners Dog. Fosdick is the sire of Ch. Danby Belziehill Olde Blue, who was bred by Mrs. Hornbrook, and is owned by Pat Fowler and Barbara Wolferman. Olde Blue was the winner of the 1972 YTCA

Int. Ch. Wildweir Keepsake P.C.

Am. Mex. and Can. Ch. Wildweir Keepsake, P.C., sire of 29 champions. Bred by Wildweir Kennels and owned by Anne Goldman, Calif. (The P.C. suffix stands for *Perro Companero*, the Mexican equivalent of the Novice Obedience degree.)

Ch. Starfire Gold Bangle, bred by Carmen Greenameyer and owned by Anne Goldman.

Sweepstakes at New York City.

Other kennels which have based their breeding on the Mayfair-Barban line are: Chelsea Kennels, owned by Nina McIntyre in Dallas, Texas; Fred Wolpert's Kennels in West Chester, Pa.; Morgangem, owned by Mr. and Mrs. Wm. Reed, Dover, Del.; Durrisdeer, owned by Virginia Bull, Blairstown, N.J.; Suma Cum Laude, owned by Ann and Jim Summa, Naugatuck, Conn.; and, in part, Joe Joly's Joly Kennels in Danvers, Mass. and Ylva Nordin's Jessamine Kennels in Washington, Va.

Mrs. Anne Goldman's Starfire Kennels, founded in 1960, is situated in Santa Monica, Calif. Thirty-four champions have won their titles for Starfire, of which 29 have been sired by Am., Mex. & Can. Ch. Wildweir Keepsake (Ch. Wildweir Pomp n' Circumstance ex Wildweir Emperor's Waltz). Keepsake is the top producing child of Pomp n' Circumstance's 95 champion children. His dam was a granddaughter of Ch. Star Twilight of Clu-mor and Ch. Little Sir Model.

Keepsake's daughter, Ch. Starfire Gold Bangle, bred by Carmen Greenamyer and owned by Mrs. Goldman, was the top winning Yorkie on the West Coast in 1968 and placed in the Top Ten Yorkshires for that year. Bangle won nine Group placings.

140

Other Keepsake daughters who have won top honors are: Mrs. Goldman's Ch. Starfire for Keeps, winner of the Sweepstakes and Winners Bitch at the 1971 YTCA Specialty at Atlantic City, N.J.; Mrs. Jean Rauch's Ch. Starfire Queen of Hearts, Winners Bitch at the 1973 Specialty at New York City; and Jean and Glen Fancy's Ch. Starfire Dragon Lady, BOS at the 1968 Specialty.

Keepsake's son, Am. Can. & Mex. Ch. Starfire Mitey Model, owned by Mrs. Margery May, is the sire to date of six champions. Another son, Ch. Starfire Titan, sired Lee and Richard Sakal's top winners, Am. & Mex. Ch. Camelot's Little Pixie and Ch. Camelot's Little Sir Hector. The Sakals owned the Heaven-Lee Kennel in Los Angeles during the late 1960s. Little Pixie was the top winning Yorkshire in the U.S.A. in 1970 and placed 3rd in the ratings of all Toy Dogs that year. She was the winner of 3 Bests in Show, 14 Toy Groups, 10 Group placings and 30 Bests of Breed. Hector, her litter brother won a Toy Group and 5 Group placings.

Titan was also the sire of Vic and Lorraine Berry's Ch. Precious Posy, a top winner in 1969. Mr. and Mrs. Berry own the Doodletown Yorkshire Terriers, in Newport Beach, Calif. Doodletown was established in 1963 and owned or bred 11 champions.

Helen Stern owns the Carlen Kennels in Brooklyn, N.Y. which were started in 1960 when her daughter presented her with a tiny Yorkshire puppy in a shoebox. The puppy grew up to be Ch. Kanga's Stinger of Carlen (Kanga's Braggin Bandit ex Kanga's Cuttysark Crumpet). Stinger was bred by Swen Swenson, owner of the Kanga line in New York City. Mrs. Stern owns seven other champions.

Ch. Kanga's Stinger of Carlen (at 13 years of age) with daughter Daiquiri of Carlen (at 10 years.) Owned by Helen Stern, N. Y.

Ch. Wildweir Ballerina, bred by Wildweir Kennels, and owned by Maybelle Neuguth.

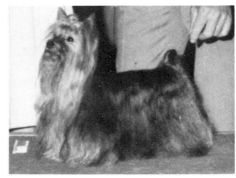

Am. Can. & Mex. Ch. Wildweir Ten O'Clock Scholar, sire of 20 champions. Bred by Wildweir Kennels and owned by Kay Radcliffe, Ill.

Ch. Rob Roy of Castlethorpe, bred and owned by Blanche Dunbar, Calif.

Ch. Kirnel's Jump for Joy. Bred by Nell and Kirill Fietinghoff, and owned by Valerie Kilkeary and Judy Tyma, Calif.

Nancy Donovan of Kalamazoo, Michigan started breeding in 1960 when she purchased Ch. Wildweir War Bonnet from Wildweir. War Bonnet was a son of Ch. Flook of Achmonie ex Wildweir's Merry Widow. Since then Mrs. Donovan has bred or owned 12 champions.

Her Toy Group winners are Ch. Wildweir Belle of the Ball (Moonrose's daughter by Ch. Wildweir Pomp n' Circumstance) and Ch. Wildweir Katherine the Great (Ch. Wildweir Weekend Warrior ex Kajimanor Shady Sadie). Katherine won Winners Bitch at the 1972 YTC of Greater St. Louis Specialty. Ch. Wildweir War Bonnet, Ch. Wildweir Harbor Lights, and her homebred Ch. Wildweir Wise Councilor have all placed in Toy Groups.

At the 1973 Specialty of the YTC of Greater St. Louis, Mrs. Donovan carried off Winners Dog and Best of Winners with her homebred Wildweir Fairly Obvious (later Champion), and Best in Sweepstakes and Winners Bitch with homebred Ch. Wildweir Fairly Respectable. They are littermates sired by Ch. Wildweir Fair n' Square ex Wildweir Piccalilli, a daughter of Ch. Royal Picador and granddaughter of Ch. Buranthea's Doutelle. Mrs. Donovan's dogs are based entirely on Wildweir breeding and are always registered with that kennel name.

Helen and Merrill Cohen of Baltimore, Md. have also always registered their Yorkshires with our kennel prefix, as their breeding stock is based entirely on Wildweir. Mr. Cohen is a licensed judge of both Obedience and conformation. Helen and Merrill's Mar-del's Terrence, C.D., C.D.X., U.D. is one of the 14 Yorkshires that have won their Utility Dog titles.

Ch. Wildweir Prim n' Proper (Ch. Wildweir Pomp n' Circumstance ex Wildweir Time n' Tide) was the No. 2 Yorkshire in the United States in 1970 and won 1 BIS, 16 Toy Groups and 44 Group placings. Her son, Ch. Wildweir Briefcase, sired by Ch. Royal Picador, was Best of Breed at the 1971 YTCA Specialty at Atlantic City, N.J. Briefcase placed in several Groups and is the sire of four champions. Ch. Wildweir Rosette (Ch. Wildweir Pomp n' Circumstance ex Wildweir Scarlet Ribbons—the dam of 10 Champions) is a Group placer and the dam of two champions. Ch. Wildweir Dynamite C.D., bred by Wildweir, has sired a champion and is a Group placer, as is their homebred Ch. Wildweir Super Girl, C.D.

Mrs. Nancy Wehr is the owner of the Windy Hill Kennels in Baltimore, Md. and has based her breedings on Wildweir dogs.

Tykil, owned by Valerie Kilkeary and Judy Tyma, is located in Hammond, Indiana. Their top winner, Ch. Kirnel's Jump for Joy (Ch. Wildweir Dinner Jacket ex Ch. Wildweir Good Tidings) was bred by the Fietinghoffs.

Jump for Joy, bred to her son, Ch.Tykil Rythm n' Blues, who was sired by Tykil's Ch. Kirnel's Sportin' Life (Ch. Wildweir Coat of Arms ex Ch. Kirnel's Yum Yum) produced Ch. Tykil Psychedelic.

Edyce and Melvin Kenniston, owners of the Ken-Klair Yorkies, own Ch. Tykil Psychedelic, who was BOS at the 1972 YTCA Specialty in San Francisco.

Sportin' Life's daughter, Tykil Begin the Beguine, is the dam of three champions for her owner, Darshire Kennels.

The Darshire Kennels, owned by Harriet and Darrel Karns of Clarksville, Tenn., started in 1963 and has bred or owned 10 champions. Their top stud dog, Ch. Darshire Corrigan (Ch. Wildweir Darktown Strutter ex Ch. Wildweir Tipperary) has sired 9 champions. His litter sister, Am. & Can. Ch. Darshire Something Special, is the dam of three champions.

Corrigan's son Ch. Suwilla Johnny Jump Up, bred by the Suwilla Kennels of Mrs. William Mainard in Memphis, Tenn. is a Group winner.

The Karns also own Tykil Trade Secret, a bitch bred by Tykil Kennels who has produced four champions, and Ch. Darshire Tomorrow the World, sire of three champions.

The R'Town Kennels of Lynne Richardson in Covington, Tenn. are based on dogs of Darshire and Tykil breeding.

Mrs. Maybelle Neuguth started her Maybelle line with Wildweir Liberty Belle C.D. (Ch. Wildweir Cock of the Walk ex Ch. Aoife of Adelaide) in 1960. Belle won her C.D. title in 1962.

Mrs. Neuguth lost her life in 1970 when, after rescuing her grandchildren from a fire, she attempted to rescue her beloved dogs.

Mrs. Neuguth's breeding was closely tied to Wildweir and the dogs that she planned to keep for breeding usually carried both the kennel names of Maybelle and Wildweir. Ch. Wildweir Ballerina (Ch. Wildweir Poppycock ex Wildweir Heavenly Body) was her top winner, winning 5 Toy Groups, 10 Group placings and 22 BOB.

Her top stud dog was her homebred Ch. Wildweir E. Major of Maybelle, sired by Ch. Wildweir Pomp n' Circumstance out of Maybelle's Memory of Adelaide, a daughter of Wildweir Liberty Belle, C.D. and Ch. Buranthea's Doutelle. Major sired 10 champions, and was a litter brother to Chs. Wildweir Waltz and Ch. Wildweir Duet of Maybelle.

The top brood bitch of the Maybelle line was Wildweir Hot Fudge (Ch. Yorkfold Chocolate Boy ex Ch. Wildweir Ticket to the Moon), dam of four Champions.

In all, Maybelle Neuguth bred or owned 18 champions.

Ch. Ozmillion Playboy. Bred by O. Sameja (England) and owned by Windsor-Gayelyn Kennels.

Ch. Windsor-Gayelyn Robin. Bred and owned by Windsor-Gayelyn Kennels.

Ch. Gayelyn Pentroad Jemina Do, bred and owned by Annette Edwards.

Ch. Lord Pickwick of Oxford, owned by Windsor-Gayelyn Kennels.

Am. & Can. Ch. Leprechaun's Nik Nak and Am. & Can. Ch. Antiqua's T.N.T. of Leprechaun, Am. Can. & Berm., C.D., pictured winning Best Brace in Show at Eastern Dog Club, 1970, under judge Louis Murr. Owned by Betty Dullinger.

Ch. Newsham's Wish Come True. Breeder-owners, Mrs. Beth Newsham and Gary Newsham.

Ch. Mr. Wonderful, bred by Mrs. Charles McLennan, owned by Betty R. Dullinger, Maine.

Raybrook Kennels, owned by Ray Ryan and Ken Thompson, are situated in Cleveland, Ohio and were started in 1960. Their Ch. Stirkean Spring Star (Eng. Ch. Stirkean Chota Sahib ex Stirkean Anne Marie of Winpal), a Group winner, was imported from Edith Stirk's Stirkean Kennels in England.

Ch. Raybrook Palladin (Ch. Raybrook Rear Admiral ex Raybrook Happiness) was Best of Winners at the 1971 YTCA Specialty and has placed in a Toy Group. Raybrook has bred or owned 14 champions. Its breeding has been based primarily on Stirkean, Catherine Miller's Kasam line, and Devanvale.

Mr. Ryan is a licensed judge of the breed and, in 1972 judged the North Counties Yorkshire Terrier Club Show in England. Mr. Ryan was the first American judge ever asked to judge an English Yorkshire Specialty, and the show had the largest entry of the breed at an English or European show.

Hazel Thrasher, of Kansas City, Mo., founded her Zelden line in 1960. Ch. Whitecross Gay Jester and Ch. Whitecross Tom Pinch were imported from Mrs. H.I. Knight, owner of Whitecross in England. Tom Pinch (Whitecross Mendip Lad ex Whitecross Blue Steak of Stoneycroft) won 3 Toy Groups, several Group placings and placed No. 4 in the Top Ten U.S. Yorkshires in 1966. Tom and Jester each sired three champions. Whitecross traces to Ch. Splendour of Invincia, Ch. Harringay Remarkable, and Ch. Mr. Pim of Johnstounburn.

Zelden has bred or owned 18 champions.

Carol Fencl of Wheaton, Ill. started the Ka-jo Yorkshires in 1960. Her first champion was Ch. Kajo's Barlu Bonnie Lass C.D., who finished in 1962. Lass was a great-granddaughter of Ch. Twinkle Toes of Soham.

Am., Can. & Bda. Ch. Kajo's Wendy on the Go (Ch. Wildweir Pomp n' Circumstance ex Kajo's Lynbrook Rebecca) was Best of Opposite Sex at the 1970 YTCA Specialty at Chicago. Wendy is a Group winner in Canada and has placed in a number of groups in the United States. Am. & Can. Ch. Kajo's Starlight Debutante and Ch. Ka-Jo's Candyman are both Group placers.

Betty Dullinger's Leprechaun Kennels, started in 1961, is now located in Kezar Falls, Maine, and is active in both conformation and Obedience. Ch. Leprechaun's Alexander, bred by Kathy Dullinger, is the only Yorkshire to hold a conformation title and C.D. titles in the U.S., Canada and Bermuda, and has sired two champions. Alexander, through his dam, Doris of Capricorn (the dam of 2 champions) is a grandson of Ch. Marjorie Lane Futfut.

Am. & Can. Ch. Antiqua's T.N.T. of Leprechaun (Ch. Leprechaun's Alexander ex Antiqua's Lady Luck) was bred by Zola Last, of the Antiqua Kennel in Silver Springs, Md. Ch. Leprechaun's Nik Nak (a homebred sired by Ch. Mr. Wonderful) and T.N.T. have set a breed record for Best Brace in Show awards, having won 12 in the United States and 4 in Canada.

Ch. Mr. Wonderful, who was bred by Mrs. Charles McClennan, owner of the Cowpens line in Maryland, sired four champions. Mrs. Dullinger's Green Isle Man For All Seasons (Ch. Wildweir E. Major of Maybelle ex Tammy of Green Isle), bred by Wm. Carsidona, traces to Irish breeding and has sired a champion.

Mrs. Dullinger served as YTCA President in 1968 and 1969. Leprechaun has bred or owned nine champions.

Ursala Taintor and Sharon Ames, Woodbridge Kennels in Dover, Mass.; Trold Kennels of Betty Waggonis in Westfold, Mass.; and R. Wayne Gurin and Margot Dwyer's in Cresthill Kennels in Southboro, Mass. are all founded in whole, or in part, on dogs of Mrs. Dullinger's breeding.

The Shareen Kennels, located in Fort Lauderdale, Fla. and owned by Margaret (Spilling) Inman, started breeding in 1961.

Ch. Shareen Mr. Tee See (Ch. Shareen Pride of J.B. ex Ch. Shareen Pixie Punkin) is the top winner and top producer at Shareen. Tee See was the winner of 1 Best in Show, 12 Toy Groups, 34 Group placings and 86 Bests of Breed. He has sired five champions to date including Mrs. Inman's Group Winner, Ch. Shareen Golden Boy. Golden Boy, bred by Lucena Gluck, is out of Ch. Gaybrook Star of Belziehill.

Windsor-Gayelyn was originally two separate lines that became a partnership in 1969. In 1975, the partnership was dissolved, with each partner resuming on her own.

Gayelyn was founded in 1962 when the late Barbara Welch and Marilyn Koenig purchased Stirkean Bright Star from Beryl Hesketh, who had imported her from Mrs. Stirk, of England. In 1963, Ch. Heskethane Rob of Lilactime (Tzumiao's Limelight of Lilactime ex Gay Request of Lilactime) joined the kennel. Rob was bred by Violet Howgill, owner of the Lilactime Kennels, Eng. Limelight, Rob's sire, is the sire of six American champions. Rob became the foundation stud of the Windsor-Gayelyn line and has sired seven champions.

Windsor was founded in 1963 when Kathleen Kolbert purchased Ch. Windamere Dolly Dewdrop from the Windamere Kennels in Indiana.

Mrs. Welch died in 1968 and in 1969 Windsor and Gayelyn joined forces, locating in Oxford, Conn. in an old homestead built in 1714. A total of 28 champions were bred or owned by this kennel. Their first homebred champion was Ch. Darn Toot'n of Gayelyn, who was sold to

Family type. Ch. Wildweir Sugar Daddy and Ch. Wildweir Little Ol' Winemaker being shown to Best Toy Brace at Hoosier KC 1967 show under judge Joseph Faigel. Handled by owner Dorothy Naegele.

Am. Can. Mex. & Berm. Ch. Northshire's Mazeltov, sire (to date) of 13 champions. Breeder-owners: Wally and Dotty Naegele, Illinois.

Am. & Can. Ch. Wildweir Patty of Northshire, owned by Dotty and Wally Naegele.

Ch. Wenscoe's Whynot of Shaumar winning Best in Show all-breeds at Santa Ana Valley KC, 1970, under judge Kay Finch. Handler, John Thyssen. Bred by Wendy Whiteley, and owned by Betty Conaty, Calif.

Ch. Wenscoe's Whizzaway of Tzumaio, sire of Whynot. Bred by Elsie Gilbert (England) and owned by Wendy Anne Whiteley.

Ch. Wenscoe's Whizz Bang, bred by Wendy Anne Whiteley and owned by Doris Craig, Virginia.

Mel Davis of New York City, who also owned Toot'n's sire, Ch. Tabordale Pepperpot, a Group winner in 1962. Darn Toot'n won 5 Toy Groups and 25 Group placings, and is the sire of three champions. Darn Toot'n's dam was Troubadour's Germaine, who is a top producer with 8 champion offspring.

Am. & Can. Ch. Windsor Gayelyn Robin (Ch. Heskethane Rob of Lilactime ex Sugar Plum's Plumb Beautiful, a daughter of Ch. Wildweir Poppycock) is a homebred. She was a Group winner and was BOS at the 1972 YTC of Greater St. Louis Specialty.

Six of the Windsor-Gayelyn studs have produced one or more champions. Ch. Ozmillion Playboy (Eng. Ch. Heavenly Blue of Wiske ex Ozmillion Tender Touch), bred by Mr. O. Sameja, was imported in 1971.

Ch. Lord Pickwick of Oxford (Gayman's Blue Tango ex Ch. Sugar Plum's Big Bow Wow) has placed in several Groups. Ch. Windsor-Gayelyn Silk n' Satin was WB at the 1970 YTCA Specialty and, since becoming the property of Mr. and Mrs. Joe Sampaio, of Rio de Janero, Brazil, has become an International Champion. Ch. Windsor-Gayelyn Stitch n' Time won the Sweepstakes at the 1973 YTCA Specialty at New York City.

Mrs. Annette Edwards of Weston, Conn. owns the Pentroad Kennels, which started in 1965. Ch. Gayelyn Pentroad Tom Tiddler (Ch. Gayelyn Tom Foolery ex Gayelyn Pentroad Eliza Do) was WD at the 1972 YTC of Greater St. Louis Specialty. His litter sister, Ch. Gayelyn Pentroad Jeminado, was WB at the 1972 YTCA Specialty.

Kay Radcliffe's Kajimanor Kennels, started in 1963, are located in Rockford, Illinois. Her first Yorkshire, Carrie of Yorktown, is the dam of three champions.

Kajimanor's top stud and top winner is Am., Can., Bda. & Mex. Ch. Wildweir Ten O'Clock Scholar (Ch. Wildweir Pomp n' Circumstance ex Wildweir Dilly Dally), who has sired 20 champions and won 5 Toy Groups, 19 Group placings and 41 Bests of Breed. His son, Am. & Bda. Ch. Kajimanor Olde Blue, has won 4 Toy Groups, 16 Group placings, 35 Bests of Breed and sired three champions. Another son, Ch. Kajimanor Misty Moonlight won 6 Group placings and has sired three champions. Ruthie dePlata Pina, imported from Hazel Berkerry's DePlata Pina line in Ireland, was the dam of six champions. Ten bitches, bred or owned by Kajimanor, have produced one or more champions.

The Northshire Kennels of Dotty and Wally Naegele in Mount Prospect, Ill. are founded primarily on Wildweir lines and are the home of eight champions. Northshire was started in 1963 when they purchased Ch. Wildweir Patty of Northshire (Ch. Wildweir Pomp n' Circumstance ex Tzumaio's Mazurka) from her breeder, Mr. and Mrs. Steve Kessel. Patty was the first Group winner for Northshire and won 3 Toy Groups and 15 Group placings.

Am., Can., Bda., & Mex. Ch. Northshire's Mazeltov (Ch. Wildweir Darktown Strutter ex Northshire's Fire n' Brimstone) has won Toy Groups in the United States, Canada and Bermuda. In all, he has won 10 Toy Groups, and 27 Group placings. In 1974 he was BOB at the YTC of Greater St. Louis Specialty. He is the sire of 13 Champions including Ch. Gait-moor Lucinda, a great-granddaughter of Ch. Wildweir Pomp n' Circumstance, by Francis Snoop n'telle ex Brandy of Wandel, and Ch. Gait-moor Little Big Man, who has won 3 Toy Groups and 6 Group placings.

Melody Lane Kennels, founded by Mrs. Mary Purvis in 1968, is located in Centerville, Iowa. Ch. Melody Lane Mini Trail, a Mazeltov son, has placed in 6 Groups. Mini Trail's dam, Melody Lane Patti Marie, is the dam of three champions sired by Mazeltov. Mrs. Purvis has owned or bred 13 champions.

Mazeltov's litter brother, Northshire's Toast of the Town, is owned by Gary Newsham and his mother, Beth Newsham, of Omaha, Nebraska and is the sire of Ch. Newsham's Golden Promise. Fancy Mcbrale of Ashley (Ch. Wildweir Sugar Daddy ex Dansel Mollie Brown) is the dam of Promise and of Pomp n' Circumstance's daughter, Ch. Newsham's Wish Come True. Both Promise and Wish have placed in Toy Groups.

Mrs. Doris Craig started the Gaytonglen Yorkshires in 1964 in Richmond, Virginia, and has bred or owned ten champions. She is the breeder of Mayfair Kennels' top winning dog, Ch. Gaytonglen Teddy of Mayfair. Mrs. Craig's first champion, Ch. Drax Fleurette (Drax Star Talisman ex Ch. Drax Blue Mist), was purchased from Mrs. Felix Drake's Drax Kennels in Hialeah, Fla. Gaytonglen is also the home of three champions from Wenscoes, including Mrs. Craig's stud dogs Ch. Wenscoe's Wee Freddie and Ch. Wenscoe's Whizz Bang. Gaytonglen's Golden Tamie is the dam of "Teddy".

Mrs. Wendy Ann Whiteley, owner of the Wenscoes Yorkies, began breeding in England where she finished Eng. Ch. Wenscoes Wendoline before moving to LaJolla, Calif. in 1964. Since coming to this country, she has bred or owned 13 champions.

Mrs. Whiteley's top stud dog has been her import Ch. Wenscoes Whizzaway of Tzumaio, bred by Mrs. Elsie Gilbert (Tzumaio's Swanky Boy ex Tzumaio's Mona Lisa of Teddy Town.) Whizzaway has sired 12 Champions.

His best known offspring is Betty Conaty's Ch. Wenscoe's Whynot

Ch. Lorill's Fire Festival, bred and owned by Mr. and Mrs. William Jordan, Calif.

Ch. Jeremy's Kid Kelly of Mr., bred by Louise Jeremy, and owned by Mr. and Mrs. William Jordan, Calif.

Am. Can. & Mex. Ch. Starfire Mitey Model, Canadian Best in Show winner. Owned by Mrs. Margery May, California.

Am. & Can. Ch. Topaz Cufflink, son of Mitey Model. Bred by Margery May and owned by Marjorie James.

Ch. Wildweir Cloud Nine, bred by Wildweir Kennels and owned by Barbara Clark, Texas.

Ch. Wynsum Midnight Star, bred and owned by Dorothy Truitt, Texas.

Left: Ch. Wildweir's Skater's Waltz, a top winning bitch in the East in the mid-60s. *Right:* Her grandson, Ch. Cottleston Chalk Talk. Both bred and owned by Ruth L. Cooper, Illinois. - *Photos, Tauskey.*

of Shaumar, winner of a Best in Show, 3 Toy Groups and 3 Group placings. Whynot's litter sister, Ch. Wenscoes Miss Whizz, who is co-owned by Mrs. Whiteley and Dustine Bitterlin, also won a Group in 1971. Another daughter, Ch. Wenscoes Whisper, Mrs. Whiteley's first American champion, was BOS at the 1967 YTCA Specialty. Whisper has placed in several Groups and was among the Top Ten Yorkies in 1966. Ch. Wenscoes Whip it Quick sired three champions. His daughter, Ch. Wenscoes Wishbone was Best of Winners at the 1969 YTCA Specialty.

Whizzaway is the sire of the Group-placing Ch. Moonglow of ChinSe, owned by Inez Graf, owner of Chin Se Kennels in Stockton, Calif.

Wenscoes Gin Fizz of LaNores is the dam of three champions including Ch. Whynot.

Bridlebar is owned by Barbara Clark in Boerne, Texas. Mrs. Clark started with the kennel name of Francis, but Bridlebar is the name the American Kennel Club accepted for registration. The Bridlebar line is based on the Bridle line bred by Margaret Riley in England and on Wildweir.

Bridlebar's first champion and top winner was the import, Ch. Gold Sherrie of Bridle (Bridle Blue Rebel ex Lady Julie of Bridle) winner of 17 Group placings and 22 Bests of Breed.

Ch. Wildweir Cloud Nine, sire of six champions and Ch. Dansel Doutelle, sire of four champions, were both sired by Ch. Wildweir Pomp n' Circumstance. Cloud Nine is a son of Wildweir Victoria, a grandaughter of Ch. Star Twilight of Clu-mor, and Dansel Doutelle is a son of Wildweir Time Marches On, a Ch. Buranthea Doutelle daughter.

Ch. Francis Doutelle Time Bomb is the sire of eight champions including Dr. Ellen Brown's Canadian Group winner, Ch. Todwil's Fearless Fosdick. Time Bomb is owned by Glen Wills of the Todwil Yorkshires in Carbondale, Illinois.

Mrs. Clark's Ch. Francis Rebel Blu the Top has produced two champions, as has her Francis Picador Firecracker. In all, Bridlebar has owned or bred 17 champions.

Mrs. Dorothy Truitt of Fort Worth, Texas owns the Wynsum Kennels. Her Ch. Wynsum Midnight Star (Francis Cloud of Gold ex Haywire Yuletide Holly) placed in several Groups and was the dam of a champion.

Mrs. Ruth Cooper is the owner of the Cottleston Yorkshire Terriers in Glenview, Ill. Her homebred Ch. Wildweir Skater's Waltz (Ch. Wildweir Pomp n' Circumstance ex Wildweir Best Bib n' Tucker) was the top winning Yorkshire on the East Coast in 1964 and '65, winning 6 Toy Groups and 38 Group placings. She was also a top producer, being the dam of five Champions. Our Ch. Wildweir Stuffed Shirt was Waltz's litter brother and sired four champions including a Best in Show winner.

Waltz's son, Ch. Cottleston Culprit (now owned by Mrs. Naegele) won the 1967 YTCA Sweepstakes. Waltz's daughter by Ch. Wildweir Brass Hat, Ch. Wildweir Waltzing Matilda, placed in several Groups and was the dam of two champions including Ch. Cottleston Chalk-Talk who won 2 Toy Groups and 9 Group placings. Mrs. Cooper also owns Ch. Wildweir Rags to Riches (Wildweir Sassenach ex Wildweir Gold Lace). He was a full brother to our Wildweir Scarlet Ribbons, dam of 10 champions.

The Lorill Kennel of Janice and William Jordan is in Los Gatos, Calif. The kennel was started in 1965 and they have owned or bred seven champions.

Mrs. Jordan is the co-breeder, along with Mrs. Edwin Morrie of Ch. Edlyn Hanky Panky. Mrs. Morrie is the owner of the Edlyn Kennels in San Jose, Calif.

Besides the Group-winning Ch. Jeremy's Kid Kelly of Mr., the Jordans own Ch. Lorill's Fire Festival, whose sire is their top stud dog Ch. Sun Star of Halldera n' Lorill (Wildweir Sunshine n' Shadow ex Ch. Wildweir Ribbon of Moonlight II). Sun Star, sire of 3 champions to date, was bred by Betty Hall, owner of the Halldera Kennels in Belmont, Calif. Mrs. Hall's Ribbon of Moonlight was Winners Bitch at the 1965 YTCA Specialty. Sun Star's litter brother, Sun's Shawn of Halldera, won WD at the 1969 Specialty.

The Topaz Kennels of Margery May were first situated in Scarborough, Ont. Canada, but moved to West Los Angeles, Calif. where they are now located. Twenty-one champions have been bred or owned by Mrs. May.

Mex., Am., & Can. Ch. Kirnel's Topaz Medallion (Ch. Wildweir Coat of Arms ex Lady Candy Barr) was purchased in 1965 from the Fietinghoffs. Medallion has sired seven Champions. His daughter, Mrs. Marjorie James' Ch. Topaz Twinklet, won the Sweepstakes at the 1972 YTCA Specialty in San Francisco.

Medallion's son, Am., Can., & Mex. Ch. Highland Dinner Jacket, is owned by the Highland Kennel of Mrs. DeForest Simmons in Highland Creek, Ont. Canada and sired the Robert Irvines' Canadian Best in Show winner, Am. & Can. Ch. Mister Tom Thumb of Highland. Ch. Blue Magic Flash of Highland, won Winners Bitch at the 1968 YTCA Specialty.

Ch. Green's Lydia of Durgin, first Yorkshire Terrier to win a title in Alaska (1958.) Bred by Myrtle Durgin and owned by Melba Green.

Ch. Minipoo's Blu Tiffany, Group winner. Bred and owned by June Fisher, Hawaii.

Int. Am. Can. & Mex. Ch. Arriba of Arriso, owned by John and Dorothy Leonard, Cal.

Yorkies are becoming very popular in Japan, too. Grand Champion Trinket's Trisha II, Best Yorkshire in Japan 1974. Owned by Tom T. Yamamoto, Saitam-Ken, Japan.

Eng. & Am. Ch. DeeBee's Bee Bee, winner of the Toy Group at Crufts (world's largest show, held in London) 1972. Bred by Mrs. Pitcher (England.) Owned by Gloria Lipman, N.Y.

Ch. Quarnhill Fusspot, bred by Mrs. E. Lamb (England) and owned by Gloria Lipman.

Ch. Viclar's Heesa Dandy. Bred by Vivian Foster and owned by Nancy Lee Webb, Pa.

Ch. Windshaven's Camille, bred and owned by Nancy Lee Webb, Pa.

Am. & Can. Ch. Topaz Cufflink, bred by Mrs. May and owned by Mrs. James, was Best of Winners at the 1972 Specialty. Mrs. James also owns his full sister, Am. & Can. Ch. Topaz Vikki's Verity, who was BOW at the 1973 YTC of Canada Specialty. Their sire is Am., Can. & Mex. Ch. Starfire Mitey Model, a son of Am., Can. & Mex. Ch. Wildweir Keepsake out of Twin Oaks I'm Betsy, a Ch. Wildweir Dinner Jacket daughter. Mitey Model has won Best in Show in Canada, as well as Toy Groups in the United States, Canada and Mexico. The dam of Cufflink and Verity is Mrs. May's Beegee's Sue's Victory, dam of four champions.

Victory was bred by the George Schildgens of Long Beach, Calif. The Schildgens have been breeding since 1960. Their Melissa Lee (Ch. Wildweir Coat of Arms ex Gwenny of Bourland) is the dam of three champions including Ch. Beegee's Sweet Blue Laurel, the Schildgens' Group winner in 1972.

Mrs. Bonita Hewes owns the Radnor Yorkshires in Elverson, Pa. This line started in 1966 with Ch. Faience Lord Lovejoy, who traced to the Hintonwood line in England, and was bred by Russell Jackson of Collegeville, Pa. The top winner of the Radnor Kennel, Am. & Can. Ch. Apollo Radnor, has won several Group placings. Radnor Kennels have owned or bred eight Champions.

Mrs. Hewes co-owns Silverwind's Spirit of Apollo (Ch. Wildweir Fair n' Square ex Ch. Wildweir Candytuff) with his breeder, Elissa Taddie, owner of the Silverwind Kennels in West Chester, Pa.

Ch. Pete's Tiger, owned by Dorothy Scott of Austin, Texas, is a Best in Show winner. He was bred by Mrs. Victor Schupp out of Ch. Peter Pan of Wayside, a grandson of Ch. Mr. Kipps of Grenbar. His dam was Rosemarie of Wayside.

Fred Wolpert started breeding in 1967, basing their line primarily on Mayfair-Barban and on Maybelle Neuguth's breeding. Their Ch. Frojo's Blue Buttons of Maybelle (Ch. Wildweir E. Major of Maybelle ex Kella don Shanadora) is the dam of four champions. The Wolperts have bred or owned 12 Champions.

Frances C. Geraghty's Yorkfold Kennels are located in Louisville, Ohio. This kennel is based on dogs of Mrs. D. Rossiter's (English) Yorkfold Kennels and Mrs. Palmer's Winpal line in England.

The first Group winner shown by Yorkfold Kennels was Ch. Gayfold Lorelei (Ch. Yorkfold Gold Teddy ex Ch. Don Deigo's Sweetie Pie), bred by Mrs. N. Quillen.

Ch. Bella Donna of Winpal (Eng. Ch. Yorkfold Wrupert Bear ex

Winpal Queen Bee), bred by Mrs. Palmer, won her first Toy Group in 1967. In all, she won 8 Toy Groups and 11 Group placings. Am. Ch. Yorkfold Bruno Bear, shown by Mr. Geraghty and owned by Mr. E. Hitchin, won 1 Best in Show, 8 Toy Groups and 14 Group placings. Bella Donna was the dam of four champions.

Am. Ch. Yorkfold Jezebel, bred by Frances Geraghty, is a daughter of Bella Donna. Jezebel's sire, Eng., Am. & Can. Ch. Yorkfold McPickles (Eng., Irish & Jap. Ch. Buranthea's Saint Malacky ex Gold Dinky of Arcady). Jezebel was the winner of 1 Best in Show, 7 Toy Groups and 17 Group placings.

Ch. Yorkfold Witchhunter (Ch. Yorkfold Benjamin, a son of Jezebel's ex Ch. Bella Donna of Winpal) is the winner of 5 Toy Groups and 31 Group placings. He was the winner of the 1972 YTCA Specialty, and is sire of a champion. Witch Hunter's brother, Ch. Yorkfold on Target, has placed in 5 Toy Groups.

Beatrice and Rex Kramer started the Beerex Yorkshires in 1967 and have bred or owned eight champions. The Beerex dogs are based on the Progresso line. Their first champion was Ch. Progresso Busy Bee, who is the dam of Beerex's top winner and sire Ch. Beerex Rajahd. Rajahd has won 5 Toy Groups and a number of Group placings, and 41 Bests of Breed. He has sired three champions.

Nancy Lee Webb began Windshaven Kennels in Broomall, Pa. with two top stud dogs. Ch. Yorkfold Wags to Witches (Eng., Am. & Can. Ch. Yorkfold McPickles ex Ch. Bella Donna of Winpal), bred by Mrs. Frances Geraghty, has sired 8 champions. Ch. Viclar's Heesa Dandy, bred by Vivan Foster of the Viclar Kennels in California is by Am. & Can. Ch. Viclar's Sompin' Special (a son of Ch. Wildweir Keepsake) out of Aine of Plata Pina (an Irish import from Hazel Berkerry's line) and he has sired six champions.

Ch. Wynsippi's Candid Lass (Ch. Gay-Lee's Rise n' Shine ex Lorely Bonnie of Wynsippi), purchased from Virginia Knoche, won Best of Opposite Sex at the 1971 YTCA Specialty at Atlantic City, N.J. Lass was bred by Mrs. L. Anderson.

Mrs. Webb has bred or owned 14 champions. Her Ch. Windshaven Incredible sired Evelyn and Frances Malone's Mal-O-Bar's Reckless Robert, winner of the 1973 YTCA Sweepstakes at San Francisco. The Malones Mal-O-Bar Kennels are located in Contati, Calif.

Ch. Lamsgrove Pinnochio (Eng. & Jap. Ch. Pagnell Peter Pan ex Whitecross Daisy Belle), bred by Mrs. E. Lamb and owned by Pearl Trojan of Chesterton, Ind., was a top U.S. winner in 1967, winning 1 Best in Show, 2 Toy Groups and 2 Group placings. He has sired champions.

Ch. Ladylair Fancy Pants.
Breeder-owners: Fay and
Chuck Hudson, Ill.

Ch. Marie of Glengonner.
Bred by D. A. Peck, Scotland.
Owned by Mr. and Mrs. Robert Pricer, Va.

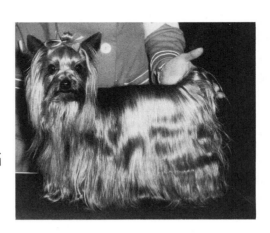

Ch. Doton's Blue Prince.
Breeder-owners, Dotty and
Tony DeMaula, N. J.

The Nikko Kennels of Gloria and Stanley P. Lipman at Great Neck, Long Island, were started in 1969, and have won titles with 17 Yorkshires.

The Lipmans' Ch. Aga Lynn's Alfie (Judlu's Jethro ex Aga Lynn's Jenny), bred by Agnes Wegaman, was Winners Dog at the 1972 YTCA Specialty.

Ch. Quarnhill Fusspot (Eng. Jap. Ch. Murose Storm ex Quarnhill Quality), bred by Mrs. E. Lamb, England, was imported by Mr. and Mrs. Gordon Duffy of Rush, N.Y., owners of Stonybrook Kennels, and sold to the Lipmans in 1971. Fusspot is a Group winner and has sired five champions.

The Lipmans purchased Eng. & Am. Ch. Dee Bee's Bee Bee (Dee Bee's Bumble Boy ex Polly Fisher of Whitton) from Mrs. Dorris Beach, of the Dee Bee's Kennels in England. Bee Bee was bred by Mrs. Pitcher, Eng. and was a top winner in England, winning the Toy Group at the world famous Crufts show, as well as a Best in Show and a Yorkshire Terrier Specialty. In the United States, she has won 4 Toy Groups and 10 Group placings.

Mrs. Ruth Jenkins is the owner of the Jentre Kennels in Issaquah, Washington. Mrs. Jenkins owns Am. & Can. Ch. Clarkwyn Jubilee Eagle, winner of 2 Toy groups and 9 Group placings. Jubilee was Best of Breed at the 1973 YTC of Canada Specialty in Toronto, Can. Mrs. Jenkins' Can. & Am. Ch. Jentre's Tia Tia, a daughter of Ch. Heart G's Spunky Sparky, has placed in several Groups.

Tony and Dorothy DeMaula own the Doton Kennels in Mattituck, N.J. Ch. Doton's Blue Prince (Ch. Loughlann's de Plata Pina ex Doton's Little Miss Muffet) was their first champion. Doton is based on dogs of Hazel Berkerry's DePlata Pina Kennels in Ireland.

Charles and Fay Hudson, of North Lake, Ill. own the Lady Lair Kennels. Their Ch. Handy Andy of Hillcrest is a son of Ch. Lamsgrove Pinnochio, and has sired three champions. Lady Lair has owned or bred seven Champions.

Mr. and Mrs. John Leonard own the Dorchester Kennels in Berkeley, Calif. They own the only two American Yorkshires we know of that have won the International titles awarded for winning either C.A.C.I.B. or F.C.I.'s: Int. Am., Can., & Mex. Ch. Stirkean's Tiny Tim of Kingsmere has won 4 Toy Groups in Mexico and a Toy Group in Canada. Int. Am. Can. & Mex. Ch. Arribo of Arriso has won a Toy Group and 4 Group placings in the United States, and the same in Canada.

162

5

Introduction to
The Standard

PRESCRIBED standards are useful things. They can help us buy clothes to the right fit, measure the ingredients for a cake, and even set values for a monetary system. In purebred dogs, the word *standard* identifies the written and approved concept of the ideal dog of the breed.

Most breeds were originated to serve mankind in some specific way. The Yorkshire Terrier stems from the little rough terriers of Great Britain—little terriers who killed rats around the farmyard and caught small game for the master's table. This little dog worked in water, over hills and dales, and underground, to bolt small game. He was small enough to carry in a pouch and saddlebag, and got along on small rations.

By degrees, breeders became interested in not only keeping this ratting ability, but in preserving a specific *type*. A local keeper of a public house, looking for some way to improve his patronage, would provide a place where a gathering of fanciers could show off their specimens—not only in action, but in form. Thus conformation became a consideration, and rules were drawn up. The criterion brought to light desired points, and soon, from this touchstone, the breed had—in a rough way—developed a standard.

However, a hitch has developed too. Through the years, word meanings change. For example, today we speak of people "doing their own thing." But back in the time of the Vikings, a "thing" was a place for an assembly or council.

The Yorkie standard has many words that make true sense only if we take the pains to interpret them as intended by the establishers of the standard. To do this, we must take into account the dog's origin, its use, and the literal meaning of the words. We must keep in mind, too, that the points desired for the breed are tied genetically to other points in the breed. The standard abides as a guard. If we lose the concepts tailored by those who originated the breed's identity, we wind up with dogs that—albeit sound—are lacking in the qualities that distinguish them as Yorkshire Terriers.

Therefore, before going on to today's AKC-approved standard, let's look back at some of the first full Yorkie descriptions on record.

Among the earliest descriptions of show or breed type comes this, from *The Dog* by Idestone in 1872. In his chapter on "The Broken-Haired Fox Terrier," Idestone writes:

Manchester has produced a sort of late years called Scotch Terrier, with a long silky forelock covering the face and eyes. These are invariably Blue-grey, Tan or Black-Tan and they are large or toy size. I imagine they are manufactured from those for which Peter Eden was famed. I have seen—I think at Middleton—the stock dog from which most of these dogs come, and the best class I ever saw was produced at that exhibition; for these men in rags refused offers of twenty or thirty guineas from the London dealers, and they were not far wrong, as the breed has become exceedingly fashionable and second-rate specimens—first-rate ones are never in the market—readily fetch twenty or thirty guineas each. A good blue, a rich tan, length and silky texture of forelock, symmetry and clearness of marks, are the great points of excellence, whilst the prevalence of the blue tinge is never passed over, and generally carries the day.

These dogs require constant attention, and are carefully brushed, combed and cultivated, as one lump of felt is soon succeeded by another, and a tangled coat is fatal to all chances of success. Great roguery is committed by the dishonest in the dressing and staining of these dogs, but the chicanery has hitherto never escaped detection as judging takes place in daylight and even heightened color is transparently visible to a practiced judge.

Dogs of this breed are generally cropped, but it does not add to their beauty as the ears are scarcely visible. The coat is profuse on the body, the tail is not very bushy; the feet are short-coated; the eyes rather full; the mustache moderate; the tan is profuse and blended into a black saddle, and the general texture is soft and silky; the back should be silvery, with a mixture of slate or blue; this should prevail on face and legs.

The dog is hard to describe and difficult to judge, requiring a practiced eye, acute observation, and adroit comparison. The oldest dogs are generally the most taking; none are thoroughly coated until they are over two years old, and much allowance must be made for age. They are also called Yorkshire and Lancashire Terriers, and the best I have seen have come from the latter county, with the exception of Mr. Foster's.

Though this is not a standard, we feel it would take more than practice, acuteness and adroitness to sort out. The general picture of a long-coated Toy dog with soft, silky hair of a blue and tan color is taking form. Already the distinct facet of his being is his coat and color.

The next approach to a description of a show Yorkshire Terrier comes from, *"Dogs: Their Points, Whims, Instinct and Peculiarities,"* edited by Henry Webb and published in 1872.

From the pages of this book, voices trail down from the past offering us a description of Crab and Kitty's grandson; a dog who appears in Huddersfield Ben's pedigree as a great-grandparent, a great, great-grandparent and a great, great, great-grandparent. Which should blow to the four winds the voices that offer us the theory that the Yorkie just blew like a falling leaf into the world of dogdom. This type of breeding can only be called controlled in-breeding.

The dog mentioned in Mr. Webb's treatise was "Old" Sandy who was registered by The Kennel Club as a Yorkshire Terrier, though his great-grandson Huddersfield Ben beat him into the registry.

Mr. Webb says in 1872:

Mr. Spink's Scotch Terriers are well known and we have great pleasure in being able to give photographs of his most celebrated dogs; Old Sandy (commonly called Huddersfield Sandy) was unfortunately stolen on his way home from Brighton in 1866, after winning the first prize at the dog show. His weight was seven pounds, a very rich tan, golden head, deep blue and a very straight, rather strong, hair, but very bright. Illustrated by photo are: Silk, also a prize dog; Doctor; and Punch, who has won a large number of prizes. Mr. Spink says that the Scotch Terrier should be bred as follows:

"The head rather long, with hair falling down considerably below the jaw, golden color at the sides and on ears, also on the muzzle and mustachios; hair on the back long and perfectly straight, good rich blue and very bright; legs and feet well tanned and not too much feathered; tail perfectly straight and well carried; shape firm and compact, not too long on the legs, broad chest and tanned; there must be no white on any part of the body, not even the slightest suspicion of curl or wave on the coat, and the hair fine and bright in quality. The blue and tan should contrast so well as to please the eye, rich and decided in color, and not a sickly silver color all over."

Slowly the rules that would model the Yorkshire Terrier were being laid down, rules that make him a distinct member of the family of purebred dogs.

The next informant on the Yorkshire Terrier's points is Hugh Dalziel from Mr. Walsh's book, *"Dogs of the British Islands,"* published in 1878. His description of their general appearance leaves one feeling that he wasn't too keen on the breed.

The photo montage of Mr. Spink's Scotch Terriers referred to in the accompanying text. These are believed to be the earliest photographs of Yorkshire Terrier ancestry known. The numbers identify: "Silk" (47); "Doctor" (46) and "Punch" (48.)

He may be described as the newest goods of this class from the Yorkshire loom; with the greater propriety that his distinctive character is in his coat—well carded, soft and long as it is and beautifully tinted with 'cunning Huddersfield dyes' and free from even a suspicion of 'shoddy'.

Visitors to our dog shows, who look out for the beautiful as well as the useful, cannot fail to be attracted by this little exquisite, as he reclines on his cushion of silk or velvet, in the centre of his little palace of crystal and mahogany, or struts round his mansion, with the consequential airs of the dandy that he is; yet with all his self-assertion of dignity, his beard of approved cut and color, faultless whiskers of Dundreary type, and coat of absolute perfection, without one hair awry, one cannot help feeling that he is but a dandy after all, and would look but a poor scarecrow in dishabille and, possibly too, on account of his dwelling, or reception room, in the construction of which art is mostly set at defiance, one is apt to leave him with the scarcely concealed contempt for a Scion of the 'Veneering family' who, in aping the aristocrat, fail as *parvenus* do. Such as he is, however, there can be little doubt that should ever a canine Teufelsdröckh promulgate a philosophy of clothes for the benefit of his species, the Yorkshire Terrier will represent the dandiacal body: Whilst, in striking contrast, those everyday drudges, the Irish Terriers and Scotch Terriers, with their coarse, ragged unkempt coats will be exhibited as the 'bog-trotter' and 'stock-o-duds' sects of the doggy family.

Mr. Ash then quotes Mr. Dalziel as giving the breed's points in 1878:

The head is small, rather flat on the crown, and together with the muzzle, much resembles, in shape, the Skye Terrier. The eyes, only seen when the "fall" or hair of the face is parted, were also small, keen and bright. The ears, when entire, are either erect, with a slight falling over at the tip or quite pricked.

The legs and feet, although scarcely seen, were to be straight and good, or the dog would have a deformed appearance.

The tail is usually docked, and shows abundance of feathering.

The coat long, straight and silky; must not have any appearance of curl or crimping, and, if wavy, it must be very slightly so; but many excellent specimens have the coat slightly waved.

He writes that he does not know the utmost extent to which the coat has been grown, but supposes it to be 10 to 12 inches.

The colour is one of the most essential things to be looked for in the Yorkshire Terrier; so important is it and so fully is this recognized by exhibitors, that it is said some specimens are shown at times not quite innocent of plum bags and things judiciously applied. They are really blue and tan terriers, and the blue ranges from the clear silvery hue of a deep sky-blue and a blue-black. All dogs, I believe, get lighter in color as they age. The tan on the head should be golden, and the 'fall', or hair over the face, gets silvery towards the ends; the tan is deeper on the whiskers and about the ears and on the legs.

They vary in size considerably, so much so that I advocate most strongly making two classes for them, for it is utterly absurd to class any of this breed as a broken-haired terrier, as The Kennel Club does, regardless of the plain meaning of the words. What can be more stupid than to give one of these terriers a prize in his own proper class and proper designation, and his own mother a prize in the broken-haired toy class?

He gives the weights and heights of some of the leading dogs:

"Smart" (Mrs. Foster's), age 3 years, weight 10 lbs.; height 12 inches; length from nose to set of tail, 22 inches.

"Sandy" (Mrs. Foster's), age 2 years, weight 4¾ lbs.; height 9 inches; length from nose to set of tail, 19 inches.

Six years run between the two 1872 descriptions and Mr. Dalziel's of 1878. During this period the specification of points desired had increased even to the point of criticism. The Yorkshire Terrier had now acquired a criterion for head, eyes, muzzle, ears, legs, tail and size. Yet the emphasis remained on his shining glory—the distinction that places him apart from other canines—his required coat color and silken long coat.

This emphasis can be seen in the Yorkie's description given in 1887, in *The Dogs of Great Britain, America and Other Countries* written by Stonehenge, together with chapters by American writers. It goes:

As they are always shown in full dress, little more than outline of shape is looked for; the eye, except when the hair is tied up is invisible; the tail is shortened, and the ear is generally cut. When uncut, it must be small and is preferred when it drops slightly at the tip, but this is a trivial point, and sinks into insignificance before coat and color; the coat must be abundant over the whole body, head, legs and tail, and artificial means are used to encourage its growth; length and straightness, freedom from curl and waviness being sought for; the body color should be clear, soft, silvery blue of course varying in shade; with this is preferred a golden tan head, with darker tan about ears, and rich tan legs. The style in which the coat is arranged for exhibition is beautifully shown in the sketch of Katie; but that stage of perfection is not attained without much time, trouble and patience. When the pups are born they are black in color, as are pepper Dandie Dinmonts and others; at an early age, the tip of the tail is nipped off to the desired length, the ears, if cut at all, not until the age of six to eight months, and before this the coat will be changing color, getting gradually lighter. To prevent the hair being scratched and broken, little or no meat is given.

From these beginning sketches, the costuming came into play. By degrees, his general appearance was brought to the fore. Reference was made to body shape and action. Rules were drawn, models fixed and the breed characteristics established. Words set down as descriptions of early show Yorkshire Terriers have descended to us as part of our present standard.

Drawings of Yorkshire Terrier by Arthur Wardle for two different printings of Rawdon Lee's *Modern Dogs*. The top drawing, done prior to 1895, shows cropped ears; the lower version was drawn in 1896 after ear cropping was banned in England.

Hunting for a positive date for the first accepted Yorkshire Terrier standard leaves one trailing through contradictive testimony. Mr. P.H. Coombs, in a book copyrighted in 1891, includes a standard he says was accepted by the Yorkshire Terrier Club of England in 1890. Mrs. Munday, Mrs. Swan and Colonel Whitehead in their respective books—*The Yorkshire Terrier*—hold with the standard being accepted by The Yorkshire Terrier Club in 1898, with no mention of the former Club. Other English writers say the first accepted standard was drawn up by The Y.T.C. in London at a general meeting January 5, 1911. And littering up the trail further, Mrs. Mallock includes in her American books—published in 1907 and 1925—what she claims to be the standard.

Mr. P.H. Coombs has his version of the first standard in *The American Book of the Dogs*, edited by G.O. Shields, copyright 1891 (Yorkie Article by Coombs):

Quantity and color of hair on back	25
Quality of coat	15
Tan	15
Head	10
Eyes	5
Mouth	5
Ears	5
Legs and Feet	5
Body and General Appearance	10
Tail	5
Total	100

General appearance. This should be of a long-coated pet dog, the coat hanging quite straight and evenly down each side, a parting extending from the nose to the end of the tail. The animal should be compact and neat, the carriage being very "sprightly" bearing an important air. Although the frame is hidden beneath a mantle of hair, the general outline should be such as to suggest the existence of a vigorous and well-proportioned body.

Head. This should be rather small and flat, not too prominent or round in skull, rather broad at the muzzle, with a perfectly black nose; the hair on the muzzle very long, which should be a rich deep tan, not sooty or gray. Under the chin, long hair about the same color as the center of the head, which should be a bright golden tan and not on any account intermingled with dark or sooty hairs. Hair on the sides of the head should be very long and a few shades deeper than the center of the head, especially about the ear-roots.

The Eyes should be of medium size, dark in color, having a sharp, intelligent expression, and placed so as to look directly forward but should not be prominent. The edges of the eyelids should be of a darker color.

Ears, cut or uncut. If cut quite erect; uncut, small, V-shaped, and carried semi-erect. Covered with short hair. Color to be a deep, dark tan.

The Mouth should be good and even; teeth as sound as possible. A dog having lost a tooth or two through accident not the least objectionable, providing the jaws are even.

The Body should be very compact with a good loin, and level on top of the back.

Coat. The hair as long and straight as possible (not wavy), which should be flossy, not woolly. It should extend from the back of the head to the root of tail. Color a bright steel-blue, and on no account intermingled with fawn, light or dark hairs.

Legs quite straight, of a bright, golden-tan color, and well covered with hair, a few shades lighter at the ends than at the roots.

Feet as round as possible; toe-nails black.

Weight divided into two classes, viz; under five pounds and over five pounds, but not to exceed twelve pounds.

Referring to the standard, Mr. Wilkinson says: "Personally, I confess a weakness for color over quantity of coat, as I contend it is quite possible to produce a vast quantity of coat on a specimen otherwise indifferent. From boyhood, I remember my father (now deceased) being a great breeder and fancier of Yorkshire Terriers, and he could not tolerate a dog without the rich golden tan, and I certainly inherit his weakness, and think points most difficult to obtain should be thought most highly of when they are produced. I am rather afraid that, of late years, too much thought has been given to length of coat in preference to good color and moderate coat combined. A lot of hair with a dog attached does not constitute a perfect Yorkshire Terrier."

Mr. Bootman also says with relation to this point: "Richness of tan on head and legs should, to my mind, be more cultivated than at present. This property was highly prized by the old breeders. The craze for length of coat has in great measure been the means of reducing the quality of tan."

In *Toy Dogs*, by Lillian C. Raymond-Mallock, published by Dogdom Publishing Co., Battle Creek, Michigan, in 1907, only a few changes appear. She goes on: "Coat, which should be glossy like silk (not woolly)". She also adds: "not intermingled the least with fawn, light, or dark hairs."

Mrs. Mallock then puts a description of the tail into the standard: "Tail—cut to medium length, with plenty of hair on, darker blue in color than the rest of the body, especially at the end of the tail and carried a little higher than the end of the back."

Luckily there are clues spread around that make it evident what transpired and why; Mr. Coombs and Mrs. Mallock held to a standard that did not conform to the one accepted by The Kennel Club and the American Kennel Club.

In *The Twentieth Century Dog (Non-Sporting)* published in London in 1904, the author, Herbert Compton sheds a great deal of light with the following excerpts:

What the Whippet is to the miners of Northumberland—what the Bulldog was reputed to be the horny-handed sons of toil—that place the Yorkshire Terrier fills in the cottages of the weavers and workers in certain manufacturing districts. Although it has been taken up by fanciers of light and leading, and by dames of high degree, it is really a working man's pet, and his ewe-lamb in a way.

And now for a description of the subject of this article. I am happy in having two at my disposal, and as there are differences of opinion in the fancy, I have no hesitation in giving them both.

Mr. F. Randall: "In my opinion the type of Yorkshire Terrier now shown in London and the South cannot be improved. I consider the dark, steel-blue (not silver) a great improvement on the pale-coloured dogs, which seem to generally be preferred in the North, and are easier to breed than the darker ones."

Mr. Fred Poole (representing the North): "I am quite satisfied with type, as I think a good specimen of today is as near perfection as it is possible to get. My club, the Halifax and District Yorkshire Terrier Club, is the oldest society in existence of its kind and going very strong, with plenty of members. All the Champion dogs of the past and present owe their origin to Halifax, such as Halifax Marvel, the sire of these three noted dogs, Ch. Ted, Ch. Merry Mascot and Ch. Ashton Queen.' "

Then Mr. Compton continues: "The following are the points of the Yorkshire Terrier Club, an institution belonging to the South of England; in the North, the points vary somewhat, especially in color."

Rather than give the whole standard that Mr. Randall provides Mr. Compton, we will just give those points that differ from Mr. Coombs. Under *General Appearance*—"the carriage being very upright, and having an important air." Head had now changed measurement from breadth to length, as it says; "nor too long in muzzle" and added to *Head*, "on no account must the tan on the head extend on to the neck." All references to dark, sooty or gray being intermingled with the tan have been collected and phrased as, "nor must there be any sooty or dark hairs intermingled with any of the tan." No mention is made of the hair under the chin.

"*Ears*—small V-shaped and carried semi-erect. *Eyes*—have acquired a "sharp terrier expression," rather than "a sharp intelligent expression."

"*Coat*—The hair on body as long as possible, and perfectly straight (not wavy), glossy like silk, and of a fine silky texture. Colour, a dark steel-blue (not silver-blue) extending from occiput, or back of skull, to the root of the tail, and on no account mingled with fawn, bronze, or dark hairs." Thus, the texture has been described in fuller length. 'Flossy' has become 'glossy' and 'not woolly' has been dropped. The wording has acquired a highbrow tone by adding "occiput."

Legs have added a new measure: "Tan not extending higher on the fore legs than the elbow, nor on the hind legs than the stifle." *Tail* follows Mrs. Mallock's description.

Inserted as a separate clause: "*Tan*—All tan hair should be darker at the roots than in the middle, shading to a still lighter tan at the tips."

"*Weight*—Three classes: 5 lbs. and under; 7 lbs. and under but over 5 lbs.; over 7 lbs." The point value given:

```
"Quantity and length of coat ........................... 15
 Quality and texture of coat ........................... 10
 Richness of tan on head and legs ..................... 15
 Color of hair on body ................................... 15
 Head...5, Eyes...5, Legs and feet ..................... 5
 Tail, carriage of...5, Mouth ........................... 5
 Formation and general appearance ................... 10
```

Now the gentleman from the North held with the points as "Symmetry and general appearance, 20; quality and quantity of coat on head, 15; quality and quantity of coat on back, 15; tan, 15; head, 10; eyes, 5; mouth, 5; ears, 5; legs and feet, 5; tail, 5."

The Northerners also stuck with a standard running generally as put forth by Mr. Coombs. The texture has become "which should be glossy like silk (not woolly)." Their dogs, from the birthplace of the Yorkshire Terrier, remain bright steel-blue. Both Mrs. Mallock and Mr. Coombs imported their stock primarily from the North and obviously held with the breed's originators and early fanciers.

Mr. Compton finishes off his article with: "The Yorkshire Terrier fancy is well supplied with specialist clubs, including The Yorkshire Terrier Club, The Halifax and District Y.T. Club, The Y.T. Club of Scotland, The Bolton and District Y.T. Club, and The Manchester and District Y.T. Club. Mr. F. Randall is the Honorary Secretary of the first named, which was formed in 1897, and has done a great deal for the breed, especially in giving a healthier tone to the show ring. It is under the Presidentship of the Countess of Aberdeen, and has passed from the beaten track by recently electing two lady members as judges."

The workers and weavers were about to find their social class carried little weight as the Dames of high degree and fanciers of light and leading took up their pet.

The Manual of Toy Dogs and Their Treatment, by Mrs. Leslie Williams, copyrighted 1904, and updated 1910, third edition 1913, has the: "Points of the Yorkshire Terrier as laid down by the Yorkshire Terrier Club, Secretary Mr. F.W. Randall, 'The Clone', Hampton-on-Thames." It is the same as given by Mr. Compton except that it now states: "Colour, a dark steel-blue (not silver blue)." And then before "the value of points in judging", comes: "*Silver Yorkshires*—points identical with those of the standard Yorkshire, as described above, except colouring, which should be as follows: *Back*—silver. *Head*—pale tan or straw colour. *Muzzle* and *Legs*—light tan. *Ears*—a shade darker tan.''

Silver was never a desired color as can be demonstrated by the early write-ups of winning dogs. When bright steel blue was replaced by dark steel blue, one of the breed's original rules established by the originators of the breed was violated. A course was laid that would lead to black Yorkies with tans intermingled with sooty, grey or black hairs. For the use of 'dark' was to define the depth of color desired. The point remains that 'bright' more lucidly illustrates what was originally desired. Bright gives illumination to steel blue showing that it should reflect light.

It would seem likely that the General Meeting of the Yorkshire Terrier Club in London, January 5, 1911, was a very lively encounter. When the last of the old guard fell before a hail of words from the new recruits to the breed, a new standard was drawn up. The pet dog of the north, became the Toy dog of the south.

The same standard accepted and approved by the Kennel Club was accepted and approved by the American Kennel Club from 1912 until April 12, 1966. It continues as the standard approved by the Canadian Kennel Club.

AKC Standard from 1912 to 1966

General Appearance—Should be that of a long-coated toy terrier, the coat hanging quite straight and evenly down each side, a parting extending from the nose to the end of the tail. The animal should be very compact and neat, the carriage being very upright, and having an important air. The general outline should convey the existence of a vigorous and well-proportioned body.

Head—Should be rather small and flat, not too prominent or round in the skull, nor too long in the muzzle, with a perfect black nose. The fall on the head to be long, of a rich golden tan, deeper in color at the sides of the head about the ear roots, and on the muzzle where it should be very long. The hair on the chest a rich bright tan. On no account must the tan on the head extend on to the neck, nor must there be any sooty or dark hair intermingled with any of the tan.

Eyes—Medium, dark and sparkling, having a sharp, intelligent expression, and placed so as to look directly forward. They should not be prominent, and the edge of the eyelids should be of a dark color.

Ears—Small, V-shaped, and carried semierect, or erect, and not far apart, covered with short hair, color to be of a very deep rich tan.

Mouth—Perfectly even, with teeth as sound as possible. An animal having lost any teeth through accident not a fault, providing the jaws are even.

Body—Very compact, and a good loin. Level on the top of the back.

Coat—The hair on body moderately long and perfectly straight (not wavy), glossy like silk, and of a fine silky texture. Color, a dark steel blue (not silver blue) extending from the occiput (or back of skull) to the root of tail, and on no account mingled with fawn, bronze or dark hairs.

Legs—Quite straight, well covered with hair of a rich golden tan a few shades lighter at the ends than at the roots, not extending higher on the forelegs than the elbow, nor on the hind legs than the stifle.

Feet—As round as possible, and the toenails black.

Tail—Cut to medium length;with plenty of hair, darker blue in color than the rest of the body, especially at the end of the tail, and carried a little higher than the level of the back.

Tan—All tan hair should be darker at the roots than in the middle, shading to a still lighter tan at the tips.

	Points
Formation and terrier appearance	15
Color of hair on body	15
Richess of tan on head and legs	15
Quality and texture of coat	10
Quantity and length of coat	10
Head	10
Mouth	5
Legs and feet	5
Ears	5
Eyes	5
Tail (carriage of)	5
Total	**100**

With exception that a specification of "Weight up to 7 lbs." has been added, and the point specifications at the end of the standard have been dropped, these remain the requirements called for in the English standard today.

In 1966, the Yorkhire Terrier Club of America drew up a new standard, approved by the Board of Directors of the American Kennel Club, and this standard—reproduced on the pages that follow—is the one that applies in this country today. It was the hope of dedicated fanciers of the breed that the updating and rearranging of some of the wording of the old standard and the adding of specifications on the color of puppies would benefit the breed. With hindsight, however, we now see that these hopes have not been materialized. It remains, alas, that to fully comprehend the standard, one must be aware of the meanings behind its words.

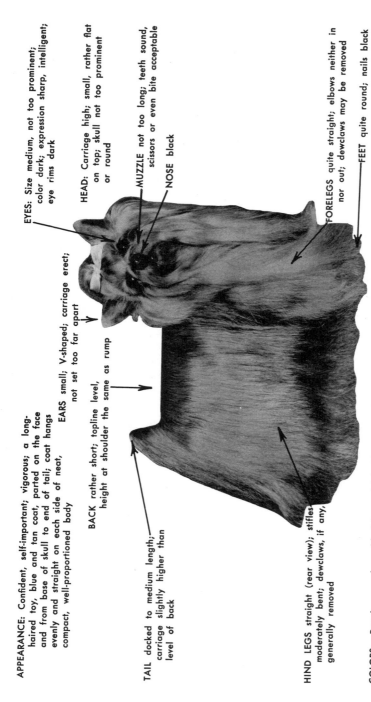

APPEARANCE: Confident, self-important, vigorous; a long-haired toy, blue and tan coat, parted on the face and from base of skull to end of tail; coat hangs evenly and straight on each side of neat, compact, well-proportioned body

EYES: Size medium, not too prominent; color dark; expression sharp, intelligent; eye rims dark

HEAD: Carriage high; small, rather flat on top; skull not too prominent or round

MUZZLE not too long; teeth sound, scissors or even bite acceptable

NOSE black

EARS small; V-shaped; carriage erect; not set too far apart

BACK rather short; topline level, height at shoulder the same as rump

FORELEGS quite straight; elbows neither in nor out; dewclaws may be removed

FEET quite round; nails black

COAT quality, texture and quantity of prime importance: Texture glossy, fine glossy, silky; body coat long, straight (not wavy); may be trimmed to floor length; the headfall can be tied with one or two bows; muzzle hair long; hair on ear tips trimmed; hair on feet may be trimmed

WEIGHT: Must not exceed 7 pounds

TAIL docked to medium length; carriage slightly higher than level of back

HIND LEGS straight (rear view); stifles moderately bent; dewclaws, if any, generally removed

COLORS: Puppies are born black/tan. Adult blue is steel blue (not silver nor mingled with fawn, bronze or black hairs). Tan hair is darker at roots, shading lighter to tips (no sooty or black hair with tan). Blue extends over body from back of neck to tail root. Hair on tail darker blue, especially at end. Headfall rich, golden tan, deeper at sides, ear roots and on muzzle. Ears a deep, rich, tan (tan should not extend down back of neck). Chest, legs, a bright, rich tan, not extending above elbows or above stifles

Visualization of the Yorkshire Terrier standard.—Courtesy, Dog Standards Illustrated, Howell Book House Inc.

6

Official AKC Standard
for the Yorkshire Terrier

General Appearance—That of a long-haired toy terrier whose blue and tan coat is parted on the face and from the base of the skull to the end of the tail and hangs evenly and quite straight down each side of body. The body is neat, compact and well-proportioned. The dog's high head carriage and confident manner should give the appearance of vigor and self-importance.

Head—Small and rather flat on top, the skull not too prominent or round, the muzzle not too long, with the bite neither undershot nor overshot and teeth sound. Either scissors bite or level bite is acceptable. The nose is black. Eyes are medium in size and not too prominent; dark in color and sparkling with a sharp intelligent expression. Eye rims are dark. Ears are small, V-shaped carried erect and set not too far apart.

Body—Well proportioned and very compact. The back is rather short, the back line level, with height at shoulder the same as at the rump.

Legs and Feet—Forelegs should be straight, elbows neither in nor out. Hind legs straight when viewed from behind, but stifles are moderately bent when viewed from the sides. Feet are round with black toenails. Dewclaws, if any, are generally removed from the hind legs. Dewclaws on the forelegs may be removed.

Tail—Docked to a medium length and carried slightly higher than the level of the back.

Coat—Quality, texture and quantity of coat are of prime importance. Hair is glossy, fine and silky in texture. Coat on the body moderately long and perfectly straight (not wavy). It may be trimmed to floor length to give ease of movement and a neater appearance, if desired. The fall on the head is long, tied with one bow in center of head or parted in the middle and tied with two bows. Hair on muzzle is very long. Hair should be trimmed short on tips of ears and may be trimmed on feet to give them a neat appearance.

Colors—Puppies are born black and tan and are normally darker in body color, showing intermingling of black hair in the tan until they are matured. Color of hair on body and richness of tan on head and legs are of prime importance in *adult dogs,* to which the following color requirements apply:

BLUE: Is a dark steel-blue, not a silver-blue and not mingled with fawn, bronze or black hairs.

TAN: All tan hair is darker at the roots than in the middle, shading to still lighter tan at the tips. There should be no sooty or black hair intermingled with any of the tan.

Color on Body—The blue extends over the body from back of neck to root of tail. Hair on tail is a darker blue, especially at end of tail.

Headfall—A rich golden tan, deeper in color at sides of head, at ear roots and on the muzzle, with ears a deep rich tan. Tan color should not extend down on back of neck.

Chest and Legs—A bright, rich tan, not extending above the elbow on the forelegs nor above the stifle on the hind legs.

Weight—Must not exceed seven pounds.

Approved April 12, 1966.

7

In-Depth Study of the Standard

THE YORKSHIRE TERRIER'S type is embodied in the points of the standard that distinguish him from other purebred dogs. The English standard is slightly different in wording from the American standard—differences we shall note further on in this chapter—but both desire the same type of Yorkshire Terrier.

In the United States, it is the present American Kennel Club approved standard that we—whether breeder, exhibitor or judge—must accept as guide. The question of whether it is a good set of rules, clearly worded, setting forth the ideal model, will remain. A new standard, or revision of the present, might steady the breed's flow, but past experience doesn't present an airtight case for such thinking. Our better course would seem to lie in looking into the reasons and thoughts behind the wording of the standard.

The points in *General Appearance* are more clearly defined in the rest of the standard. It is well, however, to place them mentally before us before going further into the master-plan of the Yorkie's framework.

General Appearance: That of a long-haired Toy Terrier whose blue and tan coat is parted on the face and from the base of the skull to the end of the tail, and hangs evenly and quite straight down each side of body. The body is neat, compact and well-proportioned. The dog's high head carriage and confident manner should give the appearance of vigor and self-importance.

A true Yorkshire must meet these requirements—if he fails, it is pointless to study him into the finer points of the standard. They contain in themselves the general description of the breed's characteristics—though words have been shuffled—that has served since the first specifications were set down to differentiate purebred dogs from run-of-the-mill canines.

To begin with, he is a Toy Terrier. The word "Toy" does not mean he is a plaything, even though all Yorkies enjoy playing. Toy here explains that he is to be small—diminutive—but still a Terrier.

His body is sketched in—neat (trim, tidy, orderly), compact and well-proportioned.

His color, with no ifs or ands, is Blue and Tan. His hair is long and quite straight down each side of the body. Only a silk-satin textured coat will fill this rule.

Finally, there is his temperament. He carries his head high, showing pride. His confident manner gives him an appearance of self-importance and pride.

Head

If we look back to Mr. Dalziel's description of 1878, and *Standard and Points of Judging the Yorkshire* of 1891, we find excellent examples of how rules laid down in the early stages still form part of the present standard.

Dalziel: "Head is rather small, rather flat on the crown."

Coombs: "Head should be rather small and flat, not too prominent or round in skull, rather broad at the muzzle."

The topline of the Yorkshire Terrier's small head—as viewed from the side—descends from the highest point of the occiput over the skull to the muzzle ending at the nostrils in a rather flat line. The Yorkshire Terrier does not have a pronounced stop—he does have a slight one.

The standard specifies "the skull not too prominent or round"— meaning that it is not to be a bumpy skull, nor is it to be apple-headed.

At one time in his patterning, the problem facing Yorkshire Terrier breeders was the length of the head. The long and short of it has now been resolved with muzzle "not too long". Luckily, although the words have gone through shifting positions, the Yorkie's head description has held pretty close to the original rules laid down by his originators. It is rare to see an apple-headed Yorkie with its accompanying very short muzzle—the so-called "doll-faced" Yorkie. Nor are there very many with the long muzzle, which are generally down-faced. The men who established the points of the breed were aware that early ancestors of the Yorkies carried these unwanted points, and with maintenance of their rules the genes for these faults have been nearly retired from his makeup.

Faulty—down face, long muzzle.

Good head, sparkling with sharp, intelligent expression.

Correct head—young dog, not yet in full coat.

Correct head—adult dog, in full coat.

The Yorkshire's muzzle is not snipey, it is definitely wider than narrow. A snipey muzzle is pointed and weak. On this point, you can tuck away information that has been dropped out, breadth does play a part in the shape of your Yorkie's foremost extension.

The Yorkshire Terrier's earlier definitions called for a level bite, but as the realization came that the type of bite can be inherited, breeders felt that this was teetering on the rim a little too close. To control (as much as possible) the inheritance of bites being neither overshot or undershot, scissors bite *or* level was allowed.

The best test for your Yorkshire Terrier's bite is the line and meeting of the animal's upper and lower jawbones. The jawbones, when the mouth is closed, should fit together in a straight line forward. The upper jawbone should fit closely over the lower jawbone. If the jawbones do not fit together, or the upper jawbone does not overlap the lower jawbone as it extends forward, you will obtain a wry mouth, lower jaw tilted from one side to another.

If the front teeth of the lower jaw are overlapping or projecting beyond the front teeth of the upper jaw when the mouth is closed, you will have an undershot bite in the manner of a bulldog. If the front teeth of the upper jaw are overlapping the front teeth of the under jaw when the mouth is closed, you have acquired an overshot bite à la "Andy Gump."

Subtracted from the standard in 1966 was a section most breeders would like to see restored: "An animal having lost any teeth through accident not a fault, providing the jaws are even." (This is still in the English standard.) In fact, most knowledgeable breeders would be happy to carry this one step farther and have it say: "Teeth lost through age or accident not a fault, provided the jaws are even."

Before one hastily cries that either instance is a result of negligence, one should know the facts. Nobody every told the Yorkie that he wasn't a sure-footed mountain goat. A number of Yorkies have found themselves on the floor with happily no more damage than a hole in their dentition. And have you ever tried to break up a Yorkie battle? The little silky-coated demons can hang on until one loosens a tooth. This doesn't stop their fight, but it leaves one party with a missing tooth.

Good care of a Yorkshire includes keeping their teeth free of tartar. But sooner or later, as they age, they'll need to have their teeth cleaned by a veterinarian. With their small jaws, this usually means an anesthetic to protect the Yorkie from ending up with a dislocated jaw. All Yorkshire Terrier owners approach the thought of an anesthetic with trepidation. Ninety-nine and 9/10th of the time all is well. But the one-tenth, the time that you're told *your* dog didn't come out of the anes-

Beautiful head.

Large ears, poorly set.

Faulty—bat (round) ears.

thetic, just doesn't make you remember all that have. Therefore, the risk of having an older dog's teeth cleaned or allowing them to fall out, should be strictly the exhibitor's choice. Some fine dogs—dogs that in appearance were models of what the breed should be, or who represented excellent potential as breeding stock—have been lost to future generations through the Yorkie's delicate approach to anesthesia.

At the same time, it must be recognized that a rotting tooth can be risky to the animal's health. An obvious case of poor care should be considered a more serious fault than a tooth lost through accident.

Nose

"*The nose is black.*" The only change from the old standard in this is the dropping of the word "perfect" from in front of black. A dog whose nose is not black shows the breakdown of pigmentation and should be strongly faulted. Because of the strong emergence in recent months of this heretofore unreported problem, breeders, judges and buyers should be especially watchful against these animals.

Eyes

"*Eyes are medium in size and not too prominent; dark in color and sparkling with a sharp intelligent expression. Eye rims are dark.*"

In one earlier standard, a specification called for the eyes to have a "sharp terrier expression"—a requirement of rather, questionable utility. For example, the Bull Terrier wants "a piercing glint" and "well sunken," while the Dandie Dinmont standard calls for an eye that is "large, full, round."

A round eye gives a Yorkie a quite woe-begone expression, far from what is wanted. And a well sunken eye will not show a Yorkie's mischief, deviltry and keenness. The Yorkie's eyes minus their sparkling sharp intelligent expression take away a large piece of the breed's identity.

In Yorkshires with an extremely red-haired head one is likely to find the lighter eye rim and, almost always, light eyes. Dark eyes, medium in size, help to give him his keen, bright expression and all should steer clear of light eyes or light eye-rimmed dogs.

Eye placement was dropped from the new standard. The previous standard contained wording, still in the British standard, that specified: "And placed so as to look directly forward." It would be good to reinsert this, for it is one of the terrier characteristics of the Yorkshire Terrier.

184

Ears

The standard concludes Head specifications with: *"Ears are small, V-shaped and set not too far apart."* Such a short sentence, but what a load underlies it. The genius that added the beastly word "too" should be made to realize that too many toos have too often led to too much woe. Before the present standard, the specification had simply been "not far apart." The British standard still has it that way. The addition of the word "too" changes the whole picture by allowing for any kind of interpretation.

The Yorkshire Terrier should have small V-shaped ears. They should not be round at their tips, nor bat-shaped like a French Bulldog's. They are carried erect, and when excited or at attention, carried higher. Many Yorkies, when gaiting, will flick one ear rearward, keeping a mental check on what foe might be advancing on them.

Although this is not covered in the Yorkie standard, the ears should have quite thin leather (outer cartilage of the ear), though with enough strength to keep them erect. Thick leather leads to semi-erect or drop ears.

Low-set ears take away from a Yorkshire Terrier's alert expression, one of the breed's identifying points. Tying long hair from them into the top-knot to make them appear higher set, or not too far apart, should not fool anyone. The animal's ears remain stationary and useless.

The size of the ear should receive a good deal of appreciative regard. Yorkies' ears were cropped until cropping was outlawed in Great Britain in 1895. The ancestors who went into the production of the Yorkshire Terrirer all had large ears and they are dominant genetically to small ears. While in a well-cultivated adult Yorkshire, with ears properly trimmed and dressed with golden feathers, the shape of the ear is barely visible, no breeder should ever forget that the ears do add up in the total of a prosperous look to the head.

Body

The standard calls for *"Body: Well proportioned and very compact. The back is rather short, the back line level, with height at shoulder the same as at rump."* (To this add the description of "neat" from General Appearance.)

The use of the word "rather" before "short" is quite senseless. How can he be "very compact" if he is *rather* (defined as "in some degree") short backed? The Yorkie's body is well-proportioned; the word picture projected should be one that portrays the terminology of the body's description, namely that the topline is to be perfectly level.

185

Well-proportioned head and body.

Bad topline—down faced.

Correct topline.

The length of the back is to be in relation to the height at the shoulders and the rump so that the animal appears basically square.

A common mistake that is made is illustrated by this quote from a magazine: "A Yorkie should look square, which means that the legs should be the same length as the back, giving room for length of coat." Such a dog has either no body between his back or legs, or he has a long back to equal his leg length and overlooked body. It is the Yorkshire's body AND leg length that square him against his short back.

The Yorkshire's back is a straight, level line from his shoulders to the set-on of the tail; i.e., the rump. The less loin between the back rib and the hip bones, the better. With a short loin, he is more likely to achieve the desired level topline.

The short loin should have breadth and well-developed muscles. The loin is the dog's pivotal point, and strength aids in the ability to make rapid changes in direction—whether forward, reverse, up or down. An under-developed, long, narrow loin shows up as a weak point in a topline.

The lay of the shoulders is not mentioned in the standard but, as they underlie his back, they need to be considered. Good shoulders, well placed, are very necessary to obtain freedom of movement, which will show in the straightness of a Yorkie's backline when he is gaiting or posing. Good shoulders form the correct foundation for a sound forefront. They help to shorten the back and form the correct base for the neck to flow smoothly into the backline.

Looking down onto a Yorkie's back, the topline seen from side to side is reasonably broad. His chest should have a good spring of ribs. This curvature of ribs, along with a comparatively wide front and depth between his forelegs, allows for good heart and lung capacity. This latter point was very important when he was used as a ratter or varmint hunter and often went underground or swam through water. Though few Yorkies engage in such activity now, they are a very vigorous and robust breed and still need the heart and lung room.

Legs and Feet

An unsoundness of legs, fore or hind, will detract from the Yorkshire's general carriage and topline, in motion or when he is standing at attention, most likely wondering whether the onlooker knows as much about him as he is sure he knows about himself.

The Yorkshire Terrier belongs to the digging Terrier family. His forelegs are straight, with the elbows close to the chest, neither in nor out. The lower forelegs do toe out slightly, like a Cairn Terrier, so that

187

Looking down on correct topline.

Topline remains level at shoulder and rump, even with head down.

when digging the dirt will fly out to the sides and not pile under him. The forelegs should be medium in length and strongly muscled.

The Yorkshire's hindlegs, whether in motion or standing still, are straight, with the hocks parallel, not close together or cow-hocked.

His hindlegs are broad across the pelvic area. If the pelvis is narrow, the Yorkie's rear gait will make it look as if both hindlegs were attached in one place. The upper thighs should carry a firm muscular pack.

The Yorkie is to have a moderate bend at the stifles, viewed from the side. Lack of angulation at the stifle causes lack of drive and short strides increase wear and tear on the "kneecaps." Medium strides that bear the rear-end at an equal level with the fore-end are your desire.

The hocks on the Yorkshire Terrier should be well angulated to give him power and good movement. They, along with the back pastern, should be short. Ideally, the hocks should come to just about a line drawn down from the rear-most point of the animal's body. Hocks too far to the rear give a loss of control in the rear-end action.

Good movement and soundness are primarily dependent upon having bones of the right size, and in the right place. The bones in his legs should be medium in girth, taking into measure that what fits a two pound Yorkie is not suited to a seven pound Yorkie.

With proper hindlegs, a Yorkie will move with verve, and pose without upsetting the level line of his back. His height at the rump will be the same as at the shoulders and he will retain his neat, compact and well-proportioned aspect.

The majority of Yorkshires have front feet larger than their rear feet, as do several of their Scotch cousins. The feet are round and should be tight, with the toes not spread apart. The pads should be well-formed and firm.

The toenails are often overlooked, but should be checked to see that they are black. In the hazy past of the Yorkie's ancestry, some animal contributed white toenails to his get. The men who drew up the rules for the breed knew it, and made a point to include specification of black toenails in his pattern. It's a minor point, but should be of concern to breeders, awakening them to the fact that he has this gene in his storehouse. (Quite a few Yorkies are born with one or more white toenails, but by maturity they will have turned black. If not, you have a clue that you have an animal with the ability to pass on white markings.)

This section of the standard states that dewclaws are generally removed from the hindlegs, and may be removed from the forelegs. Remove them on all legs, or you are likely to catch a comb on one and have a sore-legged Yorkshire Terrier while the damage heals.

Neck

Before continuing our journey through the approved standard, we note that there is one part of the Yorkshire Terrier's body that is not referred to, and that is his neck. Like all quadrupeds, he *does* have a connection between his head and shoulders.

When he was first being established as a separate part of the canine sphere, it was his ratting ability that was extolled. The little Yorkshire Terrier of the working man grabbed the rat and, with a quick snap of his head, dispatched the rodent. It takes a neck to move the head in this snatching action.

The Yorkshire of today still carries this ability, though his chances of being entered in a ratting contest are almost nil. Still, he does shake his toys in the same manner, and a specimen with a thin, long neck is likely to find himself indisposed with displaced verterbrae—a sort of doggy whiplash.

Under these circumstances, the best type of neck for a Yorkshire should be a muscular one, without coarseness. Moderately short, but not so short as to appear clumsy. He should have sufficient neck length to carry his head proudly, adding to his elegant appearance and contributing to a well-proportioned square body. The neck should flow smoothly into the neckline.

Do not be deceived into believing that the Yorkshire standard calls for "a long, elegant reach of neck." The change in the standard from "the carriage being very upright and having an important air" to "The dog's high head carriage and confident manner should give the appearance of vigor and self-importance" has led some people astray. This change only signifies that he is proud, bold and forward in his carriage.

Tail

To resume with what *is* in the approved standard, we come to: *"Tail—Docked to a medium length and carried slightly higher than the level of the back."*

Many a Yorkshire worthy of sympathy has found himself looked at with disfavor for having too short a tail when, in reality, it is not his fault at all. Whoever docked it, either made it too short or—having no guide to go by—docked it to what was medium of the length of the tail with which the puppy arrived into this world.

Obviously, medium meaning middle, one wants a tail that is neither too short or too long. Most long-time breeders have their veterinarians dock tails to 1/8 to 1/4 inch past the tan on the underside, giving a tail length that at the animal's mature size will vary from 1 1/2 to 2 1/2 inches (from the set-on of the tail to its tip).

190

The set-on of the tail is actually a greater concern, for this he is born with. A Yorkshire Terrier's tail-set should be high on the croup (the back part of the back, above the hindlegs). The tail is the extension of the vertebrae that make up his spine. In an animal where it is desired to have a level back, the croup is nearly parallel to the horizon. A rounding-off of the rump, with a low tail-set, makes for a roach-back appearance.

The standard prescribes that the tail be carried "slightly higher than the level of the back." A Yorkshire with his tail tucked between his legs looks like he is cringing and fearful of the world, or belongs at home in a sickbed. Your Yorkshire is a stiff gentleman. When encountering a newcomer, he brings his tail upright while the question of territorial rights and friendly relations are established—an accord reached or the battleline drawn!

Avoid breeding together dogs with low tail-sets; you want a Yorkshire that can carry its tail above the topline while gaiting, or drop it straight down in repose. You will, of course, be chancing a too-gay tail. But better an animal with gay tail whose general appearance suggests the standard's prescription of "confidence, vigor and self-importance" than one whose sightless tail makes it appear shy, weak, and of no consequence.

Coat

The Yorkshire Terrier becomes a unique breed of dog by virtue of its outer covering—its cloak of shining blue and bright gold silk, whose general outline conveys the existence of a vigorous and well-proportioned body carried with self-importance. The dressing of the head's long, bright gold hairs allows the Yorkie to parade its sharp, intelligent Terrier spirit.

The Yorkie is alone among purebred dogs in its demand for metallic colors of gleaming radiance displayed through hairs of lustrous spun silk. A Yorkie with impure, weak colors—hair incapable of naturally reflecting light rays, or hair of thicker grade—can never achieve the unique, glowing coloring that truly typifies a model of the breed.

The prime points of a Yorkie's coat are its texture and its colors. The two are equally important, for without one or the other, the Yorkie has lost type. The texture and colors cooperate to produce the animal desired in the standard.

We will here explore these points in four sections: texture, colors, transition from newly-born to adult, and how the color is acquired.

Puppy (3 1/2 mos.) with thick heavy coat—will not attain correct visual colors as an adult.

Silky coated puppies (4 and 3 mos.) Their coat appears thinner as puppies. As adults, they will have thick, long coats of correct fine, silky glossy texture.

Wavy coats are visible at an early age, and in general portend a light silver adult. This dog's wavy coat is still silky (note reflected light.)

Straight, fine silky coat.

1. *Coat Texture*

The standard states "Quality, texture and quantity of coat are of prime importance." The Yorkshire's "quantity" of hair is long—and of a density that hangs flat, evenly against the body. The long hair should never be so thick as to completely hide the outline of the underlying body. Its length should not impede the dog's ability to show off his carriage. To this purpose, the body coat—if desired—may be trimmed. If the owner does not trim, he assumes the risk that the impediment may deter chances of higher placement in showing his dogs.

The long hair falls from all parts of the head and is longest on the muzzle. The hair on the skull is tied up so as to better show the sharp intelligent eyes and the ear carriage that help express the Yorkie's character.

The hair hangs straight and totally free of wave. In the specification under General Appearance that the coat hangs "quite straight," the word *quite* is used in the sense of *completely*. In middle English, quite meant "free, rid of" and in Latin "freed".

The factor necessary for straight hair is inheritable. When seen through a microscope, cross-sections of individual hair strands look round, oval or flat. A round-shaped hair is straight. Scientists have found that curly hair is usually a dominant trait; straight is usually recessive because it is masked by a more dominant characteristic.

The undesired waviness is usually found in the light silver Yorkies, but has begun to be seen in black woolies and gray cottony-coated Yorkshires, too. In this reference to waviness we are not talking of the little left over from poor grooming when the "crackers" (i.e. wraps) are removed, but one that runs through the coat in long, horizontal, wavy lines.

The feet and ears grow an equal quantity of hair, but are trimmed. The standard states that feet *may* be trimmed for neatness. The movement of a Yorkie's legs is often only visible in the placement of the feet, and long hair on them can cause false illusions. Also, untrimmed feet can often harbor foreign objects that can cause injury or infection.

The ears should be trimmed on the tips. The standard does not leave this point open to personal choice. The trimmed ear shows the shape, size and ear placement. An untrimmed ear subtracts from the head's total appearance, and from a structural point of view — long, heavy hair growth on the ear tip is likely to bring it down to a drop or semi-erect ear.

The long "quantity" of hair is recessive to short hair. A Yorkie with hair that is short due to neglect or illness is one matter, but a Yorkie with a short silky coat should be considered as uncharacteristic.

The length of the hair depends (aside from care) on its quality. The correct individual hair strands of a Yorkie are of a *fine* grade.

Hairs are produced by glands situated in the inner layers of the skin. These glands secrete the protein called *keratin* that forms the hair. The hair has an inner and outer core. The quality of the hair (fine, medium or thick) is determined by the hair producing glands and the manner in which the hair passes through the hair follicle cells. Hairs with thick outer cores are heavy and dull, for the extent to which they can refract light is diminished by the thickness and roughness of the outer layer.

The Yorkie's coat is made up of fine, silken hairs. In this era of man-made fibers, few know the true feel of silk as spun by the silkworm munching its way through mulberry leaves. Silk is cool and strong. This coolness can still be felt in the desired silken-haired coat; when the hair is laid over your hand, it will feel cool, and not warm your hand as will the wrong-textured coat. It was because of this cooling quality that clothes for tropical countries were made of silk rather than wool. As for its strength, this can be tested by taking a thread of silk, a strand of wool, and a thread of 100% cotton, and trying to break each in half. The wool will part first, and then the cotton, but you may cut your hand before you part the silk thread. The strength of the fine, silky hair (as opposed to the wooly or cottony coat) allows it to grow to proper length with the quality that maintains it without snarling, matting, or splitting.

The Yorkie's fine silky coat is *glossy* in texture. Around 1876, Dr. Gordon Staples wrote:

> There are one or two things remarkable about the coat and feathers of a well-bred Yorkshire. First, its extreme length. Secondly, its great straightness. The least approach to a curl of a Yorkshire would prove fatal to its success in the show ring. Thirdly, the quality of the feather. It is soft and silky—it is flat down to the sides. And, as the little things sport and frolic about the carpet and engage in mimic warfare, the feathers ripple upon them and this combined with its sheen and color gives these toys the appearance of being clothed in little jackets of flowing water.

Originally, the word used in the Yorkie standard to describe the surface of its coat was *flossy*, which comes from floss silk. This silk is described as "soft, downy and made of the untwisted thread from unreelable silk fibers."

The word in the standard has been changed to *glossy*, defined as "having luster or shine, polished." Luster in turn is "to shine or have sheen with brilliancy, especially from reflected light."

The Yorkie coat should look like satin, a smooth silk woven with a glossy face. A coat that does not have a polished, shining surface is not a glossy-textured coat. It cannot reflect and refract light, essential re-

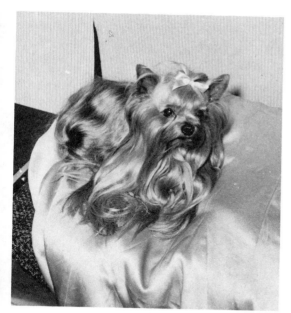

Beautiful fine silk coat displayed on satin.

Correct fine silky coat, reflecting light glossily. Picture is of Eng. Ch. Blairsville Most Royale, winner of the Reserve Best in Show at the 1974 Crufts Dog Show at London, the only Yorkie to ever win this honor. Breeder-owners: Mr. and Mrs. Brian Lister.

quirements for providing the visible metallic gleaming colors of a Yorkie.

The hair's length, fineness, silkiness and glossy qualities are all factors in the transmission of its colors to the human eye.

2. Colors

Adult Coat Color

The coat color for the adult Yorkie is set down in the standard as:

"Color of hair on body and richness of tan on head and legs are of prime importance in ADULT DOGS to which the following color requirements apply:

Blue: Is a dark steel blue, not a silver blue and not mingled with fawn, bronzy or black hairs.

Tan: All tan hair is darker at the roots than in the middle, shading to still lighter tan at the tips. There should be no sooty or black hair intermingled with any of the tan."

The difficulty in determining what the colors specified in the standard look like, and how they are produced, has been a major stumbling block in the understanding of the Yorkie's adult coloring.

Defining color is based on the eyes of the beholder. It is determined by the individual's perception of light rays reflected to his eyes.

All interpretations by an individual are the net result of his environmental learning and binocular efficiency. In childhood, you learn that leaves are green, the sky is blue, newly-fallen snow is white and moonless nights are black. Color names follow the current fads: last year's "dusty rose" becomes this year's "gray-pink." Your occupation, hobbies and place of habitation all influence your name for each color hue.

The individual's discernment of color involves *hue, brilliance, saturation,* and depends on the light source. In speaking of color, various terms such as *dark, medium,* or *light* designate differing degrees of vividness of hue. This vividness is also determined by the light's radiancy.

The standard specifies that the adult (over 12 months, i.e. one year) Yorkshire Terrier's body coat is a dark-steel blue, darker on the tail, especially on the tip. The *hue* required is the primary color blue. The saturation point of the blue is *dark*—that is differing in degree by being higher or lower than medium blue, but minus any approach to blackness.

The word steel is used to show *brilliance.* The dark blue is to reflect light rays. Black, for example, is destitute of light, or incapable of naturally reflecting it. The blue color is to shine, to have luster, gloss, a metallic sheen—as of a piece of polished steel.

196

Dam with 2½-week-old puppies. Note tan points on rear ends.

Coat showing blue color all the way through.

This is a cross-your-fingers; coat should indicate color change at this age. Coat texture is wooly, does not reflect light.

Darker blue on tail.

As a slight diversion here, it is interesting to note some of the images that "dark steel-blue" has brought to mind. Here's one:

"The old timers said it was the color you saw when you looked down a clean gun barrel. That's all right for Sheffield, where they make gun barrels, but we don't have the same opportunity down South (England), and as far as I'm concerned, the last thing I'd do would be to look down a gun barrel."

Our sentiment exactly! Anyway, modern gun barrels are made out of alloyed steel. Here's another comparison, less lethal:

"A deep shade of metal like the blade of a knife, not stainless steel but the old-fashioned knife we used to have—the blade of which when polished gave a blue shade."

Can you imagine a group of Yorkie fanciers encircling a judge, making their point with a flourish, that their specimen most closely resembles the knife they are wielding?

The standard prescribes that the adult Yorkshire Terrier is to have a headfall that is *"a rich golden tan, deeperest color at sides of head, at ear roots and on the muzzle, with ears a deep rich tan!"* Chest and legs are *"a bright rich tan."*

Thus the *hue* required is the color termed tan (red-yellow in hue, of high saturation). The degree of vividness varies from deep to bright. The saturation point of the tan is *rich,* that is abundant in color as opposed to pale in color.

The word "golden" is used to show that the tan is to show *brilliance,* with a high degree of ability to reflect light source rays. Refined and polished gold has a metallic gleaming brightness.

The Yorkshire's adult colors are given placement. *"The blue extends over the body from back of neck to root of tail. Hair on the tail is a darker blue, especially at end of tail."* The requirement for this darker blue on the tail and tip is a safeguard to keep the tan on the underside (not top or sides) of the tail. It also maintains a visible sign that the pigment supply for the blue is kept strong and not weakened, thus, allowing the tan to run up into the blue body from the breeches.

The deeper color of the golden tan on the muzzle, sides of head (also above the eyes), base of ears, is at the areas that were tan marks at birth. Their deep richness in tan pigment is necessary to maintain a golden tan throughout the Yorkie's lifespan, and to pass on the genetic ability to supply this need in succeeding generations. Even the palest golden tan should always show this shading of darker gold deposits at these placement points.

The ears are the deepest golden tan. The insides of the ear should always be a rich golden tan. The hairs on the outside of the ear leather are very dark rich golden tan. Close observation on many Yorkies will

198

show an intermingling of blackish, red-brown (sooty) hairs. If these hairs predominate, or if they are black-hued hairs, the transition from black to gold will never develop completely. The dog will invariably fail to assume any visible-to-the-eye blue hue. The best it will do is a grayish-black body color. In some it will extend on to the skull, and even reach down around the eyes, forming a black mask.

The tan *"should not extend down on back of neck."* The tan on the chest does not extend into the blue body. On the legs it is not to extend *"above the elbow on the forelegs, nor above the stifle on the hind legs."*

These placements make what is termed a saddle pattern. In the case of the Yorkie, this description is of a complete body saddle.

The Yorkshire Terrier standard is deficient in its failure to mention that the average Yorkie's blue color extends from the body around the lower throat and the upper top of the forechest, while the tan covers the underside of the tail, around the vent and the breeching.

On the underside of a Yorkie, on the brisket and midway along the pelvic arc, there are blue sections. The rest of the underside is usually tan, lightest at the arm pits and belly.

An adult Yorkie may not be a silver-blue, silver being defined as a neutral (minus any approach to whiteness) gray—that is, midway between black and white. The blue body coat may not be intermingled with hairs that are fawn (red-yellow in hue), bronzy (brown, yellowish, red-yellow in hue) or black (devoid of light-reflecting ability, or so dark as to have no distinguishable color). Overlapping of blue-black and reddish tan hairs in the blue coat produce the bronzy coat appearance.

The adult Yorkie's tan may not be intermingled with sooty (brownish-black) or black-hued hairs. Hairs that are grayish-black (lighter pigmented black) are not golden tan and fall under the edict of no black hairs intermingled. Any amount of mingled hairs, other than golden tan hues, takes away from the brilliance of the golden color. Mingled black hairs that form any visible group are obviously signs of impurity of the golden color and should be considered a very bad fault in breeding, or showing.

The adult Yorkie's blue should be a uniform shade of blue. It should not appear patched, striped or half light and half dark. A scratched or injured area will appear darker in its new outgrowth, but is perceivable by its shortened length. For the desired correctly colored Yorkie, the base of the hair shaft is a darker shade of the coat's blue color and this darker shade will show at any parting down to the skin.

The adult Yorkie's tan hair should be darker at the roots than in the middle, shading to a still lighter tan at the tips. This requirement can only be met when the hair is of the required fine quality.

Coloring of the adult Yorkshire Terrier, as prescribed by the standard. Arrow indicates darker color at the tail.

Coloring of the adult Yorkshire Terrier as it actually is. Arrow indicates darker color at tail.

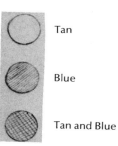

Tan

Blue

Tan and Blue

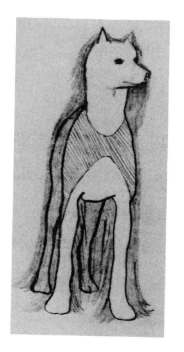

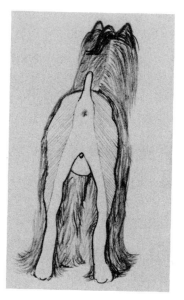

Adult Yorkshire Terrier coloring, front and rear, as it actually is.

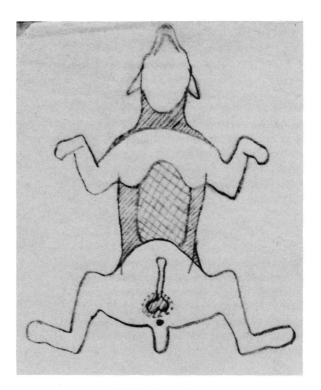

Upside down view.

Adult Skin Color:

The underlying skin has pigmentation of the same color hue as the hair. The head, chest and legs have skin pigment that is light yellowish pink to moderate reddish, orange-yellow. The inside of the ear is the same, but the outside pigmentation of the ear leather is a reddish-brown. The body's skin has a pigment that is a light grayish-blue to medium grayish-blue. The pigmentation on top and sides of the tail is medium gray-blue to dark gray-blue.

There is a nearly clear-cut line between the pigmentation on the head at the back of the skull, on the forelegs at the elbow and on the hindlegs at the stifle. On the tail, the line divides the blue, leaving the tan on the underside of the tail.

There maybe a band of light, grayish-blue pigment on the lower forechest above the shoulder points and across the underside of the rib cage. This pigmentation will not be a clearly-defined area, and may be interspersed with reddish-yellow colored skin.

On the rear end, the Yorkie has reddish-yellow skin pigment on the tail's underside, around the vent, rear of the upper thighs, the breeches and down the outer edge of the inside of the rear legs. The hocks and all other underside areas not already mentioned are light reddish golden-yellow to medium golden red-yellow.

When the golden pigmentation extends beyond or is mixed into the body's pigmentation, the body color will have intermingled fawn hairs.

Darker patches of blue pigmentation will have outgrowing patches of darker blue-hued hairs.

If the skin is injured, the hair scratched or torn out, the healed skin with the early hair growth will be a darker area until it returns to normal.

Very bluish-black, or dark grayish-black, skin pigment will have hairs that are black or less heavily-pigmented grays.

If the body color extends out of its lines into the golden tan areas, the tan will be intermingled with hairs varying from light gray to black.

3. Transition from Newly-Born to Adult

The Yorkshire Terrier is usually born black with tan-points, the tan being on the following places: on the puppy's muzzle; above each eye; base of ear; ear rims; inside of ear; underside of tail (extending midway out from body on uncut tail) around the vent and edge of breechings; on the outside of forelegs, feet and a small way up pastern; on the inside of the forelegs extending from armpit slightly onto the chest wall. There is tan on the outside of rear legs, on paws, and partially up pastern; a fine line extending up to stifle on front; and part of hock on

Tan changing and clearing on puppies—9 mos. and 5 mos. respectively. Puppies owned by Jeanne Grimsby.

Clear tan. Ch. Kelsbro Half Sovereign, owned by Iola S. Dowd.

Clear rich tans. Silverwind's Ode to Love (10 mos.), Ch. Wildweir Candytuft, Silverwind's Spirit of Apollo, and Silverwind's Fanstasia. Owner, Elissa Taddie.

rear side. The inside of the hindleg is tan except for a small blackish "V-shaped" patch on each upper inside thigh joined by a black bridge across the pelvic arch.

The rest of the underside, except for a black girth around the rear chest and brisket, is tan. The underside of the jaw (though there may be a black patch in the middle of the underside of the lower jaw) and the underside of the throat is tan. The forechest has a rosette at each shoulder point, or a horizontal stripe between them in the black.

The tan on a young Yorkie puppy is a light pale golden tan to a dark rich golden tan. All tan marks may be more or less in extension. They may be perfectly delineated from the black, or be slightly intermingled with blackish hair.

There may be a white star or a small blaze located on the forechest in the tan, or across the black and tan. This is a much looked-for point, as it is an indication that the puppy will probably be a good coat grower in quantity, though not necessarily in quality. It is also an indication that there will be no melanism, or over-supply of pigment.

It is not unusual to find small white marks on one or more toes, or a fine white line on lower forejaw. These will not be visible as an adult. Any such marks should therefore be noted wherever you keep such records, as one is apt to forget which puppy had them after they grow up.

A large amount of white marks, on chest, paws, jaws or skull, places a Yorkie into a tri-color classification and it is very wise to guard against this possibility.

The newly-born Yorkie has a nose that is mostly gray, showing a small amount of pink on the edges of the nostrils. The nose should be a dark gray at around 21 days and definitely black by two months. It is very unusual to see a mismarked nose in a Yorkie and it should be considered a very bad problem.

The toenails are gray at birth, with an occasional white one. Any that fail to become black by two months are indicative of the availability of non-pigmented skin and hair.

The eye rims will be a light reddish-brown to reddish-brown at birth, but should be a dark red-brown by two months. Very orangy red-gold tans will usually have lighter colored eye rims. This is not particularly desirable, but a sad fact of life. Unfortunately it also spoils the eye's expression.

Yorkshire Terrier puppies can be born of colors that automatically deprive them of the necessary qualities to become the proper colors of the breed. They can be born all black; all tan; tan with black-points, tri-color: black, white and tan; all blue; bluish grey with tan-points, and so remain, or change to another shade of their newly-born colors.

These mismarked Yorkie puppies are not the result of mis-alliances, or throwbacks but are rather the net product of incorrectly inherited genes, which have failed to activate the pigment glandular system to providing what they require to be in accord with the Yorkshire Terrier's breed standard.

Puppies incorrectly colored, or marked, should not be sold as "rare gold," "rare blue" or any other such gilded deceits. They should not be registered as Yorkshire Terriers, but should simply be found a loving home if one cannot bring oneself to having them put down.

The transition from newly-born puppy to adult Yorkshire terrier is a very confusing period. Any attempt by a novice to come to grips with this period by reading opinions of Yorkie breeders can only add perplexity to confusion. No one agrees. This fact alone offers the greatest hope to any breeder. The answer lies in the fact that a bloodline generally follows a course, but it never holds entirely true for all members of the bloodline.

Each Yorkie puppy commences its transition from the newly-born black-and-tan to the adult blue-and-tan by its own inherited and constructed glandular system. The combination of its inherited genes from its sire and dam at conception, and the development of the fetus into a thriving new born puppy, determines the health and makeup of the glandular system that supplies the pigment for the hair, skin, eyes, eye rims, nose and toenails.

The black tan-pointed, newly-born puppy must change into an adult with a pure clear golden tan and a pure even dark, steel-blue. Not all puppies achieve this goal. Some fail because their coat texture is unable to provide a means for light rays to be refracted and reflected to the human eye. Others fail because their systems fail to provide the necessary amount of pigment particles to the hair strands. Some fail because they inherit incorrect pattern placements. No matter what the cause, the result is that the Yorkie is unable to visually match the standard in desired colors at specific areas.

To correctly match the standard the Yorkie puppy must remove all black or blackish-brown hairs from its golden tan. This is first noticed on the skull which may go from black to tan at the hair roots, with any new outgrowth of hairs being tan. Or the hair on the skull may go from black to gray, with roots almost white, and any new outgrowth a very pale weak tan. In this last case, as the black intermingled hairs diminish the roots and new outgrowth will gradually assume a richer golden tan.

The black on the muzzle, sides of head, front ear-base and around the eyes generally achieves a richer golden tan at the roots and new outgrowth as the black intermingled hairs diminish. These areas are always a darker shade of golden tan.

The chest and legs follow the same program as the skull. All early tan marks are always a richer tan.

206

Litter brothers, Sorreldene Tangerine and Sorreldene Orange Boy—at 7 months.

Ch. Sorreldene Tangerine and Ch. Sorreldene Orange Boy at 18 months of age.

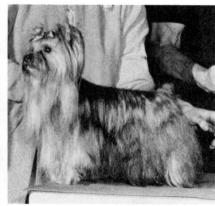

At 18 months.   2 years and 4 months.

3 years and 4 months.   4 years.

How proper coat develops in the Yorkshire Terrier, as seen in pictures of Ch. Wildweir Fair N' Square, bred and owned by the authors.

10 years.

In the case of a very light pale golden tan (creamy colored) there is usually no distinction between these early tan marks and the newly grown tan hairs.

The rear of the ear leathers are the last to surrender from the black's hold. They should be a deep rich warm golden tan minus any blackish hue. Failure of the ear to achieve a dark golden tan from the puppy black is very indicative of a Yorkie who will never clear its blue or clear its tan of black-hued hairs.

Most breeders in speaking of any Yorkie of any age, ask first about the tan. Puppies with early golden tan ears excite much envy.

The tan should never run out of its boundaries or this will give a fawn or bronzy appearance to the blue coat. This will be visible in a youngster at the shoulders, occiput and tail-set. Many a puppy reaching adulthood has slid past onlookers as having a broken blue when in reality it had a running tan.

The blue commences its transition from black to blue just above the hair roots and in the tips of the new growing hairs. It may be visible first at the shoulder, loin, rump or the entire blue body, but it is visible on each and every hair in the area. It is not necessary to search through the coat. It can be easily seen by looking down onto the Yorkie who will be obviously acquiring a bluish cast to its coat.

Yorkies who have black coats as adults may often have diluted-black colored coats on the lower parts of their bodies, and digging into their coats will uncover this fact. However they are not blue but grayish-black and when looked down onto, they will never be bluish in cast.

The newly-born to adult's skin pigment is identical in color transition as the outgrowing hairs.

The greatest block to a Yorkie's complete assumption of the desired colors is the failure of the coat texture. The newly-born puppies have flat, smooth, short-coated hairs. Only as the hair grows can texture be felt. It may be wiry, woolly, cottony or silky.

A wiry coat can develop the visually correct colors, but it will not attain great length. Most wiry coated Yorkies do change coat texture prior to one year. The hair at the roots commences to grow out a finer grade and thus becomes silky. Such puppies are, of course, an anathema to Terrier breeders, especially Scottish, Cairn and West Highland breeders.

The puppies with woolly and cottony coats, although growing great length and heaviness fast, never attain the correct visual colors. Their qualities—thick, heavy, downy and soft—deters or dulls any light rays from proper play on the hairs.

Wavy coats are visible in Yorkie puppies at a very early age and in general portend a light silver adult. A slight waviness on the upper hindquarters is not unusual in many Yorkies, but should be watched.

"Breaking" Patterns

As no two Yorkies ever seem to follow an exact transition pattern, or "breaking" as it has come to be termed, we have included the most general facts of this trying time:

A puppy that is about three to four weeks of age that shows gold hairs on the top of its head when the black hairs are parted, will as an adult have a clear golden tan. If the coat texture is silky, the blue will have no intermingled colors.

A puppy that has a wiry coat texture, with a tan that is a very bright red gold by four to five months, will as an adult do one of two things: First, if the puppy as it approaches five or six months, or at least by nine months, shows the transition from black to blue, the coat texture will soften to a silky texture. If the black coat does not show this transition to blue, the adult dog will retain the wiry coat which will never attain any great length.

A puppy that has a bright orange-red tan by four or five months, will as an adult have a bright steel-blue, which may have areas of lighter or darker blue. This coloring shows the greatest tendency to have the tan placements run into the allotted areas for the blue. The texture will be silky.

A puppy whose coat appears sparse or thin will, as an adult, have a thick, long coat of the correct fine silky, glossy texture. This coat's growth is like a human's hair, in that it is born with very little but by adulthood has an abundance of hair, the quantity having doubled and redoubled all during puppyhood (or childhood). Both colors will be totally clear.

A puppy of around four months, that has changed the color on its head from black to gray to a very pale sooty color, will as an adult enrich all the tan areas to a clear golden tan. The blue will follow the correct manner of transition from black to blue starting to do so around six months. The coat texture will be the correct silky type.

A puppy whose tan has been cleared of all the intermingled black or sooty hairs by four month age, and whose texture is fine and silky, will as an adult have correct colors. The tan of this puppy will probably enrich to a darker shade as an adult.

A puppy approaching adulthood with a thick, heavy coat that has pale cream colored legs, sooty head colors, with intermingled black hairs in tan at sides of head and on the ears and ear fringes, may as an adult diminish some of these black and sooty hairs. Its desired blue area may eventually achieve a transition from black to grey but it will never have a clear golden tan, nor a dark steel-blue. The coat texture is either a woolly or cottony.

A puppy approaching adulthood that has a black stripe in the center of its head, intermingled into the whiskers, sides of head and up into the top-knot, with ears that are more visibly black than rich dark golden tan, will as an adult have a tan that is never totally cleared. As the years pass some of the black and sooty hairs will diminish, but a check of the pigment under these intermingled areas will show that it is a dark gray which will never lighten. The black on this dog will show a few hairs that will some years hence go from black to gray, especially at the lower hips and lower shoulders, when the hair is parted down through the upper layers. The coat texture will be woolly or cottony.

A puppy approaching adulthood that has intermingled sooty or black hairs at the sides of its head running up into the top-knot, with a sooty area between the eyes, and whose ears are a sooty tan, will have a gray body coat by around three years. The gray will be lacking a blue hue. The tan will always have some intermingled sooty hairs especially at sides of the head, ear fringes and between the eyes. There may be some black or sooty hair on top of the muzzle but not in the foreface furnishings. The coat texture is cottony.

A puppy of three to four months that has a very pale gold tan and whose black has gone to light silver-blue, will as an adult be a light silver-blue. A check of this puppy's pigment will show that it is incorrect, as it will be light-gray flesh color. The texture will be silky.

A puppy that shows coarse white hairs intermingled in the blue will usually shed most of these as it approaches adulthood.

A puppy approaching adulthood, (or over a year), that has an inch wide stripe from the hair root out, then blue, with the tip and last inch or two still showing its transition from black to blue, will with age lose the blackish tips on the end as they are worn off or cut off as the coat achieves floor length. The dark stripe will remain although it may lessen in width. It shows that the pigmentation of the hair is extremely dense at its beginning and does not diminish until it reaches this point. The tan will be clear, and the coat texture silky.

A puppy that at some stage in its puppyhood shows a brownish cast to its blue or black body coat is passing through a stage in which there is a hormone imbalance. This condition will normally right itself, as it is purely a growth stage.

All these are generalities and any puppy may follow a different path.

4. How the Color Is Acquired

What makes dogs have different colored coats of hair? Hair gets its color from pigment just like any other colored substance. Pigment is a coloring matter, either a powdered substance mixed with a suitable liquid, in which it is relatively insoluble, or any of various coloring matters in animals and plants.

Authorities believe that dogs have two major types of pigments. Dr. Clarence Little in *The Inheritence of Coat Color In Dogs* (Howell Book House, 1967) states:

> Like other laboratory mammals, dogs appear to have two major types of pigment in their coats. One of these is yellow, the other dark (brown or black). The color varieties of dogs have to be formed by various genes controlling the amount, extent and distribution of these pigments both individually, in combination or in competition with one another.
>
> Pigment granules can be distributed in various amounts and patterns in either or both the outside layer (cortex) or the inner portion (medulla) of the hair. Variations in such processes produce different optical color effects resulting in the different colors in different varieties of dogs.

A new book on the study of horse color by Dr. Ben Green, *Color of Horses* (Northland Press, Flagstaff, Arizona 1975), is interesting reading for anyone wishing to understand what makes the numerous individual hair colors.

Without resorting to complicated genetic terms, the process whereby hairs acquire colors and hues of that color are described. Though no similar study has been conducted on dogs, all mammals have the same system of hair coloration.

In horses there is only one pigment (melanin) and it is produced by glands situated in the hide of horses. The pigment, and the secretion it is suspended in, appear a brown color to the eye under a microscope. The pigment migrates into the hair shaft where it is arranged in varying patterns. The pigment granules, along with the refracted and reflected light rays directed from them, account for the visual multiple, different colors.

Hair is formed by the hair glands and may be divided into three parts. *The root*, situated in the inner skin layers, is flared. *The follicle*, above the root beneath the hair shaft, is a bulb-shaped cell containing a cavity. *The shaft* growing out of the follicle, consists of a clear outer wall and an inner core.

Pigment is secreted by glands in the inner skin layers and is picked up as the hair root moves in the layer. It is forced by its own electrons through the follicle and is forced out through the opening at the top of the follicle into the hair shaft. When the pigment granules force themselves through the follicle opening into the shaft, they form a pattern and migrate to the farthest outgrowth of the hair shaft in this pattern, unless there is an obstruction or diversion in the shaft.

The patterns are always the same for different hues of a color. They are thicker or thinner in the number, or size, of the granules making the pattern. The pigment in their patterns are deposited in many forms, perpendicular to the shaft, in geometric designs the length of the center

212

of the shaft, in specific areas such as tip, along one inner wall, smeared against an inner wall, or in circular formation inside the wall of the shaft with an open core, etc. The light rays are thus refracted, reflected, deflected, entirely or partially and their courses redirected to the human eye.

Several shades of one color may show in varying areas in one animal, as a result of differing sizes or density in the pigment particles. More than one color pattern may overlap, creating a dual coloring.

Horses born black change colors because the hairs are situated in different skin layers. As the fine pigment glands in a layer cease to produce, the hairs are unpigmented, appearing white. Mingled with the black hairs the optically visual color is grayish, or mouse blue. The more unpigmented hairs mingled, the lighter the visual color will be until all skin layers cease producing sufficient pigment for the hair shaft, and the horse is whitish all over.

Sooty appearance derives when the tips are so constricted as to have a heavy concentration of pigment. Movement of the animal brings them together, giving the dirty blackish-brown smudged look.

In blue horses (Grulla), construction of the hair shaft is very complicated. It has a thin dense line of pigment granules which run the length of the center of the hair shaft. Stretching out from it to the walls are thin curtain-like partitions carrying pigment granules. This allows light to play directly on the inner line and the light is incompletely refracted from one wall of the shaft to the other, due to the partitions. The light is reflected back with a haziness which is perceived by the human eye as light blue or gray.

In golden colored horses, such as the Palamino, the follicle is so constricted that the pigment granules flow through in a very fine line which is deposited as a smear on the inner wall of the shaft. Light rays penetrating through this smear are refracted and reflected in a glowing golden haze.

The people who wove the description of the Yorkshire Terrier into a breed standard were very adept at animal husbandry. For nearly one hundred years their knowledge, which gained them advancement in the days of carriage trade, has stood to the advantage of the Yorkie in maintaining the breed's distinguishing points.

The new scientific understanding of color pigmentation of hair can be used to ensure us better Yorkies. It must be realized that we can no longer think only in terms of Mendelian genetics, where we have simple dominant and recessive effects governing the development of a trait.

We are dealing with multiple genes affecting the hairs coloration. Each pair of genes (alleles) contribute to the desired trait. Each has a recessive and dominant form, but it is the number of gene pairs and their independent behavior from the other contributing genes during the process of recombination at fertilization that makes for the attainment of the Yorkies' desired prime important points of coat color and texture.

A Yorkie will not have a coat that is dense long and straight, unless the hair glands produce many, pliable, even hairs. Thick outer walls of the hair shaft impede the penetration of light. Rough, uneven surfaces of the outer walls deflect light rays.

The desired fine, silky texture gives the hair a thin outer wall that is strong and translucent. The hair is soft, clings to the body and feels cool to the touch. Woolly and cottony textured hairs have walls that dull the reflection of the pigment granules. The hair is rough, stands out from the body and feels warm to the touch.

A Yorkie minus the correct production (in extent, amount and distribution) of pigment granules can never achieve the desired lustrously glowing metalic colors of polished gold and steel-blue. The smooth surface of coat texture combined with the colors works in complete cooperation to produce the dog as visualized by Theo Marples in his first edition of *Show Dogs:*

"Beautiful to look at, active as a kitten, vivacious as the most 'Perky Pom', the Yorkshire Terrier is the acme of Toy Dog virtue and perfection, looked at from every angle."

Size

From the beginning to the end of the AKC-approved standard, you are informed that the Yorkshire Terrier is a small dog. In the beginning: *"long-haired toy terrier"*—and at the end: *"Weight—must not exceed seven pounds."*

One is continually amazed to still read that it took many years and much crossing of breeds to being the Yorkshire down to its Toy size. In the 1860s, they were shown in *Toy Terriers—under five pounds.* By 1878, one top winner weighed in at ten pounds, and another top contender weighed four and three-quarter pounds. In 1891, weight was divided into two classes: *"under five pounds and over five pounds but not to exceed twelve."* Came 1904 and weight had become three classes: *"five pounds and under," "seven pounds and under but over five pounds,"* and *"over seven pounds."* One is not only amazed to read that it took many years to bring him down in size, but whoever passed judgment on what dogs fitted into *"seven pounds and under, but over five pounds"* has our congratulations.

It remains a fact that the animals that went into the production of the Yorkshire Terrier were small. Few exceeded twelve pounds in weight.

214

It was never the question of the Yorkie being bred down in size. It is his cousins that have been bred *up* in size. Most of the early descriptions given of Skye and Scottish Terriers, etc. give weight at twelve to sixteen pounds.

When the standard was rewritten in 1966, seven pounds was settled on. All the breeders and exhibitors belonging to The Yorkshire Terrier Club of America weighed their stock. The general agreement was that no one bred from animals over seven pounds. This weight would allow the larger bitches, who made the best brood bitches, to be shown without being penalized.

It was also settled that there would be no reference to sex. No one wished to penalize a male dog that carried the prime points that distinguish the breed—correct coat color and texture. Still, the desire was to keep the breed a small Toy dog. For this reason, the rule for weight simply specifies "*must not* exceed seven pounds."

The Yorkie is a small dog. Eng. Ch. Martywyn's Wee Teddy, owned by A. H. Coates (England.)

215

—Drawing by Melba Green.

8

Grooming

THE CARE that is given a Yorkshire Terrier's coat is all important. To keep a Yorkie groomed as a house-dog is a fairly simple matter—a good brushing five minutes a day will do the job, with a bath given when needed, or desired. The top-knot can be caught up in a wrap, ribbon, barrette or even cut short. But the care necessary to conditioning a show dog, and keeping him in show condition, is time consuming and requires patience. It is a demanding job that allows no time off. Your one reward is that your Yorkie's perfection of a full floor length mantle of gleaming gold and blue silken coat will reflect the amount of care it has been given.

The amount of coat that a Yorkshire grows depends on several things. First, the grooming must be done properly. Next, the dog must be healthy and happy. However, without the inherited ability to grow a long coat nothing is going to make the coat grow. If you wish a show dog then be sure that the dog you buy has the inheritance to grow a long coat.

Washing

Washing a Yorkie has improved some since the following description was written in 1893 in *Kennel Secrets* by "Ashmont." However, because a lot of it is still timely we've included it. Obviously, since some of the same ideas for bathing have lasted this long, they must be important:

> While as a rule to wash a dog properly is not difficult, the washing of Yorkshire Terriers is an entirely different matter, and here the novice would

217

be all at sea; in fact he should never attempt it on a good dog, for many a "crack" has been ruined in the tub; consequently for him should be given full directions.

A foot pan is as good as anything to do the washing in. Place this on the table. Put in as much lukewarm water as will nearly reach to the dog's elbows. Mix in the soap until you have suds—never rub the soap on the dog. Now take a brush, a hairbrush that has a handle and long bristles, dip it in the suds and brush from the center of the back down, and always one way. The head must be washed in the same manner; brush from the center downward; in fact use the brush just as you do when not washing.

When you are sure you have reached all parts and the hair and skin are thoroughly clean, pass the hand from the center of the back downward and force out as much of the soap and water as you can; then use the sponge in about the same way. This done, lift the dog out and put him into another tub, which is all ready on the table, containing clean lukewarm water, and brush him just as you did with the suds, until the soap is out. With the hands and sponge get out as much water as you can. Remove him from the tub and stand him on the table, put over him a cloth or towel and pass the hands over it with gentle pressure, that it may take up some of the water that remains in his coat; but on no account must the hair be rubbed or ruffled.

Now after combing him with a comb that has widely-set teeth, begins a long and tedious process of drying. For this you must have two or three brushes; while one is being used, the others must be drying in front of the fire.

This drying will occupy a full hour. When completed, take a little fine oil in the palm of the hand, rub the hands together and pass them over the coat. This done, tie up the "bang" with a piece of ribbon or tape to keep it from the eyes.

Some dogs, in fact nearly all, will "fiddle"—scratch themselves — especially the very heavy-coated ones, which in hot weather may become heated and restless; and these must have "stockings" for the hind feet. The thumb of an old glove will fill the bill. Put the foot into this and tie with a piece of narrow tape around the leg.

Let the dog run about in the room, provided you can watch him, for an hour or so. Then draw the brush over him a few times and "cage" him. But do not oblige him to lie on plush, or velvet cushions, for they are far from suitable. A linen cover is the proper thing for a cushion, for it cannot stain nor does the coat adhere to it. And such a cover should be so made that it can be taken off and washed.

Even today, to prepare a Yorkie that has a full coat for a show takes time and, like growing coat, it cannot be rushed. If you don't have at least three or four hours to do your show dog's washing and grooming, don't start it. Granted, if the dog is not yet in full coat—i.e., floor length and wrapped—the length of time needed will vary per dog, but an hour at the least is needed for a young show prospect and probably more.

A well-groomed Yorkie is always a treat to the eyes. Silverwind's Ode to Love, owned by Elissa Taddie.

To wash a dog's coat for the show, you will need the following equipment:

Two hairbrushes

A comb

Toenail clippers

Scissors

Several large bath towels

A sponge or washrag

Shampoo—it should be one that is either manufactured for a dog's show coat or a regular shampoo for human hair.

A rinse—the rinse used will depend on the dog. For most Yorkies a cream rinse is best. However there are some dogs who have very oily coats and for these, a rinse made with vinegar and water, or a small amount of baking soda mixed with water.

A hair dryer.

Before washing the dog, the ears should be trimmed. The usual amount of hair to trim off is about one-half, but this is an individual matter and has to be tried on each dog. If a dog has larger ears than are desirable, don't cut off so much hair that this becomes more apparent.

A few Yorkies have round tips. They shouldn't have, but not having read the part in the standard that outlaws them, they still produce one or two that do. If your dog does have them, try and trim the hair to a point, rather than following the actual rounded tips.

Brush out all the dust, mats or snarls before you start. If the dog is wrapped naturally, remove the wraps and brush out the coat. If possible, brush the dog's coat out the day before and you'll save a little time. Once the dog is all brushed out, place the dog in the sink. Wet the coat thoroughly. If you have a spray attachment, it is a great help; otherwise you'll have to use the faucet and the sponge to get all the coat wet down to the skin. Shampoo the coat, but don't rub the hair round and round. A downward motion should be used. Be sure to wash the underside, and each leg should be shampooed separately including the pads and between the toes. To soap the long top-knot, start at the scalp and work the shampoo from the scalp to the tip of the top-knot. Don't rub it! Once you've shampooed all the coat and skin, rinse with lukewarm water until the hair has no soap left in it. Use the rinse and then, with your hand, press out as much water as you can by running your hands from the part downwards. The whiskers and top-knot—and the legs—can be gently squeezed between your fingers to remove the excess water.

Wrap the dog in a towel and pat out as much moisture as you can. It may be that you will need several towels to soak up the water. Once you've gotten as much out this way, place the dog on a dry towel and brush the coat dry in front of an electric dryer.

The coat should be brushed from the parting downward until every bit is completely dry. Be sure the legs and underside are dried completely before wrapping. A dog that is wrapped while damp will end up with a wavy coat when unwrapped. The long-knot (*fall*) should be brushed dry by brushing the hair backwards toward the tail.

Some dogs' coats look at their best right after a bath; others look better several days ahead of time, especially if they have coats that tend to be flyaway. For this reason it is best to determine on what day, after a bath, the dog's coat appears in best bloom, so that the dog can be washed that length of time prior to the show. Washing ahead of time will return some of the natural oil to the coat and make it more manageable. Very oily coats should be washed as close to show time as can be managed.

If you have any reason to feel that your dog has been in an area where it could acquire fleas, ticks, or other bugs, be sure to use a good dip for them. One flea can cause enough damage to put a dog out of the show ring for months. No one has ever actually carried on experiments to measure how fast a coat grows, but we figure that about a half an inch a month is pretty close. (The blue coat usually tends to grow a bit faster than does the gold. Young dogs' coats grow faster, except when teething, than do the coats of more mature dogs.) If your Yorkie scratches a large hole you will have to wait until it is regrown, so it is easier to dip for undesirable guests than to wish you had. During the summer months it is wiser to keep all the dogs dipped for fleas. Your veterinarian can recommend a good one; we have used "Hilo" dip for many years without any damage to the dogs' coats. It also usually helps to ward off any hot spots as well.

Oiling

If the coat is not being washed for a show, follow the above method for washing. If you are going to put the dog's coat in oil, you will find the fastest way is to use it as a final rinse. A pint of water with a teaspoon or so of oil poured over the dog will do the job nicely. One warning—use a separate brush for this process when drying your dog, and don't get it mixed up with your other brushes that you use for drying your dog for a show.

Patience is necessary in bringing a Yorkie to its top show condition. In attempting to expedite coat growth, novices are apt to try various recommended hair stimulants. Big claims have been made for many of these, but we personally have always used olive oil, or occasionally a bath oil for dry skin when a dog's scaly skin warrants it—which is usually in winter when the artificial heat and lack of humidity can cause dry skin.

Be wary of using too much oil on a dog's coat, especially during the hot summer months, even if you do have air-conditioning. Any dog whose coat is kept in oil should have the oil washed out regularly, as it tends to collect dirt and dust.

Wrapping

The questions of whether to wrap a show dog's coat, and at what age to begin wrapping, are the ones most often asked. No one has ever grown a full floor length coat on a male Yorkie without wraps, and only a very few bitches have ever achieved a full coat minus wraps. Even then the bitches usually had wraps on top-knot, whiskers, tail and breeches. Wrapping is the only way to keep a coat from being soiled and the ends of the hair from being worn and broken off. The age at which to wrap the whole coat is usually around nine or ten months, sometimes later. The top-knot should be done up as soon as it is long enough. The tail and breeches should be wrapped when they are getting long enough that wrapping will protect the hair from becoming constantly soiled. Hence the decision of at what age to wrap can only be made for each individual dog.

The other question invariably asked is how long does it take to get a Yorkshire into full coat once the coat is wrapped? It takes around two years to achieve the correct silky-textured Yorkie, although by around eighteen months you can usually begin to see appreciable results of your care. The woolly or cottony-coated dogs often have floor length coats by a year, which is probably just as well for those who show this incorrect type, because if they had to wait longer, the dog's lack of cor-

In wraps—and combed out.

Wrapped and unwrapped—as seen from the side.

rect color would be even more apparent. Again—*time, patience* and *proper care* are the best ingredients for achieving a full floor length coat.

To tie up the coat in wraps, cut pieces of paper two to two and one-half inches wide and slightly longer than the beard, top-knot or other parts of the coat. Waxpaper is used by almost all exhibitors in the United States. But other paper will do if it works for you. The paper doesn't grow hair—it simply protects the ends from getting dirty and broken.

We know of one breeder who, having lived abroad, was used to using toilet tissue, and since the exhibitor's daughter was returning from school abroad, the exhibitor requested her daughter to bring home a supply. Upon arriving at U.S. Customs, the child declared this item and the Customs' man said to her—"We do have toilet tissue in the United States." Whereupon the child turned and said, "Oh, I know that — Mom wants it for the dogs" . . . which, we're sure, finished that poor man. If the dog lives in a tropical climate where the humidity is a problem, then it has been found that either tuille or net is better for the wraps as the hair will need the air.

Brush the selected section of hair straight and wrap the paper around the hair like a tube, double it over and put a rubber-band around the folded paper, which can be folded either up or under towards the body. Size 8 rubber-bands are best for this and can be obtained from a stationary store in varying quantities of weight. Make sure the roots of the hair are not being pulled too tightly or the dog will rub to loosen them. These wraps should be brushed out and redone every second day.

If a dog is just starting on being wrapped it is best to start with the top-knot, the tail and the hair on either side of the tail, i.e., the breeches. In wrapping, anytime, be sure that the wraps do not impede the dog's movement. Sometimes Yorkies will ignore their wraps, even when wrapped for the first time; others will try to remove them. If this is a problem a drop of Bitter-Apple or Tabasco Sauce on the wrap will usually put an end to their, or their pals, removing them.

It takes twenty-four wraps for a full show coat, which means that there are six used for wrapping the head furnishings. Wrap the top-knot in one, the chin whisker and each side whisker in one—don't get the chin whiskers mixed in with the side ones. The hair on the side of the head is parted from behind the ear and up to just before the eye. The side coat has five wraps, one on the neck, one on the shoulder, two between the front and rear legs, one on the hips. Each leg has a wrap, the chest, the tail and one on either side of the tail on the breeches.

If you do have a dog that scratches, then it is best to put socks (boots) on the hind feet. Tube gauze works very well for this. You can usually buy it in the drugstore or, if not available, ask your druggist to order it for you. The gauze for large fingers and toes—size 2—is the best size. Cut a strip about six inches long, twist the strip in the middle and then tuck one side into the other. Put the rear foot into the sock and wrap a narrow strip of tape, either transparent or adhesive, around the top of the sock to keep it on, or use a piece of yarn or string. Don't wrap the tape too tight and be sure the toes have room to move freely.

Trimming

For the show ring, and for any dog to really look its best, the over-hanging hair on the feet and the hair between the pads should be trimmed. Since all dogs are extremely touchy about their feet, it's best to start trimming the paws while they are puppies. The toenails should also be kept cut back and they are easier cut right after a bath.

The paws should be trimmed as round as possible. Here again, study your dog; if the paws turn out too much, then trim the outside edge more than the inside edge—this will give the dog a better look. Shaggy-haired feet on a Yorkie detract from the dog's neat appearance and can make a dog appear to be moving incorrectly. The standard specifies that feet be trimmed as round as possible.

When the coat of a Yorkshire becomes so long that it interferes with the dog's gait, it should be trimmed. A dog that is unable to move prop-erly because he is stepping on his hair, or whose feet become entangled when gaiting, cannot present the proper picture. It's extremely foolish to assume that all a Yorkshire needs is a lot of hair. Most judges, in fact, approach a full coat with the idea that they are going to discover a fault hidden beneath the dog's flowing coat. They expect, and rightful-ly so, that the dog can and will move proudly around the ring with the other dogs who may have less coat, so don't put your dog at a disad-vantage by allowing his coat to become so long that it detracts. If the coat is too long, cut it. Most Yorkies, if they are carrying an excessive length of coat, look out of balance—extra long trailing coat can make a dog appear to be long bodied.

To trim an overly long coat, first brush the dog all the way out, re-move all the wave. Be sure the dog is not standing on any of its coat. The dog should be standing close to the edge of the table so that the coat can be brushed straight down over the edge.

When the dog gaits, the hair will tend to spring up a bit; you should trim the side coat from the rear leg forward, so that there is between an inch to an inch and a half hanging over the edge. From the rear leg backwards, trim it slightly longer like the train of a dress. Across the chest and in front of the front legs leave plenty of clearance so that the dog's gait can be seen—one-half inch over the edge is usually about

224

right. All this trimming should be done slowly and carefully. Try cutting a little and then gaiting your dog until you find the length that allows the dog a free and easy gait. If the whiskers are so long that the dog walks on them, they should be trimmed as well.

Trimming a Yorkie in full-show coat should be done by someone who knows what they are doing, never by someone who has never done work with a Yorkie's coat. Trimming a show coat is always scary as one is always sure that you're cutting too much—but even if one were to end up floor length, better that, and a dog that can gait properly, than one who cannot because its coat is too long.

Brushing

All Yorkshires need to be brushed and no show coat was ever attained without proper application of the brush. The brush should be made with pure bristles, and they should be of variegated lengths, not too soft but rather stiff. Don't use a nylon bristle or pin bursh, for the hairends will be split and the coat growth will be retarded.

It is best to either dampen the brush, or spray the coat lightly with water or a coat dressing, of which there are a number made for dogs. The hair should be brushed from the part downward. Some people prefer to brush the dog by laying the dog in their lap; however, we prefer to brush the dog while the dog is standing. Be sure to brush all the coat and to leave no snarls or tangles anywhere. A comb is used to put a part in the dog; it is not used to pull out snarls. Most important in good grooming is patience and gentleness—don't ever get mad at the dog.

Brushing out a Yorkie to get it ready for the judging at a show follows much the same process as brushing out the dog's coat at any other time. All wraps are removed. They can be all removed at one time and the whole coat brushed, or each undone separately and the coat in it thoroughly brushed out. Any wave should be brushed out so that the coat lies flat and straight and the coat should be brushed until it shines. The coat will achieve a natural shine almost immediately, that is assuming that bathing and coat conditioning has been done properly. Woolly or cottony coats never have the proper natural shine that makes the hair look like silk-satin, and when in motion "like running water." The parting down the center of the dog's back should be made as straight as you can make it. Some people use a knitting needle for this purpose, but a comb will do the job.

To put on the dog's ribbon take down the top-knot and brush it out completely. Re-do the top-knot, positioning it on your dog's head to give the dog his best expression. This is something that should be de-

Showing length of topknot.

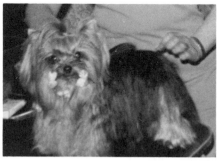

Left: Face furnishings still wrapped. *Right:* face furnishings groomed ready for ring.

cided ahead of time; a badly placed ribbon can ruin a dog's expression. Few Yorkies look their best with their top-knot pulled way back between the ears and, on a dog with a longer than desirable muzzle, tying the ribbon far back only accentuates the problem. By the same token, a dog whose muzzle is shorter than is wanted should not have his ribbon tied too far forward.

The hair that is gathered up for the top-knot is usually parted by making a slightly curving part from ear to ear along the back of the head (skull); the parting then traces from a line extending from the top corner of the ear base to the outside edge of the eye. If the skull is perhaps too broad, take up a little more hair on the sides. Unfortunately, there is no hard and fast rule about the exact position, so it becomes a matter of trial and error with each individual dog.

Having gotten the top-knot correctly positioned and rewrapped, be sure your wrap is not so tight that the eyes are pulled up; if they are, loosen your wrap before proceeding. Put a size 8 rubber-band around the hair at the base between the scalp and the wrap. Cut a length of string (kite or butcher's string is best) about six inches long and wrap it once or twice around the base on top of the rubber-band, and tie a knot, leaving the leftover ends uncut. Undo the wrap, and fold the top-knot backward towards the tail so that you make a small knob with the rest of the top-knot hanging loose down the back. Wrap the remaining string around the top-knot leaving a knob of about one-half an inch to hold the ribbon and knot the string—cutting off any extra length.

The Ribbons

Picking the color for the dog's ribbon is a matter of personal preference. But as a general rule, pastel colors (although lavender is okay), black, brown, yellow and white tend to fade the dog's colors, and do not show up well in the ring. Bright colors are best; red, blues, greens, or the variations of these basic colors. Young dogs, whose golds are not cleared all the way, tend to look best with red ribbon as it picks up the gold, minimizing the black or sooty spots. Some golds clash with the shades of red and it detracts from the gold shadings. Very light blue body coats are usually enhanced by bright shades of blue. On an adult dog of correct color, any of the bright shades look fine. Try different colors on the dog until you find the color that suits your dog's coloring best and brings out the highlights of his clear blue and gold.

The ribbon should be about one-half inch in width and, if satin ribbon is used, it should be the kind that is satin on one side only, as the double-sided satin ribbon simply slides off at the most inconvenient moments. Seam binding used for hemming clothes works very well and comes in a wide range of colors, besides being fairly inexpensive and readily available in most places. Very wide ribbon or ornate arrangements on a dog's top-knot detract from the correct Terrier expression. Two ribbons can be used, but generally the single ribbon is preferred. A Yorkie requires a very long, thick top-knot in order to do justice to the two ribbons. Some exhibitors make a bow of the ribbon ahead of time, attaching it to a rubber-band which is then placed on the top-knot ready-made.

There are a number of commercially made bows that can be purchased from various pet suppliers. These ready-made ones, however, do not look as well as a bow that is tied on the dog.

To make a bow, cut a piece of ribbon of sufficient length to work with when tying the bow. Dampen the center; it will help to keep the ribbon from slipping off once it is done up. Tie the ribbon at the base of the knob that is left, placing it on top of the string, which again helps prevent the ribbon from slipping or turning. Tie a bow so that it faces directly forward. The bow should not be so large that it interferes with the dog's eyes, or so tiny it cannot be seen. Cut off the excess ribbon and, to keep the ends from unraveling, cut a notch into the end of each side.

If there is time to wait before the judging begins, and the dog has long whiskers—gather the chin and side whiskers together and loosely wrap them under the chin, being sure to leave about two inches of hair that is not wrapped. Sometimes a string or piece of yarn is tied on each set of whiskers, so that they are out of the way. Either way, this will not interfere with his panting if it is hot, or drinking water, but it will prevent the whiskers from getting dirty, or from them getting into the dog's mouth and being chewed off or from the dog choking on them should they get into his mouth. Once a Yorkie is ready—i.e. all brushed—let him sleep until his class. If the dog has been properly groomed it takes only a minute or two to do a final brush-up just before going into the ring.

There are several don'ts that novices, and even some who should know better, should be warned of in preparing a Yorkie for the ring. No dog should be shown with hair spray, oil or lacquer in or on any part of the coat. It is not proper to use anything to keep the short ends of hair in place in a top-knot. Texture is of prime importance in the standard and it cannot be properly judged if it has been altered by any of these things. The ear fringes should never be tied into a dog's top-knot to support the ears, or to make the ears appear closer together. This looks artificial and any good judge can spot it as the dog loses the ability to properly use his ears when at attention or at rest.

Any form of artificial coloring aids should never be used; the purpose of showing dogs is to improve the breed and it is impossible to breed better coloring into breeding stock by coloring the show dogs artificially.

Water—rainwater is ideal—or one of the light coat dressings can be used to brush out the coat and to help keep it from being flyaway or even to prevent static electricity, which can be a problem in some buildings. A bottle, plastic or otherwise, with a spray attachment should be used for this purpose, with the spray being sprayed lightly on the coat or directly onto the hairbrush.

Brood Bitches

A brood bitch can be kept in show coat if she is to be returning to the ring, but it takes patience and common sense. If the bitch's coat is wrapped, it will have to be brushed every day, a little at a time, as the puppies cannot be without their mother for long periods. If the show coat is not wrapped, keep it lightly oiled with a pure oil and brush it twice a day. It is best to wrap the hair on the tail and the breeches—the hair on either side of the tail—to keep it clean. If this area gets dirty, rinse it off, dry it, brush it out and rewrap. For a brood bitch that is not being kept in a show coat, a light brushing everyday is best, or the coat can be trimmed down before the bitch whelps her puppies. Once you start giving the puppies a meal, usually at around three weeks, the bitch can have a bath, but don't use anything but a pure shampoo and light pure oil rinse. Some bitches do shed a little of their coats, but if they are brushed regularly it stays nominal.

Groomed brood bitch. Eng. & Am. Ch. Martywyn's Wee Mischief, winner of Yorkie specialty and brood bitch class.

Grooming the Puppy

The first grooming that a Yorkshire Terrier puppy gets is when the puppy's ears, paws and toenails are trimmed for the first time.

Puppies need their ears trimmed as soon as it is apparent the hair is overhanging the edges of the ears. The weight of too much hair on a puppy's ear can cause the ear to hang down, rather than remain erect or come up properly. This is usually visible around three weeks of age if the coat is extremely heavy. Very heavy hair on a puppy's ear is usually a pretty good indication that the texture is going to be either wooly or cottony. Silky-textured coated puppies do not have as heavy a growth of hair on their ears. The hair should be trimmed as far down on the edges, back and front of the puppy's ear as soon as possible if the hair is very heavy. On puppies with silky-textured coats, the hair should be trimmed three-quarters of the way down, which is further than it will be trimmed as the puppy grows.

The scissors that are used should be sharp and have a blunt point. These can be purchased at a drug store or sometimes from pet suppliers. In drug stores they are usually sold for babies. Trimming a puppy's ear takes extreme care and lots of patience. They are usually wiggling around and interfering in any way that they can. Hold the puppy in your lap, take the ear gently, but firmly, with your fingers. Feel the edge of the ear with your fingers and trim along the edge carefully. To remove the hair from the back and front, roll the leather of the ear over your fingers—the hair stands up and it is easier to trim. If you have trouble finding the ear's edge, dampen the ear and the edge is more visible. Whatever happens, treat the puppy gently and encourage him; don't frighten him by fighting with him over his wiggling. If you have to change from ear to ear, as the puppy insists on turning around, do so. If he does not get scared, he'll settle down and let you get on with the job—at least for a couple of minutes. Once the puppy realizes that he is not being hurt, you'll find that the trimming can be done quickly with a minimum of twists and turns.

The paws are trimmed by gently trimming the overhanging hair from around the paws and between the pads. Dogs are very touchy about their feet, so be careful. It may also be advisable to trim the hair under the tail to prevent the puppy from getting soiled.

Toenails usually need to be trimmed before anything else, and should be done as soon as they appear to be scratching their mother when they nurse. This can be anywhere from ten days to three weeks. Toenails that are left too long can be very uncomfortable for the mother, and long nails can catch in the bedding, causing a puppy to dislocate or strain a leg while trying to get the toenail free.

230

Bathing Puppies

Since the coat of a Yorkie demands a clean, healthy skin to grow, we usually start washing our puppies at around two months of age. The first bath should be given at a time when the puppies are their most active. Don't pick a time when they are worn out from playing and are usually napping. Don't wash a puppy if it has had an upset stomach, been ill, doesn't act just right, or had shots that day. If you have friends coming to see the puppies, wash the puppies the day before, not the day they come. Too much excitement in one day can bring on an upset. If the puppy is going to a new home, the bath should be a day ahead. The puppy is not going to get that soiled in 24 hours. If the puppy does get a little soiled, a damp washrag should do the job of cleaning him up.

For the puppy's first bath, support the puppy in your hand or with only his rear feet touching the bottom of the sink. Using a sponge or washrag, wet the puppy thoroughly; if the puppy wants to look at the sponge, the running water or sink—let him—but don't let him get scared by slipping or getting water in his mouth or eyes. If the puppy isn't frightened while being washed now, or at any later time, the whole job will be a lot easier for both of you. Having gotten the puppy wet, apply shampoo and gently wash him all over. Care should be taken around the face, but do wash it as well, including the ear leathers. Using the sponge, or washrag, rinse him thoroughly getting out every bit of soap. Wrap the puppy in a large towel and rub the coat dry. It is only for the first couple of baths that rubbing the coat dry is advisable; after that, too much damage is done by rubbing. Once the puppy is dried as well as possible, take another dry towel and, with the puppy in your lap, use a hair dryer and brush the coat to finish getting him all the way dry. After the puppy's bath, plenty of time should be allowed for a long nap before the puppies have any more excitement.

From this point on the puppies should be washed every two weeks until they are around five months, after which time we usually wash them once a week. Of course, if the dog is a house pet and its coat is not being grown for show, a bath can be given less frequently. No puppy should be allowed out-of-doors until at least several hours have elapsed from when it was bathed. And no puppy or dog should ever be washed if it is not feeling well.

Puppies should start being brushed early, but the hairbrush should not be as firm as the one used on the coat of an older puppy. Brushing should be done daily.

Grooming the Pet Yorkshire

The care of the non-show coat of a Yorkie should be much the same as of a dog being conditioned for the show ring. Both need to be brushed regularly, kept in good health and kept clean. A few minutes of brushing every day will keep the dog looking like a Yorkie should and it is really only fair to the dog. Unfortunately for the pet dog, the best of intentions sometimes deteriorate and the brushing is left un-done—until one day the owner realizes what a snarled mess the dog's coat has become. At this point they are usually at a loss as to how to undo the damage, and are too ashamed to call the breeder. Often it be-comes an ordeal for the dog and owner as the owner tries to comb out the snarls. Here, then, are a few ways that help make it easier on ev-eryone:

First off, don't try to comb out the coat. Snarls should be undone while the coat is damp. Give the dog a bath and rinse with a rinse made of bath oil (or any oil) mixed with water. Squeeze the excess water out of the dog's coat, then start brushing. When you come to a snarl, sepa-rate it with your fingers, using the brush to help break up the mats. Hold the snarl so that your fingers are above the snarl and against the skin—this way the pull is against your fingers rather than pulling against the dog's skin. The very woolly-type of coat usually mats, and if the mat is too tight it is best to cut these out if the brush and fingers cannot separate them. On the cottony-type coat, the snarls are close to the skin and present the hardest problem to undo. If—after washing and brushing—any mats remain, and with this type coat they probably will, they will have to be cut out. Being so close to the skin, too much brushing will irritate the skin causing sores. The cut places, or even if the whole coat is cut, will regrow just as human hair does. A dog with the correct silky-type coat can get snarled due to lack of care, but they never snarl as badly as do the other type coats. A bath given as above, with a good brushing, will generally remove any snarls leaving a silky-coated Yorkie silky-coated again.

An elderly dog should be brushed regularly, but should not be washed as often as younger dogs, and only when the dog's health is good. An older dog's circulation is not what it was when he was young-er, so keep a check on the skin for any sores, and don't overtire the dog by brushing him too long at one time. If you can't keep an older dog brushed, then the coat should be trimmed short.

The time and care put into your Yorkie, whether a pet or a show dog, will be repaid. His coat will not shed out so all your work will last as long as his care is maintained. Long or short, his gleaming silky tresses, tossed about in play or parade, will be your eye-filling reward.

Short cut, for ease of grooming an older dog.

Schnauzer trim.

Show trim maintained. Wildweir Forget-Me-Not, dam of 4 champions, pictured being shown to BOB at 9 years of age. Note color still holding. Owned by Vic and Lorraine Berry.

9

Showing Your Yorkshire

THE SHOWING of Yorkshire Terriers can be fun for the whole family or a hobby for a single individual. Yorkies adapt well to competition in obedience, conformation or junior showmanship—and it is not unusual for one Yorkie to participate in all three, being shown by a different family member in each.

If you have never shown before, we suggest that a first step would be to attend a dog show in your area (without your dog) and see what it entails. If you can, contact a local Yorkshire Terrier or all-breed club (your veterinarian may be able to steer you to one) for guidance. Otherwise, an inquiry to the American Kennel Club, 51 Madison Avenue, New York, N.Y. 10010, will bring you answers on shows in your area, where to contact clubs, or on the requirements for showing.

To enter your Yorkie at a show, it must be six months of age, and registered with the AKC. Assuming that you will look to local clubs or the AKC for information on the classes to enter, or how a dog earns points toward championship, we will confine ourselves here to pointers that may be of help in actually showing your Yorkshire.

It is the exhibitor's job to help make the best of his dog. The dog show ring is not the place to start training your show dog. Teach your dog to walk properly, to stand still on the table and ground, and to be examined by different people. A few seconds spent on the following things, while your puppy is under three months, will help assure that they will not be stumbling blocks in his show future:

1. Put the puppy on a table, keeping your hand close by it so that it knows you are close. The first couple of times on a table, the pup-

py may lay flat down and just look around. Next, it will slowly stand up and take a few sniffs around. A tidbit fed on the table will help. The puppy has to get the idea that it is safe up there. Just think how you'd feel if someone put you way up on something twenty feet off the floor. Some puppies are never bothered and will start off all over the table, so keep a hand near the puppy.

2. Try using a word such as "up" or "table" when you lift your puppy up to place it on the table. In this way it will be ready; otherwise that lift up can have the same effect as a fast elevator ride.

3. Don't put the puppy, or allow it to be put, on a table when being given an innoculation.

4. Once the puppy appears to accept the table and height—then start teaching it to stand.

5. Teaching the puppies to follow your feet will make leash breaking easier for everyone.

Shows are held both outdoors and indoors, so your Yorkie should be trained to walk on grass as well as on cement, dirt and rugs. Grass at most outdoor shows is anything but ideal for Toy dogs. It does help if you have prepared your Yorkie for such a circumstance. One way to do this is to first walk it in grass that is overdue to be mowed, and then walking it through mowed grass in which the clippings have not yet been picked up.

No Yorkie should be shown if it is not in condition. A Yorkie that is too fat, too thin, has a scratched-out coat, is not bathed, or is simply under the weather, hasn't got a chance of winning. A Yorkie that is not lead broken, that won't stand for the judge to examine, or that is simply scared due to not having been accustomed to strange surroundings, is not going to win. No matter how much coat, or how perfect its color, if the judge cannot see your Yorkie walking proudly, or examine it to feel its construction, or look at its teeth, he is not going to place the dog. A show dog is just that—a dog that shows itself so that the best points can be seen.

Remember that in entering your dog at a show, you are actually asking for a judge's opinion of it. Be honest with yourself in evaluating your dog against the standard. Realize that while a young dog may have a great future, if it meets up with a mature dog that is in its prime, youth will generally have to give way. Judges are required to judge the dogs as they appear on the day they are shown—not on their futures or pasts. And if you lose, but don't feel you should have, don't get upset—seek other judges' opinions at other shows.

At The Show

A lot of worry about that first show can be eliminated by knowing where, what and when. If the show is unbenched, the time to arrive depends on how many Yorkies you have to get ready. A good average is one-half hour for the grooming of each dog. Then allow time to get your Yorkie exercised, your equipment set up and a look around. If you have never shown under the judge, find where your ring is located. It is best to locate its position anyway. Trying to find it at the last minute will only upset you and your exhibit. Having found the right ring, watch how the judge manages the ring—in other words, does he gait the dogs up and down the mat, in a triangle, or in an "L" pattern? Are the dogs examined on the table and then gaited, or does he examine each dog before gaiting the dogs?

If you are the first breed in the ring at the specified hour, check to see if the judge is running on time or not. If there are other breeds listed before Yorkies at the specified hour, then you have to guess as to what time it will be. But since you came to show your Yorkie, it is better to be too early at ringside than too late. Take your crate to the ringside, and your brush, comb, leash, spray, bait and, of course, your dog. At some shows you cannot bring your crate to the ringside; if this is the case, bring a large towel to the ringside and spread it out on the floor for you and your Yorkie. If the dog is young, allow time for him to look around and see where he is while he sits in your lap or you hold him in your arms. Put him down by your feet, after being sure there is room and that there are no large dogs or children in strollers too close, and let him study the whole place from his angle—which is naturally a much lower view than we humans ever see at a show. Then get him groomed up.

Ask the ring steward for your armband and put it on your left arm with number visible to the judge. When your class is called take your Yorkie into the ring and set him up, being sure that his back and front legs are in the proper place, his back (topline) level and his coat well groomed. A judge always looks the class over, and if your dog is standing looking its best when the judge turns to look, it is going to help. The whole class is usually gaited (walked) around the ring, and then the judge will ask the exhibitor to stand his Yorkie on the table where he can examine the dog's structure, check its bite and look at the dog's coat. Usually, the dog is then gaited individually while the next exhibitor gets his dog ready on the table. A Yorkie, when gaiting, should move on a loose leash looking at his owner—a little bit of bait helps to keep him looking like he adores you. When you are through gaiting your exhibit, go back to the end of the line and tidy his coat. Set your dog up so that it is looking its very best when the judge takes a final

Breed judging at Westminster KC show, Madison Square Garden, New York City.

Ch. Star Twilight of Clu-Mor being shown in the Toy Group at Westminster 1958.

look. This is, alas, the point at which your Yorkie usually will decide to move around, sit down or climb in your lap. Take comfort in that you are not the first one it has happened to, nor will you be the last. A young dog should enjoy its first couple of shows and a few goofs won't hurt; there are lots of other shows. But not if your show prospect gets scared or upset at the start of its career. He can feel your emotions, so relax! A Yorkie that has a good time at the beginning will end up being an easy dog to show.

The judge will place the class and, if you are indicated, place your Yorkie (and yourself) in front of the proper placing marker that is at one side of the ring. Should you get first, then you return to the ring with the other first prize winners of your dog's sex when Winners class is called. If you get second, stay at the ringside because, should the dog who beat you get Winners, you will have to go back in the ring to compete for Reserve Winners. If you are lucky enough to get Winners then you go back into the ring when the competition for Best of Breed is called. Should you be in doubt, ask someone; oddly enough every exhibitor did have a first show with just as many fears and qualms, even though some exhibitors and handlers tend to forget this fact.

Learning all the ways to make the best of your Yorkie's good points and minimize its faults is best learned by watching other people show their dogs. Trial and error is very good experience. Getting a friend to come and watch you show your Yorkie so that he can tell you where you made mistakes is always a big help.

One question that invariably arises is whether to show your own dog or hire a handler. A professional handler is someone who is licensed by the AKC to show dogs (various breeds) for a fee. No one but a professional handler is legally allowed to charge money to show another person's dog. This is for the protection of both the owner and the dog. Frankly, our opinion is that any owner is as capable as a handler of doing a good job with their Yorkie so long as the owner tries. It is the owner's job to get the Yorkie into the proper show condition. An owner that is willing to learn to groom a Yorkie for the ring usually can spend more time doing it than can a handler who has a number of breeds to show.

It takes a few shows for a novice and young dog to work well together, but if an owner has the desire he can learn. A lot of people seem to feel that they cannot win unless they have a handler. This fallacy is given credence when a beginner, having failed to win with his Yorkie, hires a handler to show his dog and the dog wins. The owner immediately supports the supposition that judges only look at handlers, forgetting the obvious—that he, the owner, was making no effort to learn how to show his Yorkie, whereas the handler he hired made every effort to present and show the Yorkie to its best advantage. The second argument put forth is that handlers are the backbone of dog shows because they are professionals. Frankly, if there were no breeders, there would be no dog shows—hence, no necessity for handlers. If a person is physically or emotionally unable to show their Yorkie then, obviously, a handler is necessary. Again, sometimes, for various reasons, an owner cannot get away from home and then must employ a handler. Of the 31 Yorkies that have won Best in Show, 24 have been shown by their owners.

A question usually asked by those attending their first show with their new show prospect is "What do I need to take with me?" If one were to be absolutely technical, "The dog and a leash" would be the answer, but there are things that make the job easier. So, starting with your dog, here is a list of suggestions:

1—A crate. Actually with a Yorkie this is something that is best to purchase early in your Yorkie's life. When driving in a car, it gives your dog the same kind of protection your seatbelt affords, should you stop suddenly. If your dog is crated when you have to go into a restaurant, or stop where you cannot take the dog with you, windows can be left open for air without its getting out or someone reaching in to steal your dog. At shows, your Yorkie will appreciate the quiet security of his own place. The crate, be it a wire one, wood or whatever, should be large enough for your Yorkie to lie, stand or sit. A crate eighteen inches long is ideal. For summer, it should be open on three sides at least; and—if it is a wire crate—for winter it should have a cover, or sides that have air holes in them. There are crates made that have removable sides for the summer, which reinserted provide winter comfort for your dog. The wire crates have canvas covers you can buy, or you can make one yourself.

2—A pad, towel or rug to sleep on in his crate, or for his bench, if it is a benched dog show.

3—A padlock—for the crate, or benching, in case you have to leave him alone for a short time.

4—A chain on which to put the padlock, when locking your benching at a benched show. A big chain collar is fine for the job.

5—Grooming equipment for your Yorkie.

6—Water. It is best to bring water from home for your dog. A change can upset him and put him off his best performance.

7—A water bowl.

8—Extra towels.

9—A folding chair or chairs. Although some buildings provide these, it's easier to be sure you have a place to sit.

10—A table. A grooming table can be purchased at most shows, or you can use a TV table or card table.

11—Some kind of tidbit that your dog enjoys so you can bait it to get its attention in the ring.

12—You'll find paper towels, Kleenex or some kind of wipes a good idea to have along.

There are other pieces of equipment that are useful, but until an owner is showing more than one dog, they just aren't necessary. These include a wire pen in which to exercise your Yorkie and wheels to transport your equipment from the car to the building.

What the Judge Is Looking For:

If this is your first time in the show ring, it's kind of handy to have an idea of what the judge is looking for—that is, what the judge is doing in the course of making his (or her) decision.

First, if your dog isn't trained, you've handicapped yourself and given the judge his number one reason for not placing your dog. Do follow the directions on training your dog. In that way the judge will be able to determine that your Yorkie is the most perfect animal in the ring—just as you are sure it is.

Second, the name of the game is to determine your "perfect" Yorkie's faults and try to make them less obvious.

The judge first assembles all the class entrants in a line, and checks the exhibitors' armbands to be sure that all are present and that no one from another class is in the ring. The judge may study the dogs in their lineup or he may gait them around the ring. In this, he is trying to get a general impression of how well each dog's body is proportioned, and of the overall balance of the dog. Next, he wants to see the dog's topline, which should be level, the same height at rump as at the shoulders.

You have two possible problems here. If your Yorkie has not been in a group of other Yorkies his attention may stray to the animals in front, or behind. This will not help his topline, for he will be off-stride. Try and get his attention back on you. A tasty tidbit, small enough so that he does not have to halt while he chews it up, will help; even a whiff of it will recall him to you.

The other problem is that he may decide he'd rather judge the spectators hanging over the ringside. If it's his first show let him have a look; after all, you'd let him study things in a new room. You may give the judge a score here, but you'll gain a step at your next show.

Try and keep your Yorkie's head up—to prevent him from acting like a scent hound. When he investigates the entrancing odors of the well-used matting, his head and neck go down, he goes off-stride and to compensate, his backbone angles down, unleveling his topline.

If the weather is cold, or your Yorkie is nervous about the whole procedure, he'll probably roach his back. You can only hope that, given time, he'll level it out. Of course, if it isn't level when your Yorkie is safely home and "Lord" of all he surveys, it isn't going to level out at the show and score goes against you.

The judge, after gaiting the dogs around, motions the owners to halt, and has the first Yorkie in line placed on the table for examination. Sometimes the judge wants the dog placed on the table a certain way, so pay attention to the judge as well as your dog. In fact, pay attention to the judge at anytime he or she is giving instructions. The judge will appreciate the courtesy, and you'll score points in gamemanship.

Set your dog up. The front legs should not turn out at the elbow, but stay close to the chest. You want them far enough apart to give the apperance of his having a compact, square body, not a shelly body. Place the rear legs so that the hocks are straight down and parallel to each other, but apart. The legs should have a slight bend at the stifle. Now pray that your Yorkie stays that way while you tidy up his coat.

Hold him by his leash in front and a hand close to the tail. Please don't try the "Look Mom, no hands!" bit; you can never be sure that the table isn't going to collapse, or that a "streaker" won't cross the ring. You don't want to pick up a Yorkie with a broken leg, while you explain that the animal never jumped, or fell off, the table before. Besides, your touch on the dog gives him confidence.

The judge then examines the Yorkie. There are generally two ways of doing this. First, the judge will get the dog's attention to check his expression. A nice, dark, sparkling eye, framed by dark eye rims, is a point getter here. Small V-shaped ears, well set up on the skull, and used—when interested—help your Yorkie, (along with his eyes) display a sharp, intelligent expression. Ears tied up into the topknot are easily caught by any judge. If your dog's are low set, you'll just have to hope that the ears of the other exhibits are also, or that your Yorkie is so much better elsewhere that you won't lose more than a slivered point here. The judge looks to be sure the nose is black; that the head, viewed from the side, is a rather flat line, not a deep stop; that the muzzle is not too long and that the skull is not apple-headed. The judge then checks the bite (teeth).

An alternative procedure is for the judge to first check the dog's bite (teeth) to see if it is scissor or level. Either way, here's where you cross

242

Ray Ryan judging dogs on table.

Judging dogs on ground.

your fingers. A Yorkie's head isn't all that big and a human hand can encompass at least two thirds of it. Hopefully, the judge will not cover your Yorkies' eyes while checking the bite. Yorkies, like most animals, prefer to see what anyone is doing in their mouths and, if they can't, they back away and all your careful leg arrangement is thrown into disarray. If this happens, don't glower at the judge, just try a fast move to get them rearranged. Judges make "Brownie" points with exhibitors when they ask the exhibitor to show them the dog's bite, and it's a lot more healthy as judges do not have time to wash their hands between examining each dog. However, the judge is Captain of The Ring and you do what he or she asks.

The judge looks at the tan headfall for color—a rich, golden tan, distribution and purity from intermingled black hairs. He checks to see if it is deeper in color at the sides of the head, at ear roots, on the muzzle, with the ears a deep rich tan. He checks that the tan does not extend down on the back of the neck.

The judge checks that the chest hairs are a bright, rich tan. The forelegs are checked to be sure they have black toenails and that the bright, rich tan does not overreach itself and grab a piece of the blue's territory. The judge also looks for any stray black or grey hairs in the forelegs' tan.

The judge checks the hindlegs to be sure that the tan doesn't extend higher than the stifle. He checks the rear legs for construction and the tail set (placement). If it is a male dog, he checks to be sure the Yorkie has two testicles of even size and that they are properly descended.

Then the judge studies the Yorkie's body to be sure that it is compact, all portions properly balanced to give an overall well-proportioned Yorkie. He checks to be sure the backline, viewed from the side, is level and that it is the same height at the shoulder as at the rump; that the chest is broad enough for plenty of heart room and lung expansion, and that the loin is short and broad so that there is enough room for all the body's internal organs. He checks that the hip joints are correctly formed.

Then the outer covering of the body, its hair, is checked. The steel blue is to extend up the neck to the base of the skull and not into the tan on the skull. The blue covers over the body, onto the tail which is checked to be sure that it is a darker shade of blue and even darker at the tip. The blue is looked at to be sure that it is a pure blue minus any fawn, bronzy or black hairs in the blue. You, as the exhibitor, can only contribute to your gains here by presenting a healthy, well-conditioned Yorkie in muscle and flesh—your Yorkie's coat clean and thoroughly groomed.

The last thing, or the first thing—depending on the judge—is whether the coat texture is glossy—whether it shines. The hairs are each fine

244

and silky. This point will be scored by your dog's inheritance.

The judge, having examined your Yorkie, will ask you to gait your exhibit so he can ascertain the way the dog steps. Now you can score if your Yorkie does this with self-confidence. His leash training pays off in his ability to step along beside you on a loose leash. Each judge has his own pattern for watching dogs gait. Do it the way the judge instructed. If you don't hear, or understand, his directions, ask for clarification. You can pick up points here by calling your Yorkies' name before you execute a turn. Your dog will be forewarned of a change in stepping, or direction.

Most judges halt the dog as it returns to them. Let your dog know that he is about to come to a halt. Having gotten his attention, he'll halt in an alert manner.

The judge will indicate where he wishes you to place the animal. If he doesn't, return to the end of the line. Tidy up your Yorkie's coat. Tell your dog what a great creature he, or she, is. Make your Yorkie feel everybody is having a great time. This will inspire you, also.

Move your exhibit along as the lineup moves forward. When the judge is gaiting the last dog, arrange the coat and legs of your Yorkie. Get his attention, but let him stare at the judge if he wishes to; he may catch the judge's eye and hook a few more points for you. The judge now finishes the evaluation of the exhibits and places them. Hopefully, you're number one, but, if not, leave the ring. Tomorrow's judge may value your dog's points more, or less. Tomorrow you may get more from your dog.

Improving Your Own Well-being at the Shows

If the show is an outdoor one be sure you take proper rain gear; then, if it does pour, you'll at least be able to get about without getting completely soaked. Or if it is very hot, take along a sun umbrella; extra towels to shade the car will also help.

In choosing wearing apparel, remember that you are showing your dog's conformation, not your own. Pick clothes that are comfortable in which to kneel, do deep knee bends, run, walk, and that can survive having things spilled on them. Some exhibitors, it is true, do bring a change of clothes so that they look smart and well-groomed all day. The average exhibitor, having collected all that is needed for caring for and grooming his show prospect, doesn't seem to be able to find room for extra clothes. Anyway, at the wee early dawn hours the thought is far from cultivation!

Wearing apparel should complement your dog and that doesn't mean polka dot outfits to show a polka dot dog; we're referring to the color of your clothes. If you are kneeling behind your still black with clear-

Yorkies in exercise pen.

Yorkie on table in front of benching locked with chain collar and padlock.

Good bloodlines are available from many countries. Making up the Best Team in Show at Westminster, 1960, were: Ch. Sorreldene Charley Boy (bred in England), Ch. Gloamin Cherry Brandy (bred in England), Ch. The Duchess of Clu-Mor (bred in Ireland) and Ch. Wildweir Cock of the Walk (bred in the United States.)

ing face puppy, he won't be distinguishable from across the ring if you're dressed in black velvet. Pick a bright, light color that will show the lovely clear blue and tan of your exhibit. Your choice of clothes should take into account the rather undignified position you're likely to assume while getting the best out of your Yorkie. If it's a two piece outfit, be sure it won't do the splits as you bend to brush a piece of hair back into line. Mini-skirts look fine if you're sitting or standing, but not when bending over and it is the dog you are showing. On that thought, long skirts and bell-bottom trousers will hide your exhibit nicely from the judge if that's what you planned when you entered. Those snazzy new boots, fancy shoes, jingling chains, dangling bracelets, flapping coats or skirts—is your dog used to them? And will they upset someone else's dog?

Most of us train our dogs while dressed for comfort, wearing old shoes and certainly not necklaces and bracelets. Your Yorkie rarely gets a lesson while its owner is decked out in fancy glad rags and you'll be surprised at your dog's reaction. Put on a hat and walk into the room where your prize prospect is reclining and watch its reaction. We're sure you'll see what we mean. Those shiny boots you've chosen for your show debut are going to look to your little friend like a pair of shiny funny things stamping along beside it. So to help yourself and your show dog, if you are going to wear something new and different, let your dog see you in the outfit ahead of time and you'll both have more fun. Familiarity does not breed contempt in dogs, just composure.

Some exhibitors are lucky to have reliable dog sitters and time to drive leisurely to a show. They can arrive the night prior to the show and have a good night's rest, awake, have a good breakfast, show their dog, return to their away-from-home accommodations, have dinner, another good night's rest, and drive home the next day. They are, in these days, the lucky few. Most exhibitors, having been bitten by the show bug, get the dog to the show through blizzards, hurricanes, riots and illness. They get up at the crack of dawn, exercise and feed dogs, clean kennels and fix the evening meal for the dogs so it is ready when everyone arrives home, triumphant or not. Breakfast for the exhibitor is probably a cold cup of coffee and a grabbed roll, although a few shows, being aware of this, do provide coffee and donuts for early arrivals. Off to the show, show your dog, drive home, feed dogs, clean up and fall in bed and, strangely enough, you enjoyed it even if your tummy is hungry. Therefore, we feel that no treatise on showing your Yorkie should overlook that showing dogs takes energy. Energy comes from food, and dog shows are famous for their cold hot dogs wrapped in warm napkins.

A few shows are spoken of in awe such as "That's the chicken n' noodles show" or "Barbecued Bratwurst show." To them look thankfully, but there is no need to starve. First, hungry people are inclined to be disagreeable and this won't help you, your dogs, or your driving. The answer is to plan ahead. There are three good courses open to you: bought fixed food, the planned picnic, or the cardboard disaster kit.

In the bought fixed food, the great American enterprise of franchised foodstands is your answer. Buy that bucket of chicken the day before and take it along in your cooler. Or buy it as you pass a likely roadside stand. Someone can even be sent out for it, but if you've found a good parking spot you're not likely to give it up for your empty tummy. At one benched show that was very loath to feed its one thousand or so trapped exhibitors, we phoned out for sixty chicken dinners and pizzas from the local Southern chicken stand and friendly Italian place.

The planned picnic, whether for your family, or group, can really be a feast. Get all your friends together and let each bring a contribution, from plates to wine. The picnic can stretch to bringing your own portable grill. Be sure, though, that the charcoal will burn and set your grill so that you don't smoke the dogs in someone else's car. One extra word on picnics—plan on extras, as there are bound to be some extra hungry faces you can't resist. The group picnic is certain to help bring winners and losers back together while discussing the merits of sweet or sour pickles!

Next, the disaster kit: canned meat, fish, spreads (try them first), mustard, spices, pickles, olives, crackers, canned vegetables, cold-jellied soups, salad dressings, fruit juices and prepared desserts. Add utensils, plastic tableware and napkins. Don't forget the can opener and a garbage bag. You can always make a vegetable salad in a large dog bowl. If you want bread, an answer is to buy a hot dog, throw away the hot dog (or feed it to some dog that likes them), and then take the bun and build your own poor boy sandwich from your disaster box.

One more suggestion if you are leaving at the crack of dawn—take something to nibble on while driving, but don't load it in the trunk or way in the back of your station-wagon. Driving home can be improved by some sort of snack that is easy to eat and not too messy.

If you are taking children with you, a game box kept in the car for dog shows will keep them happy and out of trouble. Be sure you bring chairs for them and even extra clothes will help. They will enjoy showing the dog, or watching, but the long day needs diversion so a small surprise wrapped up in the game box helps. Pack a few old favorites — coloring books, small cars, dolls, etc. and maybe a new game for dog shows only.

Hopefully, bearing all this advice in mind, you can start to your first show lighthearted and concentrate on your Yorkie. A Yorkie in full coat moving along on invisible feet with a gold and blue mantle has no equal as a show dog.

Dog shows provide happy relaxation. "Holly" and "Pop" looking things over from the lap of their owner, Mrs. C. Groverman Ellis, whose interest in the shows traces back a half century.

Cookout at a dog show.

Puppies bred by Nina McIntire, Texas.

10

Caring for Your Yorkie

ALTHOUGH there are many books on dogs, both of a general nature and specifically on Yorkshire Terriers, there is one book that we feel belongs on any Yorkie owner's bookshelf. This book *All About Toy Dogs,* by Viva Leone Rickets, published by Howell Book House, Inc., has what is lacking in many others. All directions, suggested first aid care, and simple medications are figured to the correct size and dosage for Toy dogs.

The following on the psychology of the Toy dog is from *All About Toy Dogs* and so well describes our pal, the Yorkie, that we have included it here:

The Toy dog is, for all intents and purposes, a big dog in a small package, the "compact car" of the canine world. Living as he usually does in the midst of his owner's household, he becomes one of the family in behavior and in his devotion to human beings. He scorns other dogs as companions, preferring his "family," and it is doubtful if he even knows that he is a dog!

He jealously guards his domain, and he will fiercely attack any dog that comes along, whatever its size. He is not a "sissy" or a "panty-waist" as so many large-breed owners believe. The Toy dog walks tall, rough, tough and fierce in his own manner. He should be kept on a leash when outside his home, and he is likely to challenge any dog he meets, flaunting his watchfulness and guardianship over his owners.

He is possessive of his bed, his toys and of anything he considers his property. He gets along well with other family pets, as long as they do not usurp first place in the affections of his owners, for he is quick to sense the emotions and affections of his loved ones.

A Toy dog soon learns to read his owner's intentions from his actions. He is rarely fooled, no matter how elaborate the attempts of his owner to deceive him. Such an attempt will only cause him to view other attempts with

24-hours-old puppies. Note tan points on head and paws.

24-hours-old—side view.   24-hours-old—tail-end view, tail undocked.

Puppies, 1½ weeks old, Owned by Jeanne Grimsby.

3½ weeks-old-puppy—yawning.

suspicion. Let him find a pill or other medicine in a ball of food just once, and thereafter he will take apart every ball of food handed him until his suspicions are lulled.

It is not that the Toy dog is smarter than the large breeds, but his close association with his human family provides him with a "College Course" in human behavior.

Toy dogs are very sensitive to tones of the human voice, and their responses are to this aspect of speech rather than to words. It is impossible, however, for any to live closely with a Toy dog over a length of time and not become convinced that they do know and understand the meaning of many words.

His actions, whether conscious or unconscious, his behavior in relation to his sensations, his emotions and his physical conduct will, in large measure, reflect the behavior pattern of his human family. If he lives in the midst of a noisy and exciteable family, he is likely to be a noisy little dog conditioned to shrill and prolonged arguments. If his owners are on the quiet and dignified side, he will exhibit the same measure of serenity.

His feelings of closeness to his owners and of being a part of the family are the reasons he does not adapt well to being left at a boarding kennel when the family goes on vacation, or at a veterinarian hospital when ill. He feels deserted, but he grieves with a quiet dignity that human beings might well emulate. If left at a hospital for treatment of a serious illness, his inner sickness of heart may well defeat a veterinarian's best efforts.

It has been pointed out to us that not everybody thinks as we do. This does not exactly come as news. However, this section will have to be based to a great extent on our personal experiences. Indeed we were once beginners and, in our enthusiasm, have managed to fall into every bear-trap, near or far removed. Like all hobbies, these pitfalls, though grim at the time, really are experience teachers. The problems that confront the novice enthusiast are many, but as you progress you find the mountains diminish in height. Your Yorkie can be what you make of him, but first you need to know what, where, when and why.

On Buying A Yorkshire

What part is your Yorkie going to play in your scheme of life? Is it to be a show dog, obedience dog, or plain companion? There is no earthly reason why a Yorkie can't fill all three jobs at once, just so long as your choice has the looks, intellignece and disposition to so perform.

If you are going to want to breed your Yorkie, then its size must be a consideration. Whether yours will be a limited breeding program, or a larger program, can be the determinant of which sex to choose for your first puppy.

A female comes in season usually twice a year. She should never be

254

Three of this 10-day old litter became champions.

Dam and 4-weeks-old puppy.

8-weeks-old puppies.

bred on her first season, or before a year; and preferably not until after eighteen months. She needs to grow up, to mature physically, mentally and emotionally. A young bitch may make a good mother, but the odds are against this. She is more likely to have weak puppies and, minus maturity, treat them as an encumbrance rather than with maternal devotion.

If you plan to show your bitch, it is best to gain her title before breeding her. Puppies do not assist in the cultivation of their dam's coat. Instead, they treat her long tresses more as a nesting bed or play "tug of war" with it. In the case of an extremely long coat, a Yorkie puppy can become entangled and strangle; or the mother may frantically chew at anything to untangle her pup, in the course of which she may seriously injure the puppy.

A bitch that is in season may not be shown in obedience, so if obedience is your main aim a male is probably what you should consider.

The size that you desire in your Yorkie should be considered before purchasing. A large male makes a wonderful family pet, able to bear up to and enjoy playing with children past the toddler age. He is a great companion for a single person, young or old, as is the very tiny Yorkie, either male or female. However, very small Yorkies are not good pets for small children.

For breeding purposes, size is of great importance. Nothing over seven pounds is desirable. A small male, if from small heritage, is a good choice. A tiny bitch (anything weighing under three and a half pounds) should never be bred. You, as a breeder, are the controlling force in your Yorkie's life. Therefore, you have a responsibility to not purposefully endanger that life. A tiny bitch is not capable of naturally delivering a puppy. She will, in all probability, need a Caesarian Section, and with her tiny size the shock and stress may very well kill her.

The best size for breeding, showing or both is around five pounds. An oversize female will make a good brood, but her size must always be remembered in future generations, for, sure as shooting, that large bitch will turn up as an oversize male in the next generation. And let us hastily add that the very tiny stud dog will come out in future generations as a "teacup" bitch. This usually works out into one litter containing the last named bitch and the oversize male.

When your decision has been made on what you want, either show, breeding or pet, then you should really investigate and be careful of freely given advice of an adverse nature.

It is best, in our opinion, to buy your puppy from a breeder. If purchased from a breeder, you have the opportunity of seeing the puppy's dam and the sire, unless the dam was bred to a stud dog owned by someone else. You will also see other dogs, both youngsters and adults, that the breeder has bred.

In buying from a breeder, you can be sure of the environment in which your puppy was raised. You will have someone to help you with any problems that may come up. The breeder has the puppy's best interest at heart. If you do not know of a breeder in your area, you can write to the Secretary of the Yorkshire Terrier Club of America, Inc. for information on breeders, or write to the American Kennel Club, 51 Madison Ave., New York City, N.Y. 10010. (The AKC can provide you with the name and address of the current secretary of the YTCA.) If you have a local kennel club in your town, they can also advise you. It is possible that a veterinarian in your area can tell you where to look for a Yorkie.

Just like every other thing you buy, buying a "name brand" assures you of the product's reputation. A breeder has spent hours planning for the litter, days and nights taking care of the mother and young puppies. The breeder is attached to those puppies and you can be sure that selling one is almost like putting it out for adoption. Good breeders are usually extremely careful of where and to whom their puppies go.

It is best not to purchase a puppy under three months of age and, if for show, preferably not under five or six months. The time of year in which you should purchase your Yorkie, is dependent on whether it is to be housebroken or trained to use newspapers indoors. If your climate is moderate all year around—don't worry about this. But deep snow, monsoon rains, or 100° temperatures outdoors are obviously not conditions under which to housebreak a Yorkie puppy. If these climatic deterrents prevail in your area, then wait to purchase the puppy until better weather is likeliest.

Having decided where to purchase, contact the breeder and make an appointment to see the dogs. Be sure you tell the breeder what you want. If it is a pet, explain what your family is like and what you expect of the dog in the way of personality. If you want a show dog, say so. No one, in Yorkies, ever got a great show dog by buying a pet. Breeders sell dogs as pets for a variety of reasons, but, if sold as a pet, the dog is not believed show-worthy. If you want to buy a show dog, we repeat—to tell the breeder that you do, and wait until it is available. Do not, in your enthusiasm and impatience, rush out and buy the first puppy you can obtain.

Follow these few do's and don'ts:

1. Always demand proof of AKC registration, and ask for a three-generation pedigree. If the AKC registration is in process, or not available, ask for the registration number of the sire and dam.
2. Make it a straight purchase—no strings attached, such as pick of first litter, etc.

The pictures on these two pages trace the development of a Yorkshire Terrier from puppy to Toy Group winner. The dog is Ch. Doodletown Counterpoint (by Wildweir Doodletown Piper ex Wildweir Forget-Me-Not), bred by Vic and Lorraine Berry (Calif.) and later owned by Wildweir Kennels. "Counterpoint" is the puppy at right front in this photo of a 3-weeks-old litter, December 1969.

Two views at 12 weeks.

At 9 months.

"Counterpoint" at 2 years, 5 months.

At 2 years, 8 months.

At 3 years, 8 months.

FIRST IN GROUP

DUBUQUE K.C.

MARCH 24, 1974

OLSON PHOTO

"Counterpoint" winning Toy Group at 4 years, 4 months.

3. If you can only obtain the animal by making some sort of breeding arrangement, put all the terms down in writing. One copy for each party involved, and be sure the agreement is legal and binding.
4. No matter how fine the breeding, don't buy a sickly puppy, or an extremely shy puppy. Either condition may be curable, but the scars may also last the Yorkie's entire lifetime.

The New Arrival

Having picked your puppy, be sure to get its medical record, including the name of the veterinarian who has been treating the breeder's dogs. This will help your own veterinarian if any questions should arise.

Ask the breeder to give you full instructions on what the puppy has been eating, including how much, what type of dish and at what hours. A puppy used to a metal dish may refuse food from a china one and vice versa.

Upon arriving home, keep the puppy to one room. The whole new environment will be too much for the puppy to adjust to immediately. Don't give it food or water for at least an hour after it gets home. Let the newcomer meet the family, but hold off the neighbors and children's friends until the puppy has had a day to get used to its new home. The puppy is going to be tired from the excitement and change, so expect it to explore and then sleep.

Having chosen where the puppy will sleep, when bedtime comes put the puppy to bed. This should be a box, or metal bed to start with. A wood or wicker one is going to be demolished when the puppy cuts its permanent teeth. You might even consider a small wire crate for its bed. Most Yorkies like a place of their own to sleep in, to hoard their treasures in, or just to be able to watch the goings-on from. Whatever you choose for the bed, provide a towel, bathmat, rag rug, or old blanket in which your puppy can snuggle. Don't use anything made of polyester—the mat can get into the lungs, and it is toxic. Leave a bowl of clean water always available.

Sometimes a puppy, feeling lost and lonely, will whine and cry when left alone. Leaving a radio on low will give it a sound that is familiar in an environment that no longer contains its familiar sounds and smells.

We must admit that most Yorkies, be they pet or show dog, fail to see any reason why they should not share your bed—but that's an individual decision to be made by each owner. Or should that be each dog?

3 months old.

6 1/2 months old.

10 months old.

Care of The Female Yorkie

Like all dogs, Yorkie bitches vary as to when they will first come in season. The average age is between nine months and one year. Like all averages, there are exceptions and Yorkies have a great fondness for reading the footnotes at the bottom of pages concerning these exceptions. Hence they may come in season as early as seven months, or may wait till they are even twenty months old. We have found that some bitches will have a season prior to one year that is so immature that neither the owner, nor a male dog will be aware of the condition. This fugitive season will usually be noticed only by a change in the bitch's personality, and an increased amount of licking around the vulva.

Most Yorkies will come in season twice a year, but occasionally one will come in season once a year, or even every eighteen months. If your bitch deviates too much from the norm, you should discuss it with your veterinarian, as he will be the best judge of whether there is a problem. Certainly any bitch that comes in season more than twice a year should be checked.

The average season lasts three weeks and, again, there are exceptions. Often, the first season may continue longer.

We have found that almost all Yorkies will have a false pregnancy after their first season. It does not necessarily indicate that something is wrong, and these bitches generally make very good mothers.

A false pregnancy occasionally will make a bitch grouchy, disinclined to eat, or lethargic. Patience and a little tender love will help her through this period more than anything else.

Most bitches will be ready to accept a male between the ninth and fourteenth days. There is always the rare bitch who must be mated before the ninth day, or one who must be mated very late in her season.

Never force a mating! Mother Nature has a way of protecting her children and, over a period of years, we have found that Yorkie bitches who are extremely difficult to mate will have whelping difficulties, or may even run into problems during their pregnancy.

Since most females are very fastidious about cleaning themselves, an unwary owner may have the bitch in season several days before he knows it. It is best always to count back one or two days when determining the proper day for breeding.

If you have more than one bitch, be careful that they do not develop an antagonism to each other when one is in season. Some bitches, when in season, are so inclined and should be given a place of their own at this period. If you do have a group of Yorkies, you are indeed asking for a fight if you allow this kind of a bitch to stay free with your others. For safety's sake, close her away from them.

Do not allow two males to be with a bitch when she is in season but not ready to be bred. Along with the fact that your calculations may be wrong on when to mate her, the two males are very likely to fight over her. For some reason we've never understood, people find it strange that occasionally Yorkies will get into a fight when a group are run together. It is best to realize that no one would consider running five or six Terriers of any kind together, nor would they have five or six large dogs running together. Although a Yorkie is a small Toy dog, it is still a dog. Only dogs that are known to get along should be together when there is no one home. A bitch in season, a sick, or a weak dog should never be left with a large group.

Care of The Bitch Prior to Whelping

Once you have bred your bitch and she is out of season, there is no reason to change her usual life style. Exercise is necessary for her well-being. She should not be allowed to jump or climb stairs after the fourth week of her pregnancy. If she is used to traveling it won't hurt her so long as she has a crate to travel in, and you provide extra rest stops for her. Avoid travel if you can, but if you must, better to take her than to board her. Don't let her chase balls, or enter into strenuous activity.

She should be fed a diet rich in protein, and add milk or cottage cheese or calcium. Include a vitamin formula that you have discussed with your veterinarian. Most commercial vitamin preparations are calculated for ten to twenty pound dogs. Your bitch weighs less than this, so ask your veterinarian about how much. Too large a dosage with vitamins is as bad as not enough (either way you are heading toward producing freaks). Remember that anything you feed or give your bitch goes into her bloodstream, and so feeds the fetus. Don't, for Heaven's sake, work on that old theory that what you don't provide the bitch, the puppies will get from her system. T'ain't so. Mother takes first!

Don't allow her to be carried by others when she's pregnant, and as she advances in her pregnancy be sure she has a quiet, private place to rest.

Much has been written about making a whelping box, and having read some of the plans and descriptions for these establishments, we're sure that our Mothers have obviously not had luxury accommodations for their whelpings. Now if you are so inclined, and have the time and desire, go ahead with your carpentry. You can even add lace, ribbons, rattles, and pink or blue blankets and your future mother-to-be will probably love it. However, we have found that a trip to the grocery store for several paper cartons is easier and far more sanitary in the long run.

You will need at least two—one for the bitch to whelp in, and another to move her and babies into after the whelping is over. The boxes that canned goods or beer come in are ideal. Never use one that has contained detergents, abrasives or poisonous material. Cut an opening on one side, so that the box makes a basket-type bed. Leave a strip on the side about two and a half to three inches high to keep the puppies from tumbling out.

Having decided where you'd like the whelping to take place, let your future mother have the box to sleep in ahead of time. With luck, she'll agree it's a great place, rather than your bed, or under the couch. Small, easily washed terry cloth dish towels or flannel baby receiving blankets make excellent bedding for the box.

You will need for the whelping: disinfectant, clean towels to dry the puppies with, paper towels, scissors, and dental floss, which you'll find excellent for tying any cords that need to be tied. Be sure to let your veterinarian know that the whelping date is coming up.

There is no more important person in deciding to become a breeder than your veterinarian. Without him, or her, you are lost. No kennel has ever gotten to the top without a veterinarian's help. We know of no breeder who would not agree with us that without trust and respect for your veterinarian you cannot continue. It is their good judgment and patience that help us through the various trials that ensue in the course of raising dogs.

It is best to make your plans and your mind up for the night party which will probably occur when your bitch whelps. For some mysterious reason, best known to themselves, this is the most popular time for having puppies.

There are dozens of very good books, by medical authorities, on how to whelp your bitch, so we will confine ourselves here to a few comments pertaining to the Yorkshire Terrier.

Some bitches will carry the puppies beyond the expected date for whelping. If this does occur, the bitch should be taken to the veterinarian to be examined to be sure all is O.K. We have found that it is best not to wait more than twenty-four hours after the due date from the last day of mating. If she does not whelp by this time, in our opinion and from some experience, a Caesarian should be performed. Waiting longer may prove fatal for the puppies.

Once your Yorkie has started into actual labor, that is, actually bearing down and trying to deliver a puppy, you may allow two hours for the first to arrive. If this time elapses without a puppy appearing, your veterinarian should be contacted.

Alissa Todd

Care of The Puppies and New Mother

When you have a happy Mother with her litter, see that all the puppies are nursing, but, unless there is a weak puppy, keep your hands off! Leave her alone. Since Yorkies have relatively small litters, you will have enough nipples (or teats) to go around. All that fussing and cussing you hear is just one of the pups squashing everyone aside to get to its choice nipple. Puppies will pick out a favorite nipple right from birth, always heading for that special one when hungry. If you interfere by trying to have the puppies nurse on a nipple of your choice, they usually get upset, refusing to suck. If the litter is large and there is a weak puppy, then you are going to have to help and do a little pushing for this weaker puppy. But let the others get their favorite places and then give the weak puppy the leftover spot.

A loving pat and a bit of praise on her performance are all that "Mom" requires from you at this time. She should have a bowl of water and, if she has not eaten, give her a bowl of her usual food. All the books we have ever read assure us that a bitch won't eat twelve hours prior to whelping. We have found that our own bitches really cannot see any reason to pass up a meal, so they eat all meals and proceed to whelp after, between and around mealtimes.

If you are coping with a bitch that has had a Caesarian, here are a few hints that will help. We must state right here, that as we have, in our opinion, the best veterinarians in the United States, we do not have some of the problems other breeders have reported to us. Almost all of our bitches are awake from the anesthetic and caring for their puppies within two hours of the actual operation.

In a litter born by Caesarian section, remember that these pups will be slower starting. Settle the mother at one end of the box, on her side, and put the puppies in the center of the box so they can reach the nipples. Place a hot water bottle, or heating pad on 'low' at the other end of the box. This way the puppies can nurse and lie on the warmth of the bottle, or pad, thus relieving the pressure from where Mom is sore. Do everything you can to get the mother to assume her chores. She hurts and will, if given the chance, let you take on all her chores. Don't do it! Close your ears, partially harden your heart. If the pups are not nursing, gently open their mouths and gently get a nipple well into the puppy's mouth, squeezing a drop into their mouth. Leave their front feet free to pump the breast. The milk the puppies get at first will have some of whatever anesthetic was used so the puppies will be more sluggish than a natural-born litter. This first milk has the colostrum that is necessary.

A bitch who has had a Caesarian should be kept beside you for at least twelve hours and longer if she is not fully recovered and wide awake. You may have to rescue the puppies from time to time if they get behind their mother, as she may be too sleepy to move. Your bitch should be turned over every hour until she takes over moving about on her own. Ice cubes should be offered for her thirst, and, if you do give her water, be sure it is in very small amounts until she is wide awake. If she does not show signs of returning to full consciousness after twelve hours, she should be taken to see your veterinarian.

Should she be the rare Yorkie mother, or an extremely spoiled pet who wants no part of the whole thing, try placing the box with the puppies, mother and hot water bottle or heating pad inside a wire crate. Cover the top sides, but not the ends, with towels to block any drafts. This covered crate seems to give reassurance and serves to prevent that one bitch, because she is scared and sore, from leaving the babies.

As we have said, all mothers like a bit of praise on their performance, but if the bitch is your only one, be sure that you give her extra love and praise before touching her puppies. She can get jealous of her babies if she is used to being the center of attention.

The question of the temperature in the room where the litter is kept always comes up. We have found that our newborn puppies and their mothers do best if the area they are in remains at around 78°, winter and summer. This means that in summer the room is air-conditioned.

The mother and puppies should be situated so that they are not in a draft. Since not everyone agrees on what is the proper temperature, we can only suggest you discuss it with your own veterinarian.

If you have weathered the first three or four days and still have a puppy that is not thriving—one that has a high-pitched constant whining cry and is cold to the touch—you can try everything you want, but, in all probability, we hate to tell you, this one won't make it. If you wish to try your luck at hand-raising, consult your veterinarian for suggestions and instructions. However, all your fussing over the high-pitched whining puppy will upset the dam and the other puppies, so be careful. When it does go, don't blame yourself; Yorkies are little animals and sometimes Mother Nature doesn't get things put together in the right order in these puppies.

A few bitches will not eat, or eat lightly, twelve to twenty-four hours, occasionally forty-eight hours after whelping. As long as they have no abnormal temperature, and act normal otherwise, there is nothing to worry about. Once your bitch starts eating, and we must say most do once the family is settled and nursing, her appetite and her needs for calcium, phosphorus and vitamin D climb rapidly. You will need to give her a good ratio of a dietary balance of calcium-phosphorus to avoid eclampsia.

Eclampsia is caused by a temporary imbalance of the calcium metabolism and usually shows up two to three weeks after whelping. It can come earlier, or even in the pre-natal period. For three weeks after whelping a bitch needs two to three times as much nourishment as at any other period. She should receive a meal of fresh milk, evaporated milk or cottage cheese.

After nursing, most bitches are low or even lacking in calcium, and may also have depleted other necessary vitamins and minerals while producing milk. Therefore, they should be fed back into condition as soon as possible.

What type of calcium-phosphorus, vitamin D and extra vitamins and minerals are to be used, should be discussed with your veterinarian.

Tails and Dewclaws

Tails should be docked and dewclaws removed by your veterinarian between the third and sixth days after birth. (For the uninitiated, dewclaws are the extra, functionless toes on the inside of the leg.)

It is always advisable to remove dewclaws, back and front, though their presence is not a fault.Their presence can be a problem when grooming. If they are not removed, be sure to keep the nails trimmed short.

Weaning

When the puppies are about three weeks old, slide your hand (palm side up) around and under the puppies and you will find that they start licking your fingers. Now they are ready for food. Because they will not be able to stand on their feet, you need a dish that will fit under the lower jaw, but still leave room for their front feet to push at. They won't realize it at first, but this new food doesn't need pumping. With our Yorkies we have found that the glass casters that are made to put under the legs of tables or couches to protect the rugs, are absolutely perfect first dishes for the puppies. They don't slide, and the edge gives the puppies a chance to suck, slurp and finally chew the food out. To give the puppy an idea, gently push its chin and front feet into the food in the glass caster, or place a little food in its mouth so that it can get a taste of the food. If the puppy isn't interested in this treat, wait a couple of days. Don't force it. Puppies differ in their desire for food. One pup may feel that mother's milk is sufficient long after the rest of the crew consider it only sauce for their other food.

What should you start your puppies on? Well, we can only suggest what we've found successful, and that is raw hamburger. The one that the grocery sells as neither round nor chuck. Next, give them small curd cottage cheese in a separate glass caster. Cottage cheese is higher in protein than milk, and the latter is a glorious source of diarrhea in dogs of all ages.

It is unfortunately true that the raising of puppies is not all clear sailing. It is, by far, better to anticipate the condition before your puppies are too weak to be saved. Remember, that all points in the rearing of puppies that involve any change will create stress. Any indication of an infection, whether bacterial or viral, indicates a speedy trip to the veterinarian.

The times most important to watch for symptoms of stress are in the first week of weaning, especially if the dam has been totally removed from her puppies. This usually occurs when the mother's milk has soured or the dam calls it quits. Any puppy that is lying too quietly, or has loose bowel movements calls for quick action. We have found, with suggestions from our veterinarians, that a gentle deterrent, like children's Kaopectate, should be administered, with a digestible (charcoal tablets — an eighth is about right for the average three to four weeks old puppy) helping to keep down the formation of gas. One a day is the usual, but sometimes you may need a second dose. A dropper of honey, mixed with cooled, boiled water and a tiny bit of calcium twice a day, helps to bring things back right. A drop or two of a baby formula vitamin won't hurt and will probably help.

In the case of colic, vomiting or a stomach distended with gas: use an infant suppository cut down to size that will fit a puppy's rectal opening. Gently administer it; don't shove it way in. This will stimulate the puppy to relieve itself and pass some of the gas. Peptobismuth (children's), administered with a dropper in dosage of about a quarter teaspoon two or three times, and a digestible, usually brings this right. The charcoal acts in the stomach as a sponge to absorb the gas.

If the puppy's stomach is hard and distended, it is best to seek medical advice. If possible, you should have in your dog's medical cabinet medicine that will reduce the pain associated with colic. It must be approved by your veterinarian and figured for a puppy weighing as little as one pound.

While your Yorkie is cutting either its puppy (milk) teeth or adult permanent teeth, something hard to chew on is advisable. This is where the great American baby food industry is helpful. Look in the baby food section and bring home some of those "teething biscuits" or whatever the latest call name for them may be. If the puppies are turning their noses up at cottage cheese, it is wise to add your veterinarian's recommended dosage of a calcium product. *DO NOT* select your own. Too much calcium, minus the corrective vitamins, can cause more woe than you will ever wish for. As teeth cutting is a stress on the entire system of your puppy, a little extra dextrose in the form of honey, Karo syrup or even malted milk tablets won't hurt and it may help avoid the stress syndrome.

Baby vitamins, in small dosage, are helpful to the weak puppy. You should discuss with your veterinarian as to what is the right vitamin and mineral product to add to all your Yorkie's diet. Also, how much per pound of body weight and the amount to increase for pregnant bitches and weaned puppies.

A little Vaseline (petroleum jelly) smeared on the puppies' tailends will help to prevent a bowel movement from becoming stuck to the hair. Although the puppies will be able to cope with proper bowel elimination once they no longer have mother's tongue, occasionally one will get caught due to one of a number of circumstances. Excess hair, trimmed from around the rectum, will also help to prevent this problem.

How often should you feed the puppies? In the early stages we remove mother from the puppies, let the puppies who wish to eat get their fill, and then let mother back in to clean up what's left. Sometimes this doesn't work and Mom gets too much food.

It should be pointed out that a single puppy is usually slower to be weaned than are puppies from a larger litter. By the time the pups are five or six weeks old, the food should be given them and left with them. Change it after three hours or so to keep it fresh. It should not be offered at some dictated hour only. Their small systems, like those of birds, use more food for energy than their size shows. Also, each puppy differs in its ability to assimilate the food it takes in.

About this age, try offering the puppies some hamburger simmered in a small amount of water. As the days progress, add a small amount of the same food you intend to feed the puppies as adults. Do not try to feed the puppies in separate dishes. You can do this, but all they do is switch dishes, so why knock yourself out? The idea is to provide food at all times so that each puppy can get nourishment when its small body needs it.

We have always allowed the mothers to play with their pups and to let them nurse as long as Mom says it is O.K. This seems to satisfy both mothers and puppies, and allows them to gain a sense of security, as well as instruction in all matters concerning doggy habits.

Provide a bowl of fresh water for the puppies at all times. Be sure the bowl isn't so deep that the puppies could fall in and drown and it must be low enough for them to drink from.

Shots

Until your puppy has had its vaccinations, don't take it where strange dogs have been, or allow it to be played with by anyone who has influenza or common cold symptoms. Children, having infectious diseases such as measles, mumps, etc., should never be close to a puppy. After a year there may be no harm, but it is best to consult your veterinarian. There are those who feel that dogs are immune to these diseases. In our opinion and with a bit of experience, we have found that since Yorkies are agreeable to being cuddled and willing to sympathize with the invalid, that the close association may very well bring the puppy down with a virus-type sore throat. Yorkies can show an inability to tolerate permanent vaccination prior to three months of age. Therefore extreme caution should be taken if necessary to vaccinate before this age.

Canine hepatitus is not the same as human hepatitus and neither can be transmitted from dog to human or vice versa. Although leptosirosis is very rare in Yorkies, it is well to include the immunization for it.

If you do have to board your dog at a boarding kennel, it should have a booster shot in advance, so consult your vet. Don't board any puppy under six months, and, if avoidable, don't board a puppy at all. This booster shot, prior to boarding, may very well save you a case of "kennel cough" or in fancier terms, trachobronchitis. This is a cough that sometimes brings up a little mucus with it. The cough usually doesn't bother the dog as much as it worries the owner. However, if left untreated, it can get worse and can develop into a more serious ailment.

Prompt treatment by your veterinarian will usually see this cough cured in about two weeks or less.

A booster may also be wise if you are traveling with your Yorkie and this should be discussed with your veterinarian.

If properly administered and from a reputable drug firm, there should be no danger having your Yorkie vaccinated for rabies. Most states require this by law, and for your dog's protection, it is advisable. *DO NOT* use the three year vaccine which must be injected intramuscularly and is, therefore, somewhat more painful than the one year vaccine which is given under the skin (subcutaneously). There have been cases in large dogs of lameness afterwards, and the area on a Yorkie is far, far too small for this type.

Feeding After Three Months

When your puppy is around three months old, start it on food in a separate dish and get it onto three regular feeding times. As soon as it cuts its second (permanent) teeth, usually around four and a half months, the puppy should be put on two meals a day. Yorkies should remain on two meals all of their lives. Due to their small size, one meal is inadequate. With two, a Yorkie can better utilize its food.

As to what to feed your Yorkie? The manufacturers of dog foods spend millions of dollars on their products, producing tested and researched food for dogs. It is highly unlikely that anyone can make up a better balanced meal for a dog in their kitchen. The breeder, from whom you purchase your dog, will gladly explain what, when and how much your puppy is used to being fed, and suggest substitutions should the product they use not be available in your area. If you want to add table scraps to the dog food product, go ahead, it won't hurt. But you'll have a happier, healthier Yorkie if you give it dog food.

Most Yorkies are very good eaters and if they are not, there is usually a physical or emotional reason involved. On an average, a Yorkie needs one level tablespoon of food for each pound of body weight at each meal — hence a four pound Yorkie needs about four level tablespoonfuls per meal. Obviously some require more or less, depending on activity or temperament.

While your puppy is teething, it may want its food mashed up fine, or even handed to it piece by piece, especially while its front gums are swollen. If it doesn't eat a meal, don't panic — it may have a slight upset. However, if it is actually in distress, or persistently refuses food, a visit to the veterinarian is called for. Yorkies can develop extremely serious stomachs due to the stress caused by the pain, so it should be attended to if necessary. Tempting your Yorkie with roast beef and chicken is fine if your veterinarian says to do so, but making a habit of these goodies will be producing a bad eater.

Teething

Yorkies usually start cutting their second or permanent teeth at around three months. The baby teeth will start to loosen as the permanent teeth, coming through from below, push their way up. The mouth should be checked two or three times a week once the teeth start coming in, as a baby tooth can become wedged tight by two permanent teeth coming through at the same time. This can cause crooked teeth, or throw the whole bite out of line. A baby tooth often becomes capped on top of the permanent tooth, and it should be removed either with your fingers, a pair of tweezers, or dental forceps.

One of the greatest teething problems in the breed is failure to lose the first set of canines. Often a puppy will retain both sets of canines. The cause is one which traces to the breed's origin. Being rat terriers, the canines have very long roots and as the second canine comes in, it will often work as a brace preventing regular play and chewing actions from loosening the first canine. Should this happen, it may be necessary to have a veterinarian remove the puppy set, especially if they are interfering, or in any way, causing the teeth to come in so as to ruin the dog's correct bite. If they are not, we do not advise taking the risk involved with surgical removal. In time they generally loosen and can be removed by the owner, or will fall out themselves. Keep a close watch on these canines as they come in, as there is quite often a point when they are loose and can be removed before they become wedged tight.

The corner of a washrag, or a gauze pad, dampened and dipped in baking soda and then rubbed over the teeth once a week will help keep tartar from forming. Toothpaste makes too much foam for a dog's mouth, and should not be used.

Training and Socializing

Along with proper selection and breeding stock, proper mating, proper feeding and proper medical care, there is still one more "proper" left in order to arrive at a well-adjusted adult dog. That is, proper training and socializing.

A puppy that just grows, never getting more attention than being fed and cleaned, is simply never going to have the personality to be a well-adjusted companion or show dog. No matter how great a Yorkie's attributes are, if it is scared and shy, it does not represent the correct temperament for the breed.

On this, and the four pages that follow, Merrill Cohen—Yorkshire Terrier breeder and oustanding Obedience authority—pictures correct procedures in the early training of Yorkies.

One of the most important assets in "housebreaking" and in the well-being of your dog—a crate. Make sure it is not too large.

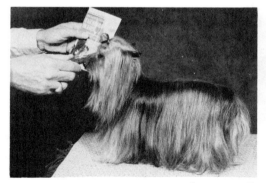

In teaching retrieving, a "chew-stick" type dumbbell as a toy helps develop interest. Praise when your dog picks up the dumbbell.

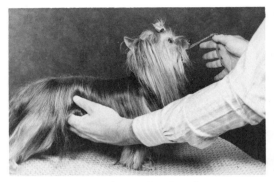

Teaching the "Stand". Lead is kept between your right hand thumb and forefinger, about 6" to 12" from your dog's nose, with the other four fingers pointing to the wall. Your left hand is really doing the work of touching the "belly."

Right: Showing how the "Stand" is done on the floor.

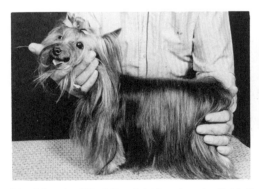

Teaching the "Sit." Put right hand under "chin" and scoop left hand behind the rear. Push back and up with your right hand—and tuck under with your left hand.

The "Sit" as it should be done on the floor. After the dog has learned "Sit", he should respond to the verbal command. If not, then as shown at right, pull up on his lead and push down on his rump quickly.

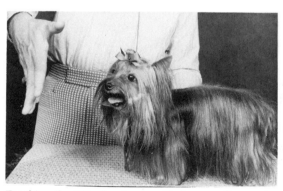

Teaching the "Stay"—*above*, with dog standing; *right*, with dog sitting. Fingers down, spread and pointed to the floor, coming toward the dog. Note that move away from the dog is on the right foot.

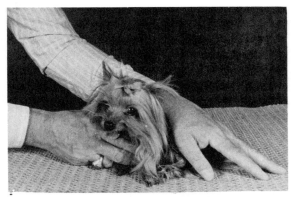

Teaching the "Down." Lift the left paw with your left hand, then the right paw with your right hand, and gently raise to the "begging" position. Let the wrist or forearm of your left arm press down on the withers as you lower both paws to the floor.

The "Down" on the floor.

Teaching "Come." Hold lead chest high, right hand out to your side. Right hand swings across and hits the lead on the order of "Yorkie come."

Heeling. Your left foot and left leg are always next to him as a guide; he follows the motion of this leg. Notice how the left hand hits the lead—then releases.

"Finish." Give the command "Heel" as you take a full step back with your left foot.

Yorkies love to play, and can easily be taught to swim. The frolicking puppy pictured below is just 8 weeks old.

A shy dog will never make a good show dog. A show dog is expected to be just that — "a dog that shows off its temperament, type and soundness". There are occasionally dogs that do not enjoy shows, who simply refuse to give their all, even though they have had every bit of proper training, or socializing.

Each puppy should have its own "call name" by six weeks and the name should be used when touching or playing with the puppies. Never give your dog a name that sounds like the word, or words, that you use to censure your dog. A dog named "Beau" cannot tell that you are not saying "No", nor can one named "Pop" tell when you're saying "Stop". It confuses the dog, and to be safe, it will fail to respond to your call.

Puppies should have small rubber toys to play with in their puppy pens. Small "Nylabones", or hard rubber bones, are good as they can chew on these when cutting a tooth.

Put the puppies out for short periods to explore and investigate the area around their pen. Be sure that nothing scares them, but don't over-protect them. Extend the time that they are out playing in the room, and let their mother play with them. She gives them a sense of security at first and, as time progresses, she'll start playing with them. Let her, even though it may look rough to you. The puppies will rough-house, engage in mock battles, and chase each other. This type of play is normal development for terriers, and should only be interfered with if one puppy appears to consistently get the worst of these games. An old nylon stocking with several knots tied in it will keep everyone busy.

Take time to play with the puppies yourself. Even if your puppy is not to be a show dog, it is still entitled to the proper development of its mind and body. Sit down on the ground and let them explore this large, friendly giant that is their boss.

As they grow up, introduce them to other areas of the house, the grass, and other outdoor surfaces. A puppy that has not learned about different surfaces can balk when suddenly confronted with a strange surface it has never seen or felt.

One of the statements most often made by those who do not know Yorkies, or for that matter, Toy dogs, is that they are afraid they'll step on them. Well that's one thing all Yorkies learn at an early age, if they've had any attention. Once they are on the floor, experience teaches them to move out of the way of advancing human feet. You can avoid having to comfort the sufferer of a stepped-on paw, by going barefoot a few times when you first put the puppies out to explore. After being bumped by your foot once or twice, they learn to get out of the way.

Because Yorkies are small, one is tempted to pick them up to pet

Keep a hand around a front leg to avoid a leap. Ruth Fields carrying Ch. Rugene's Toy Tiger and Ch. Rugene's Prince Ricardo.

Since way back, his owner's bed has been the Yorkie's favorite sleeping place.—*by Jeanne Grimsby.*

them and there is no reason not to do so. However, the chance is that, at sometime, a judge or a visitor to your home will lean down to touch your dog. If your dog has not been accustomed by someone doing this, it will probably lie down flat or shy away. So lean over the puppies sometimes to pat them, run your hand down their backs and scratch their tailends. The puppies will enjoy it and will grow up expecting such an event. After all, when you're as small as a Yorkie and it has never happened before, and a large human giant suddenly leans over toward you, you can hardly be blamed for moving away.

Because Yorkies are close to their human families, most of them will respond better if treated at home when ill. Occasionally, for a very ill dog, this may entail a daily trip to your veterinarian. But sick Yorkies feel safer and happier at home, so, if possible to make such arrangements, we can only advise that you do.

The Elderly Dog

Because of the long length of life enjoyed by Yorkies, (usually thirteen to fifteen years, and some have lived to twenty years) we have included this section.

There unfortunately comes to each of us a moment when we are forced to realize that our little one is getting old. No longer does it see as well, or hear as it did. It sleeps most of the time and it may take a touch to waken rather than the sounds that woke it easily before.

This is the time to give it that extra help — a soft bed in the center of things, where it can lie and watch its favorite world. It will feel drafts faster now, and with the stiffness in its joints will enjoy warmth. Because of the stiffness, your Yorkie will not be able to bend as well to keep itself clean. A damp rag or sponge should be used to clean up the area where it urinates. Keep its eyes cleaned with a clean damp rag, or tissue, as they will run more now. It may be necessary to wipe around its mouth after it has eaten.

Should your Yorkie develop bladder trouble, or should simple old age make necessary frequent eliminations, a thick pad of newspaper around its bed will help and make things easier for you. If your old dog makes a mistake, admonishing it will only make its troubles worse.

Short slow walks, or rambles in the yard, are good for it, but don't tire your old friend. If the weather is cold, your dog will need a sweater, or raincoat. If your Yorkie gets damp, dry it well.

Your Yorkie should have the proper kind of vitamins made for older dogs. It will need medical attention more often, if it is to enjoy life.

"Wonder if they know as much about me as I know about them."

The Yorkie is a photographer's delight.

All Yorkies curl their tongue up when panting.

Blind dogs can adjust to their problem and, often, a young dog will assist. We've seen some of our oldest dogs taken on as the responsibility of a two or three year old.

Answering the
Most Often Asked Questions

This section is a medley of useful somethings that may help in a pinch, or possibly avert a tragedy. It includes answers to the questions on caring for your Yorkie that we have found are most often asked by new owners, or would-be owners, as well as some advice.

The Yorkshire Terrier is a charming house pet but, like all animals, never feels like developing worrisome problems until the wee small hours of the new day; 2:45 a.m. to 3:45 a.m. can seem like a whole calendar year when your Yorkie has that woebegone "Please help me" look! If the problem is an obvious medical one requiring emergency care, don't hesitate to call your veterinarian.

But, sometimes, there is a question in your mind as to whether it is an emergency. If your dog is bleeding, unconscious, convulsing, in shock, paralyzed, or has an extremely high or low temperature, it's an emergency. The normal temperature, when taken rectally, is 101°. An excited dog can easily get to 102°, but, above that, your dog should see his doctor. Some Yorkies, for reasons best known to them, run a temperature between 100° to 101° normally. However, if the temperature is sub-normal, below 99°, the Yorkie needs immediate attention. Low, sub-normal temperatures usually indicate shock, or poisoning from some cause. To make things easier for yourself, take your dog's temperature when he is well and happy. Then you will know when it is above, below, or normal. Always take it before calling your veterinarian — it will help guide them in determining what is the problem.

If you are totally at a loss as to what is wrong, go ahead and call the breeder. A dedicated breeder will gladly help even if it is the crack of dawn. If it can wait till morning, fine — but otherwise, that invention of Alexander Graham Bell's will probably render immediate assistance. A breeder has probably run into the problem or, if not, he'll know someone who has that he'll be glad to call.

However, use the same common sense you'd use for yourself. Most simple Yorkie ailments will respond to the same medicines you can give, or use on, an infant.

The best way to take care of an accident is to avoid it. Therefore, before you bring your new Yorkie home, check your house for those things that can cause tragedy. Follow these few simple precautions:

Indoor Precautions

All detergents and caustic cleansers should be out of the reach of the mouths of curious Yorkies. Puppies will chew on anything and the corners of boxes fit very nicely into their mouths. Should your Yorkie chew on something of this sort, grab dog and container and call your veterinarian. Most boxes of this kind carry directions for the immediate actions to be taken.

All poisons or anything that can cause harm should, in fact, be placed in an area or at a height where they are unattainable to your Yorkie.

No problem is more urgent for any dog owner than the immediate care that needs to be given a Yorkie that has eaten a chemical poison. It may be only a matter of minutes before the systematic effects of this poisonous compound begins and permanent damage to the internal organs result.

Many chemicals which an animal may ingest can be harmful and even fatal. These products are found in rodenticides, plant insecticides, lead-based paints, gasoline, anti-freeze, amphetamine compounds, arsenical agents found in many animal bathing solutions, Kerosene products used for insecticides, mothballs, laundry and cleaning products.

Treatment of chemical poisoning needs quick action so call your veterinarian immediately. The time taken to get your Yorkie to the hospital allows time for further absorption of the poison.

Vomiting must be induced if the agent was eaten. This can be accomplished either by placing a teaspoonful of salt on the back of your dog's mouth, or giving him one or two teaspoonfuls of hydrogen-peroxide solution orally. Repeat the procedure in five minutes if no vomiting occurs.

If corrosive materials have been spilled on your dog's skin, flush the area with lots of water. If your Yorkie is hyper-exciteable, or convulsing, protect it from injuring itself. Get your Yorkie to the veterinarian, your own if possible, otherwise any veterinarian, as fast as possible.

Do not allow your Yorkie to sleep near the stove if there is a chance of hot fat spattering on the dog. Don't carry boiling liquids across the kitchen if Yorkies are underfoot. If hot fat or liquid gets on the Yorkie, turn off the stove, put the pan or container down, catch your Yorkie and flood the area with cold water while dialing your veterinarian.

All garbage should be well out of the way. There is nothing like a ramble through the contents when your Yorkie is bored. But the ramble, in addition to making a terrible mess, may well be his last. Should your dog feast on garbage, get him to the veterinarian immediately.

Medicine of any kind should also be out of the Yorkie's reach. If you

284

have any medication to take, it is wiser to place it in a drawer and shake the pills, tablets, capsules out of the container, over, and in the drawer. If one escapes your grasp, it will then fall into the drawer and not into the open receptacle below that is a Yorkshire Terrier's mouth. If, by chance, he does get one — dial your veterinarian, bottle in one hand and Yorkie in the other. If you can't get your veterinarian, call the pharmacy that filled the prescription and find out if you need to take action and, if so, what.

Never leave a Yorkie enclosed alone in a bathroom with a full tub of water. The Yorkie probably won't jump into it (unless you are in it!) but why chance it? Yorkies can swim very nicely and thoroughly enjoy doing so, but they can also panic like anyone who falls into deep water.

Any potted plant should be checked out to be sure that no part of it is poisonous. Even if placed high, leaves and blooms will fall. You may be a meticulous housekeeper, but your Yorkie is an automatic vacuum cleaner!

There are more than 700 types of plants that are poisonous or injurious to dogs. Since the list is far too long, our best advice is don't let your Yorkie eat, or chew on plants, or bushes. In some plants only part is poisonous, such as the berries, the leaves, the root or the bulb. The poisonous content may also vary with the stage of development. The amount that must be ingested to produce serious symptoms or even death varies from plant to plant.

Nor should your Yorkie drink from any water that has algae on it; if in the woods, avoid all mushrooms and any of the fungus tribe.

A new puppy should be watched to be sure that it does not decide to practice chewing on any electric plug or cords. Our feeling on this is that any Yorkie caught at this activity deserves a loud "No!" and swift slap. Those little teeth through the cord are the instant commencement of death. If the dog goes into shock, it'll rarely ever be brought around and usually the voltage will be enough to kill.

One of the most useful items to a Yorkie owner is a bottle of that pungent condiment sauce made from a species of very hot red pepper. This sauce does not stain and washes off, but clings to whatever it is applied on. Your Yorkie will have a hot mouth for a few minutes after the first try. The second try will need only a sniff. It works well on electric cords, or on anything you do not wish him to try his teething on. Although the best bet is to teach him what not to chew on, young puppies when teething or cutting their second teeth are very persistent. This method will save you a lot of breath and possible damage.

Never leave your Yorkie up on furniture alone until you are sure it can get off it safely. Whoever is on the phone, or at the door, can wait while you avoid an accident (such as a broken bone or fractured skull) by taking the time to lift your Yorkie off before answering. For the

Don't leave your Yorkie where it can jump unless it knows how to jump.

Check your house for things Yorkies can get into. Any potted plant should be checked out for danger.

same reason, do not leave a puppy alone near a flight of stairs unless you know it can negotiate them both ways — up and down.

Upstairs, downstairs and all around the house check for possible pitfalls or mishaps and you'll have no need to cry over an accident that could have been avoided.

Outdoor Precautions

Never allow your Yorkie outdoors when the lawn is being mowed. Your dog is too small for the person to see and they move extremely fast. A stone, or stick thrown out by a rotary mower could cause an injury, or fatality.

Walking should *always* be on a lead. Dogs hit by cars while accompanying their owners are, alas, always dogs that had never run into the road before.

Carrying a Yorkie in your arms should always be done with your fingers around a front leg, ready to tighten their hold in case your dog decides on a leap. A sore leg is better than a serious injury.

Don't leave your Yorkie alone in the car parked in a shopping center. Too many dogs have been stolen in this manner.

If you have a fenced yard, do not leave your Yorkies out in it alone, unless the whole yard is visible to you and you are watching. Many have been stolen in this manner, or have slipped out a tiny hole. Also, service people are unfortunately not known for their care in closing gates; for that matter, children forget too often, too.

If your dog should be lost or stolen:
1. Call the police and give them a description, etc.
2. Notify the Veterinarian Association in your area.
3. Notify all dog clubs in your area, as well as other breeders.
4. Notify your local cab, bus company, newspaper delivery service, and garbage collection service.
5. Ask your public utility meter readers to keep a look-out.
6. Place notices on bulletin boards in grocery stores and schools.
7. Ask the Boy Scouts, Girl Scouts, 4-H Clubs, etc. to watch out for your missing Yorkie.

Be sure they understand that they should notify you or the police, and that *unless* the dog comes to them they should not try to catch it. A lost dog, friendly as he may be, will panic and snap in its fear. If frightened, it may run into the path of a car.

Should your Yorkie break a leg while you are more than twelve hours away from a veterinarian, there is a simple way to protect it until you can get to a vet. Take the cardboard tube from the center of the toilet paper, or paper towels. Gently, but not too tightly, wrap the leg in cotton, or even toilet paper, leaving room for swelling. Slip the tube over the wrapped leg extending the tube so that the dog will walk on the end of it, thus putting no pressure on the leg. Try to keep it as quiet as possible until you can get to the veterinarian.

Toys

A Yorkie's toys should not be such as he is able to swallow, or that have small pieces that can be removed and swallowed. Soft rubber squeaky toys, hard rubber bones or balls, and "Nylabones" are all fine. Soft rubber balls will be demolished. All squeakers will probably be un-squeaked, but even unsqueaked they are fun.

A Final Caution

Yorkshire Terriers must be treated with extreme caution when administering any form of anesthetics. Therefore, if your dog is going to have one, be sure your veterinarian is well aware of this matter. Many Yorkies have died from overdoses of anesthetics. If your veterinarian is in doubt on this subject, ask him to consult a veterinarian who has worked with the breed. You may have to pay for a long distance call, but you'll have a live dog. If your veterinarian — and it'll be a mighty rare one — won't listen, go elsewhere.

As to the question of when should you put a dog to sleep, no one can give a positive answer. There comes a time when advancing helplessness, pain or necessity will dictate the answer. It is hard to realize, but true, that often our refusal to carry out this kindness to a suffering animal is actually a refusal on our part to face the grief that will be caused by losing our friend. Our ability to do this for our dogs is a duty given to us that we are unable to perform for some loved human that we must watch suffer in pain, and linger on when there is no possible hope.

Many people, feeling the hurt of parting from their Yorkie, shy off purchasing another. Many of these will succumb in a week or month to a new Yorkie puppy. We have found that, because Yorkshire Terriers are such individuals, the best cure for this grief of losing your old friend is a new puppy.

Traveling With Your Yorkie

The one purchase we feel every Yorkie owner should make is a crate. Many new owners look askance until they've tried it. Their feeling is that they couldn't be so mean as to close up their dog in such a thing. The truth of the matter is that they are probably being mean not to. A Yorkie is a small dog and a wire crate, or fancier one, is his haven — it is his and his only!

Traveling in the car, a crate acts for your dog's safety. Should you stop suddenly, your Yorkie will not be thrown forward, or down onto the floor. Your own attention will be on your driving, not watching your dog. If you should have an accident, your Yorkie will not be as likely to be hurt, or be running in terror down a highway if a door is thrown open. You can open the windows in your car without worrying about your Yorkie falling out. The crate provides a cool place for your dog on a hot day as it will be shaded from the sun.

A crate in a motel, hotel, or in a friend's house, protects your Yorkie from being let out of the room should you go out. Often in motels or hotels, small objects like pills, matches or small children's toys get left under beds. Our Yorkie room inspectors have pointed this out to us a number of times, as we have removed these wonderful finds from their mouths. So, if you're not present to protect your pal — crate him!

If traveling by train, your Yorkie can go with you in its crate, provided you have an enclosed sleeping space.

If traveling by plane, be warned that shipping a dog by air has many risks unless the dog is accompanied. A number of airlines will allow you to travel with your dog in the cabin of the plane if the dog is in a carrier that fits under the seat. Some airlines provide a cardboard carrier for your dog if you do not have one available. If you plan to fly with your dog, you should inquire if the airline of your choice allows it.

Dogs, like children, can get motion sickness while traveling. Most Yorkies are excellent travelers, but if your Yorkie is not one of them, a piece of an antacid tablet will often be the answer. If your veterinarian prescribes other medicine, always try it out ahead of time, while you are still at home. In this way, if your dog should respond to the medicine adversely, you will have your veterinarian at hand. Never give your Yorkie drugs that are not prescribed by a veterinarian, even if they are available in a pet shop.

When traveling with your Yorkie, the following packing tips will save worries and perhaps an upset:

1. Its water bowl.
2. Either its own feed dish, or a supply of small paper plates that can be thrown away.
3. Food that your Yorkie is used to eating.
4. A towel of its own.
5. A flashlight for walking your Yorkie at night.
6. A leash.
7. Toys that he's used to.
8. Any necessary medication and a First Aid Kit for your Yorkie, containing cures for cuts, stings, itches, diarrhea, toenail clippers and scissors.
9. A box of tissues or paper towels.
10. A sheet to put on top of the bed, if your Yorkie is a bed-sleeper. (Most of them are!)

Try to stick to feeding and walking your dog at as close to its usual hours as possible. Always take water from home for your dog. If you haven't a lot of room, but are taking a cooler, freeze some water in plastic bottles. It will act as ice for your cooler and, when thawed, you will have more water for your Yorkie. Changing a dog's water from place to place is the best way of being sure your dog will get an upset.

Nell Fietinghoff and "Winkie" leaving for show.

11

Yorkie Character

In EXTOLLING the virtues of their chosen breed, owners are inclined to wax lyrical about wonderful things it does, and to proclaim it far superior to any other. Naturally one must assume that they are slightly prejudiced, since they have chosen it above all other breeds to own. Nonetheless, it remains that once a person has owned a Yorkie, there is no doubt he will always own a Yorkie.

The Yorkshire Terrier — what can you say of him? First, he is the most adorable charmer. He always gets his way, even as he pretends to bow to your wishes. He is beautiful in his long, full mantle of blue and gold silk, with neatly placed top-knot; but he is fascinating, too, in a straggly-ragged uneven coat, casting one appealing mischievous eye between scraps of top-knot. He is happy being the doll in the doll carriage, acting lookout in a bicycle, lying contentedly in the lap of his elderly mistress (or master,) watching TV with the boss, or helping to cook dinner with the mistress, one eye cocked to the chance that a tidbit might accidentally fall, which naturally — in order to be a help — it is imperative that he immediately remove from the floor. He's delighted to strut in the show ring and show off in all his glory; or to follow your commands in the Obedience ring, even if — on occasion — he proves his independence by a performance that is his own and not exactly as you'd planned it.

Your Yorkie is happy to share with you — your bed, or anything you eat. He'll gladly accompany you wherever you go or in whatever you do.

Be he a big Yorkie or a tiny Yorkie, he is endowed with a marvelous intelligence and a most valiant spirit. He'll teach you he's bigger than any other dog, and that he owns you body and soul — even if you have been under the impression that you owned him. He is, in fact, the perfect companion for all occupations.

As a watchdog, his hearing is acute and warning will be given as soon as the normal sounds or routine are disturbed. He is not a yappy dog, but will spring to attention should a car be in the driveway, or someone at the door. We've never known anyone who owned a Yorkie in an apartment whose dog could not tell when members of the family were on the ascending elevator.

Yorkies have joined their mistresses and masters in all sorts of jobs. One of the most famous was Pasha — who took on the running of the White House when his Master and Mistress, the Richard Nixons, lived there. One traveled with his master, the captain of a freighter, all through World War II, taking his chances of being torpedoed with his boss while ferrying cargo across the Atlantic. Another has gone to court each day with a court reporter, sleeping in a basket at her feet. One goes to a hospital daily, sitting on her mistress' desk in the administration offices. Fannie Hurst, the author, always had two who slept on her desk while she wrote her novels. Yorkies have supervised gift shops, dress shops, machine shops, dental offices, bookstores, classrooms and interior decorating shops. Many actors and actresses have been accompanied by a Yorkie, both to work and around the world. Two Yorkies were among the hijacked passengers on a plane that was forced to go to Cuba, and the plane was held until Fidel Castro could see the dogs.

The list of travels and jobs that Yorkies have experienced with their bosses could go on and on, but, in truth, it is only an indication of the breed's ability to adapt itself to any situation or circumstance. The tales that follow will, we hope, give those unfamiliar with the breed an idea of what a Yorkie is; those who already know the breed, will likely find resemblances to their own Yorkie.

The breed has been used as the canine character in a number of books. The original illustrations done by W.W. Denslow in 1900 for *The Wizard of Oz* were of Toto, the artist's own dog, who was bred by Mrs. Frederick of Calumet City, Ill. Hollywood may have used a Cairn for the movie version, but the real Toto was a Yorkshire Terrier.

As to what breed the famous Greyfriars' Bobby was, we'll leave to you to decide, giving only the following quote from *Dogs: Their Points, Peculiarities, Instincts and Whims,* edited by Henry Webb, and published in 1872 by Dean and Son, London, Eng.:

Of the Scotch Terrier (Yorkies were originally called Broken-haired Scotch Terriers) we have still more to add, for Greyfriars' Bobby, the Edinburgh favorite, must not be forgotten, and we cannot do better than to give the following extract from *The Animal World* of May 2nd, 1872: "It is reported that Bobby is a small, rough Scotch Terrier, grizzled (greyish-blue) black with tan feet and nose."

Helen Hayes' dressing table.—*By Morgan Dennis.*

Illustration of "Pistache" from Albert Payson Terhune's *Real Tales of Real Dogs*, c. 1935.

First lesson. Trade card for Hood's Sarsaparilla, 1886.

Yorkshire Terriers ratting. Etching by Maud Earl, 1903.

The Yorkie As Hunter

In the early days in Yorkshire, one entertainment enjoyed by Scotchmen and the Yorkshire compatriots was rat-baiting and this tale is given in Robert Leighton's *The Complete Book of the Dog.*

The local pub was a likely place to see a good sport. As time went on, rats became less easy to obtain and it became fashionable to run handicaps. These were arranged so that the heavier the dog was, the more rats he had to kill. Various handicaps were set ranging from one rat being added to a dog's quota for every three pounds additional weight over his rival, to a rat for every pound. This was, perhaps, the favorite and it was frequent to arrange a handicap where each dog had to kill as many rats as there were pounds in his weight, the dog disposing of his quota the quickest being the winner. This put rather a premium on small dogs and breeds were developed especially for this sport. The smooth black and tan Terriers of Manchester and the rough Yorkshire Terriers were particularly good for this sport, and a friend owns a portrait of three famous Terriers ranging in weight from 5¼ lbs. to 7 lbs.

This type of competition did much to help bring down the size in Yorkie bloodlines.

Mrs. Emma Wilkinson, a well known English Yorkie breeder, owner of the Gloamin Kennels and a judge of the breed, in writing of the Yorkshire Terrier as a worker, reported: "In 1924, I had a Yorkie bitch bred by my father, Mr. J. Jensess, who was never so happy as when she was going on a ratting spree. Registered as Swanky Girl and weighing about 5 lbs. (and she had three litters), Susan used to be delighted when she was taken down to the farm. When the old steam threshing engine came to thrash corn, Susan used to sit and wait for the chance at a rat, and on one morning she killed 23 rats and was game to go again for more. Susan lived to be 14½ years of age."

To continue on with their love of hunting, here's a tale told by another famous English breeder, Mrs. Edith Stirk of the Stirkean Kennels, a breeder of many celebrated champions and a well known judge of the breed:

I have a first-hand story of one very recent Yorkie's adventures. Her name was Tidy Tiddler and she has just died at the ripe old age of 14 (written in 1967.)

I met Tidy at nine weeks when she called to see her Dad, Ch. Stirkean's Chota Sahib, and during the years I was in close touch with her activities. She had six litters all with the greatest of ease, although she was just four lbs., had a coat to the ground, lovely coloring, and was as tough as nails. She took over 14 acres of rabbit infested orchards which were like a wilderness. She bolted 129 rabbits in less than three months. On one occasion she could not be gotten out and they had to dig for her. When she was reached, there were five dead rabbits and Tidy herself was calmly sitting on a tree root ledge. Tidy must have traveled a thousand miles. On one occasion she spotted a rabbit; off she went over field and onto a brook with a covering of thin ice. Down she went but emerged on the other side, shook herself and carried on. Rats were always marked and she would not move until her owner got cracking and got it out.

Her greatest joy was a poacher, the old man of the village. They knew each other like buddies. Tidy could smell him a mile off. She would sit trembling in the window-sill waiting for his approach and the minute she saw him she would hop off her perch, dash out and jump into his pocket and off these two would go for a day's sport. Tidy always brought the dinner home for the other dogs.

Tidy's old friend, the poacher, is now 87 and still tells the story of his great poaching pal.

We have owned many Yorkies whose main joy in life was hunting. Whenever we open our summerhouse, the Yorkies have a field day catching mice, which is greatly appreciated (although it would be nice if they'd refrain from burying them in the slipcovers.) Minikin Blue Larkspur, who lived to be 15 years old, spent most of her summer days either being dragged out of a swamp or lying in the shallow water under the dock catching frogs. "Ham" (Ch. Wildweir Fair N' Square) can't be let out loose as his passion is squirrels and he'd be long gone chasing them. He has only one to his credit. He always raises one front paw in a perfect point when he spots a squirrel — on leash, of course.

The Yorkie as War Hero

Along with their hunting ability with small game, Yorkies have been war dogs. Though mention has been made of Bill Wynne's "Smokey" in other books, we feel it must be included here for no record of the breed would be complete without this proud story.

Smokey was a Yorkshire Terrier (7 inches high and 4 lbs. in weight). She was owned by Corporal Bill Wynne of Cleveland, Ohio, and served two years of active duty in the Asiatic and Pacific area during World War II before coming home to live with Bill.

Bill bought Smokey from a buddy who had found her in a foxhole near Nabxab on New Guinea in February, 1944. At first it was thought that she belonged to the Japanese, but when she was taken over to the prisoner-of-war camp and an interpreter was gotten to give her commands in Japanese, she didn't understand a word. She didn't understand English either, but her age was estimated to be just a year at that time.

Though she caught cold, shivered and got scared, she lived through 150 air raids on New Guinea, and was a crew member on 12 air-sea rescues without being airsick. Bill Wynne said she was not hard to train and came in very handy on certain types of jobs. Just how handy is best told by him:

One day while on leave in the town of Lingayen, I was running Smokey through her routine of tricks in a Nipa hut. Bob Capp, of the Communications Section, came up and eyed Smokey suspiciously. He just looked the dog over without saying a word, then finally he said quietly "Bill, we have a long pipe to run a wire through under the airstrip. It is eight inches high and seventy feet long and we are stumped as to how to get the wire through. The wire simply has to go through and we wondered if Smokey could do it. She is small enough and smart too."

We decided to let her have a go at it. Bob brought a ball of string and came along with some linesmen and we all started for the airstrip. The strip had steel matting and when trucks or planes went over it, it was like a thimble on a scrubbing board only amplified a thousand times, which was very nerve racking and ear splitting. We arrived at the bed of the creek in which three culverts, eight inches in diameter, lay side by side. The airstrip ran over the top of them. I knelt and looked through the pipes and saw that soil had sifted through each of the corrugated sections at the joinings, and in some places the pipe was half filled. I picked the one that had the least amount of soil and mold, but even at that, in some places Smokey would have only four inches of headway. I tied the string to Smokey's collar and made her sit with Bob while I ran to the other end of the culverts. I peeked through the pipe and it seemed totally black except that I could just make out Smokey's outline. The suspense of whether the little dog would do the job was reflected on every face.

She made a few steps and then ran back. "Come Smokey", I said sharply, and she started through again. When about ten feet in, the string caught up and she looked over her shoulder to Bob Capp as much as to say "What's holding us up there?" The string loosened from the snag and she came on again. By now the dust was rising from the shuffle of her paws and as she crawled through the dirt and mold I could no longer see her. I called and pleaded. Not knowing for certain whether she was coming or not. At last, about twenty feet away, I saw two little amber eyes and heard a faint whimpering sound. Those eyes came nearer and at fifteen feet away she broke into a run. We were so happy at Smokey's success that we patted and praised her for a full five minutes.

Smokey ate C-rations, Spam and took vitamin pills. Her bathtub was Corporal Wynne's helmet and her blanket was made from a green felt card table cover.

Smokey owned many decorations, and polled top place in a competition to pick the mascot of the Southwest Pacific Area. In her lifetime, she traveled 40,000 miles giving exhibitions all over the world. At twelve years of age she was still co-starring with her trainer and owner on a weekly TV show over an NBC station in Cleveland, assisting him as he demonstrated how to train your dog. Smokey could spell her name by actually distinguishing the letters and could walk a tight-wire blindfolded. Smokey's exploits are a true example of Yorkie courage.

A fact that is not generally known about Smokey is that, in addition to all her other accomplishments, she was a mother. Shortly after Bill acquired her she surprised him by whelping one puppy weighing one ounce at birth. This puppy unfortunately died at six months when disease wiped out some thirty dogs in Bill Wynne's outfit.

Another tale of the Yorkie as a war dog dates from World War I. It concerns a daughter of Eng. Ch. Armley Little Fritz, owned by Tom Hunter, who took her to France with him. This puppy lived in the trenches with Tom Hunter from 1914 to 1918 and from all accounts had a great time ratting. Mr. Hunter brought her home safely and she lived to a venerable age of twenty years.

In the Second World War, the French Resistance used many small pet dogs to carry messages as they were very clever and were not as apt to be suspected as were the large dogs normally used for this.

The Navy also had a Yorkie mascot who served on board the U.S.S. Hassayampa. This is a tale as told in *The Navy Times.*

Although most Navy ships have a dog as a mascot, the crew of this tanker is willing to bet that they have the only dog in the fleet with his own special fireplug. (He did have a square yard of sod around his fireplug, but lost it enroute to Hawaii when a heavy sea washed it over the side). He not only has his own private fireplug, but a personal life jacket and a reserved seat at the movies.

"Boots" is a 4 lb. Yorkie, born in England with a pedigree as long as your arm, and was purchased in London by his owner, the skipper of the ship, Captain M.V. McKraig. He was flown to Philadelphia where he attended the commissioning of the Hassayampa and took up billet as ship's mascot.

Since starting his sea duty, Boots has been thoroughly indoctrinated in the ways of sea-going dogs. He is first at his "abandon ship" station where he waits patiently for one of the men on watch to put his miniature life jacket on for him. He "mans" the quarterdeck when the Captain comes aboard and has never been late for chow call. He is formally listed as "Satan of Gloucestershire" with the English Kennel Club.

The Yorkie as Performer

Yorkies have played parts in many plays, movies, TV shows, the circus and vaudeville acts. As far back as 1908 there are records of their playacting. "Pingo" appeared in "The Boatman" at Terry's Theater with a St. Bernard that year. Since then they have played many parts.

"Smokey" walking a tightrope blindfolded, guided by owner Bill Wynne.

"Smokey" in her owner's helmet on New Guinea battlefield. The helmet was her bathtub.

The appealing looks and beguiling ways of the Yorkie have been featured in advertising campaigns for a wide variety of products. Around 1885 they appeared on premium cards. Premium cards first came into being in 1878 and were in full swing by 1885 with sets of flowers and animals being most popular. Hood's Sasparilla used a Scotch Terrier with pups in 1886. Since then they've helped advertise soap, clothing, rugs, stockings, and currently one is appearing in an Aspirin commercial on TV. Pogo of Taragon, owned and bred by Swen Swenson, helped Patti Page introduce the song "How Much Is That Doggy In The Window?"

Ella Gast's Yorkie played a part in Walt Disney's "Easter Parade" and several others have had parts in other movies.

In 1953, a Square Dance was performed by four Yorkies and their owners and although no one seems to have tried it since, we include it here as much enjoyment was had by all the dogs and their owners. Perhaps, someone will wish to try it again.

Yorkie Square Dance

Performed originally by:
Stella Sally Myers with "Little Peanut"
Muriel Kreig with "Ginger Lei"
Pearl J. Kincarte with "Alice"
Frances Davis with "Mike"

(All four dogs owned Obedience titles.)

Note: In the course of the square dance, every command in a trial for a C.D. title is executed.

Entrance: Heel your dogs, hurry now
             Later on they'll take a bow!

Turn—   Meet your partner, make a pair
             Go on down, don't step on hair.

End About—   Two go left, two go right
             You're all sure the dogs won't bite.

Four End—   Get to the end, form in four
             Come to the center, we want more.

Center Pivot—Two about and all go right
             Slow it down, just a mite.

End Four
Cross—   Indian File to the end of the ring
             If you're happy, you can sing.

SUCCESSFULLY WORKED.

Above: Cartoon from *Puck*,
November 23, 1887.

Right: Lithograph from
around 1890.

Cross—	First couple cross, go around the dogs Keep on moving, just like cogs.
Crosses—	Keep a square that's really true The ribbons you want are always blue. In and out, round and round Keep it quiet, not a sound.
	Go to the end, come on back Just like a hound on a track.
Center—	Come to the center, make a stop Make it pretty for Mom and Pop.
	(Everybody promenade)
	Stand your dogs and do-si-do Round and round, make a show.
	(Everybody promenade)
	Stand your dogs, just once more Wear a groove right in the floor.
	(Everybody promenade)
Ring Noses In—	Dogs to the center, all noses in Handlers out and now begin.
	Ring to the left, ring to the right Reach for the dogs, but not too tight.
Star—	Form a star that's really bright Look at the dogs, What a sight!
Figure 8—	Sit your dogs for a figure eight Don't go fast, you'll not be late.
	(Everybody promenade)
Ring Tail In—	Dogs to the center, tails in now That's so they can take a bow.
	Ring to the left, ring to the right Bend for the Yorkies, they're just a mite.
Free Recall—	Free heel now to the corners far Sit your dogs, now shoot for Par.
	Leave your dogs, to the center go When you get there turn real slow.
	Call your dogs, watch them come If they don't you'll feel like a bum.
Down—	Finish the dogs and go to the end Make a line that's nice and straight Just be sure you don't use bait.

302

Down your dogs and all relax
They'll be there when you turn your backs.
Leave your dogs and come on down
Swing around, just go to town.

Left hand swing, now the other pair
Right hand swing, go round and round
If they move, you'll call the pound.

Return to the dogs with a pretty cross
Now we'll see who is the boss.
Finish the dogs, bring them to heel
Hurry up they've earned a meal
Come to the center for a bow
Honor your partner — honor your opposite
Honor your gallery with a bow
Don't forget the dogs know how!

Devotees of a breed tend to write excessively of their marvelous attributes. We were prepared to offer here many words of tribute when it was brought to our attention that the breed has the unique ability of being able to speak for itself. Yorkshires like to write autobiographies and, unlike many would-be writers, over the years they have — with the help of fond owners — been capable of having their manuscripts published.

Starting in 1894 when Dick in "Our Dick" wrote of his life in San Francisco, and followed in 1895 when "Baba"in *The Chronicles of Baba, (the Autobiography of Manor House Fly)*, wrote the story of his life, helped by M. Montgomery-Campbell, seven Yorkies — to our knowledge — have gone into print writing of their lives. In 1899, *"Loveliness"* wrote up her very sad experiences, helped by Elizabeth Stuart Phelps. In 1934, "Nick" wrote up two years of his life in a book entitled *I'm Nick,* again assisted by an owner — Reginald Callender. In 1938 and 1941 respectively, Tapiola wrote of his adventures in two books: *Journey of Tapiola,* and *Tapiola's Brave Regiment.* In 1950 the two books were combined into one, coming out as *The Adventures of Tapiola.* Tapiola's assistant was Robert Nathan. In 1962 "Puck" wrote his story, helped by Louis Untermeyer, in *"The Kitten Who Barked".* And finally in 1971, "Mister" got his Mistress, Florence VanWyck, to get his verses about his life published in a book entitled *A Dog's Garden of Verses.* What better source, then, to learn what the Yorkshire is like, than from mouth and paws of one of these authors?

Nick in *I'm Nick* starts his book with this description:

I'm a Yorkshire Terrier, so you know what I look like. I'm only a little dog now, just about five pounds is my weight, and so you can imagine what a very tiny person I was when I first remember myself. I was about three

Yorkies get along well with most other breeds.

months old then, so I must have been a wee little thing when I was born. There must have been almost nothing of me! . . .

I was 'Pedigree' you see, and though I hadn't the faintest notion what that meant, I felt it was something important from the awestruck way in which Miss Frenchman said it to people who visited us. At first I was afraid it was a kind of disease, but I found it wasn't. So, as it seemed alright and rather a good thing to have or be — whichever it is — I thought I'd better live up to it. When I got into a fix, I'd say to myself "You're Pedigree" and it helped a lot. You can do a lot if you've got something like that to live up to.

Further on, Nick provides a perfect description of a situation that many a Yorkie has faced.

You must know that ever since I left Miss Frenchman's and my small friends there, I had felt very lonely and was always on the lookout for a companion about my own age, especially one of my own breed.

Well, one day I met one, face-to-face! He looked straight at me, and I saw the same kind of look in his eyes that were in mine, as if he too were longing for a playmate. I liked the look of him very much.

Exactly the same age and size as myself, his hair, like mine, was still short and stiff, and our coloring precisely similar — dark on the back and lighter on the head. I was prowling about the hall when I met him, nosing about, as is a way of mine, in the hope of coming across a mouse or something.

I stared at him like anything, I can tell you, and he stared at me, as much as to say, "What on earth are you doing in my hall?" But, as I have said, I rather liked him, so I "wuffed" gently to tell him so, and I saw his mouth open as he "wuffed" back, though he didn't seem to make any sound at all, which struck me as strange. Then, as is proper in making friends, I gave a playful pounce and wagged my tail, and so did he, but he didn't come any nearer as he should have done.

So I ran round and round once or twice in a circle to try and get him to chase me, but when I looked there he was, sitting down like I was, with a little bit of pink tongue hanging out as if he was out of breath too.

I ran round again, this time keeping one eye on him, and there he was running round and round, too, all by himself — when, by rights, he should have come after me!

"That's queer!" I thought, "but perhaps he's shy." So I stared at him a bit more, and wagged my tail and he copied me.

Then I thought "I will stir him up." He shall play with me! So I dashed straight at him, intending to wrestle him in a friendly way — there's nothing like a bit of a wrestle for making friends — when, Bang! something hit me hard on the forehead so that I went all dizzy, and I had to lie down for a minute.

And that's how he found out mirror images don't make playful companions!

Yorkies have a habit of getting their own way, and can think up tricks to overcome your best plans. One Yorkie always appeared with a woebegone expression, hopping forward on three legs, every time his owners wanted to go out. Having gotten away with it the first time, he would try it every time. Another one was considered too thin, so his owner put down only milk for him to drink. The Yorkie failed to drink the milk and also failed to show any signs of thirst. He was finally caught on top of the grand piano helping himself to water from a large bowl of roses. And when you scold a Yorkie severely, chances are it will end up with you on your knees begging him to please forgive you.

Dr. Gordon Staples in his *Ladies' Dogs as Companions* gives the earliest tale of a Yorkshire Terrier; his sketch of the breed is fun and still true. No Yorkie ever allowed any other breed to be head dog when he was around. The tale is titled "Wagga-Wagga".

My friends often send me hampers. I do not object to this, because they often contain what is very nice, and sometimes what is very curious. Wagga-Wagga came to me in a hamper. Wagga-Wagga is still alive and well, and may be seen any day running about the streets of Twyford, Berks. as independent as a prince.

A short sketch of him may interest and amuse my readers.

When the hamper in question came then, I hastened to undo the fastenings, when, on opening the lid, lo! and behold, Wagga-Wagga.

The first thing that occurred to me was that the doggie was wonderfully small; the second thing that occurred to me was that it was desperately wicked. N.B. — This occurred to me while the animal was holding on to my thumb, very much to his own satisfaction, by his front teeth. Having refreshed himself in this fashion, he condescended to let me put him on the table for further investigation. In size, he is capable of insertion, head foremost, into a pint pot. Color, black, with tan points. Coat, rather long (feather as hard as hairpins), weight, four pounds to a grain. Head, of the cocoanut fashion, and feathered like the body. Eyes, large and round, showing a good bit of the bull, and a large spice of the devil. Of tail, he hasn't a vestige, so there can't be a morsel of controversy on that head. He is pretty straight on his pins, but roaches his back like a cat doing an attitude of defiance. A Collie dog gave him two lines of his mind last week, and he now roaches his back much more. I baptized him Wagga-Wagga on the spot, because he hasn't a tail to wag.

The prevailing disposition of Wagga-Wagga's mind is that of morosity, combined with bad temper. There is nothing on four legs that he won't fly at, and nothing on two either.

This eulogy, written for a Yorkshire Terrier, tells much of the breed's character:

"Quite early in his puppyhood we made the discovery that we were not training him nearly so much as he was training us. He rapidly de-

Front and over sides of premium cards issued with Tiger cigarettes (Baltimore) c. 1885.

veloped into a kind master, though a very firm one. He was Rooseveltian in his good humor, once his superiority was conceded. After we had learned the meaning of about fifty growls, barks, whines, and gestures, he trained us to perform several tricks under his direction and, when he thought we needed diversion, would engage us in elaborate games. The only time he ever caught a rabbit it turned out to be a skunk, and the only time he caught a bird it was a guinea hen. He hated to be washed, but was inordinately proud of himself when he had been washed and brushed. Taking him for a walk in the city was always an adventure. He became instantly attracted to two kinds of pedestrians — men in dirty clothes and pretty girls in nice clothes — and all other strangers were treated coldly and often with embarrassing rudeness.''

Whether he lives in a palace, a pleasure dome, barn or public house; appears in movies, plays, TV, vaudeville, circuses, or exhibitions; is a character in a murder story, love story, an adventure, a child's book, or poem; is seen in magazines, newspapers or TV commercials; — be he show dog, obedience dog, or pet, the Yorkshire Terrier is, above all else, number one companion to his owner.

Family type—Yorkies of the Buranthea Kennels, England.

Family type. A quartet of English champions from the Johnstounburn Kennels.

12

Facts and Figures

THE FIRST known AKC-licensed specialty for the Yorkshire Terrier was held on February 12, 1918, by The Yorkshire Terrier Association of America. Unfortunately beyond this one fact, there are no records as to who won, who judged, etc.

The present Yorkshire Terrier Club of America has held 25 National Specialties since its official AKC recognition in 1954.

The Yorkshire Terrier Club of Greater St. Louis was the first Yorkie specialty club to gain official recognition (1972).

Other recognized specialty clubs in the United States are:

The Delaware Valley Yorkshire Terrier Club
The Yorkshire Terrier Club of Northern California
The Yorkshire Terrier Club of Hawaii
The Yorkshire Terrier Club of Puerto Rico
The Yorkshire Terrier Club of Austin.

Other specialty clubs close to recognition are:

The Yorkshire Terrier Club of Greater New York
The Bluebonnet Yorkshire Terrier Club
The Yorkshire Terrier Club of South Florida
The Evergreen Yorkshire Terrier Club

The name and address of the current secretary of the Yorkshire Terrier Club of America, or of any of the AKC-recognized affiliate clubs, can be obtained by writing to The American Kennel Club, 51 Madison Avenue, New York, N. Y. 10010.

We have tried to be as accurate as possible in these records, but we are sure that, unfortunately and inadvertently, some errors will occur. For any such errors, we apologize — and invite your letting us know, so that they may be amended in future printings.

RECORD HOLDERS

First Champions:

1st Yorkie to become an AKC champion of record:
    Ch. Bradford Harry (Crawshaw's Bruce ex Beal's Lady); wh. 1885; finished ch. 1890; Owner, P. H. Coombs, Bangor, Me.; Breeder, W. Beal (Eng.).

1st Yorkie bitch to become an AKC champion of record:
    Ch. Minnie York (Duke of Leeds ex Minnie); finished ch. 1892; Owner, Dr. N. Ellis Oliver, Chicago; Breeder, Mr. May (Eng.); Importer, Northfield Kennels.

1st American-bred Yorkie to become AKC champion of record:
    Ch. Queen of the Fairies (Little Gem II ex Fairie); wh. 1903; finished ch. 1908; Breeder-owner, Mrs. Frederick Senn, New York City.

1st American-bred male Yorkie to become AKC champion of record:
    Ch. Senn Senn King (Little Gem III ex Fairy); wh. 1905; finished ch. 1909; Bred and owned by Mrs. Frederick Senn.

Winners:

(Particulars of sire, dam, owner, breeder and records of these dogs is given in the listing of Best in Show winners that follows.)

1st Yorkie to win Best in Show at an all-breed show:
    Ch. Little Sir Model; shown 1950–1953.

1st Yorkie bitch to win an all-breed Best in Show:
    Am. & Ir. Ch. Proud Girl of Clu-mor; shown 1962–1963

1st American-bred and 1st Homebred Yorkie to win an all-breed BIS:
    Ch. Petit Magnificent Prince; shown 1953–1954.

All-time top winning Yorkshire Terrier:
    Ch. Star Twilight of Clu-mor; shown 1952–1958.

All-time top winning Yorkshire Terrier bitch:
    Ch. Wildweir Moonrose; shown 1962–1965.

All-time top winning American-bred male Yorkie:
    Ch. Gaytonglen Teddy of Mayfair; shown 1968–1973.

The first Yorkshire Terrier to be credited by the American Kennel Club as the winner of an all-breed Best in Show was Ch. Little Sir Model, owned by the authors. Model made his win on May 12, 1951 at Betlendorf, Iowa under judge James W. Trullinger. Model was again Best in Show the following day at Rock Island, Illinois, under judge Charles McAnulty.

This is what the record books show. However, back in about 1912, a Mrs. Q (that is the only identification we have been able to trace) apparently won Best in Show at the Kansas City State Fair with her Yorkie. The American Kennel Club has no record of such a show, so assumedly it was not held under AKC rules. But since we have photographic evidence of her win, we include note of it. Perhaps, even at this late date, someone will be able to produce more information as to who Mrs. Q and her Yorkie were.

In 1931, at the 2nd annual show of the Catalina Kennel Club of Tucson, Arizona, AKC records show that Mrs. M. Leighton entered her Yorkie "Misty" in the Novice class and went on to win Best in Show under judge A. J. Scott. However, the records also show that since her dog was an English import, she was ineligible for the Novice class, which was for dogs whelped in the United States, Canada, Mexico and Cuba. "Misty" was consequently disqualified by the AKC, thus losing her BIS win. Not too surprisingly, this was the first and last time that "Misty" and her owner, Mrs. Leighton, ever showed.

Here, in alphabetical order, is the list of Yorkshire Terriers that have won an all-breed Best in Show, compiled from reports in the official *AKC Gazette* through the issue of November, 1975:

Ch. Blue Velvet of Soham (Eng. & Ir. Ch. Twinkle Star of Clu-mor ex Regine of Soham); Owner, Wildweir Kennels; Breeder, Lady Edith Windham Dawson (Ire.): 1 BIS 17 GR1, 30 GR pl, 50 BOBs.

Eng. & Am. Ch. Buranthea's Doutelle (Eng. & Ir. Ch. Mr. Pim of Johnstounburn ex Buranthea's York Sensation); Owner, Wildweir Kennels; Breeder, Mrs. Marie Burfield (Eng.); 4 BIS, 29 GR1, 41 GR pl, 71 BOBs.

Ch. Camelot's Little Pixie (Ch. Starfire Titan ex Little Miss Mopsy); Breeder-owner, Mrs. Lee Sakal; 3 BIS, 18 GR1, 31 GR pl, 38 BOBs.

Ch. Carnaby Rock 'N Roll (Heskethane Jazzbo ex Ch. Carnaby Golden Honey Bunch); Breeder-owners, Terry Childs and Joe Champagne; 1 BIS, 15 GR1, 41 GR pl, 1 YTCA Spec.

Ir. & Am. Ch. Continuation of Gleno (Eng. Ir. Jap. Ch. Wedgewood's Starmist ex Joybelle of Gleno; Owner, Wildweir Kennels; Breeder, Eugene Weir (N. Ire.) 5 BIS, 28 GR1, 37 GR pl, 74 BOBs.

The unidentified Mrs. Q and her Yorkie. The inscription on the trophy reads; "Kansas City Star Trophy for Best Dog in Show, won by _____." c. 1912.

Ch. Little Sir Model winning the first all-breed Best in Show for a Yorkshire Terrier (as recorded by AKC) at Betlendorf, Iowa, May 12, 1951, under judge James W. Trullinger. Model was again BIS the following day at Rock Island, Illinois. Owned by Mrs. L. S. Gordon, Jr. (handling) and Miss Janet Bennett.

Ch. Gaytonglen Teddy of Mayfair (Ch. Progress of Progresso ex Gaytonglen Golden Tammie); Owners, Misses Ann Seranne and Barbara Wolferman; Breeder, Doris Craig; 4 BIS, 24 GR1, 47 GR pl, 100 BOBs.

Ch. Gloamin Christmas Cracker (Sorreldene Toffee Apple ex Gay Susan of Gloamin); Owner, Wildweir Kennels; Breeder, Mrs. N. Wilkinson (Eng.); 2 BIS, 10 GR1, 12 GR pl, 28 BOBs.

Am. & Can. Ch. Heart G's Spunky Sparky (Clarkwyn Lancelot ex Clarkwyn Flirtation); Owners, Mr. and Mrs. Charles Mansfield; Breeder, Marjorie R. Gunnell; 1 BIS, 5 GR1, 16 GR pl, 35 BOBs.

Ch. Lamsgrove Pinnochio (Eng. & Jap. Ch. Pagnell Peter Pan ex Whitecross Daisy Belle); Owner, Pearl Trojan; 1 BIS, 2 GR1, 2 GR pl, 5 BOBs.

Ch. Little Sir Model (Eng. Ch. Ben's Blue Pride ex Allenby Queen); Owners, Wildweir Kennels; Breeder, Mrs. M. Smart (Eг g.); 4 BIS, 31 GR1, 23 GR pl, 63 BOBs.

Ch. Mayfair Barban Loup de Mer (Ch. Devanvale Jack in the Box ex Ch. Mayfair Barban Lady Finger); Breeder-Owners: Ann Seranne and Barbara Wolferman; 3 BIS, 33 GRI, 42 GR pl.

Am. & Berm. Ch. Mayfair's Barban Yam 'n Yelly (Ch. Gaytonglen Teddy of Mayfair ex Ch. Mayfair Barban Kasha); Owners, Phillip A. and Gertrude Lanard; Breeders, Ann Seranne and Barbara Wolferman; 1 BIS, 3 GR1, 5 GR pl.

Ch. Pequa Mustang (Ch. Caprice of Pagham ex Pequa Tuffy); Owners, Mrs. Myrtle Young and Joe Glaser; Breeder, Barbara Hickey; 1 BIS, 4 GR1, 7 GR pl.

Ch. Pete's Tiger (Ch. Peter Pan of Wayside ex Rosemarie of Wayside), Owner, Dorothy Scott; Breeder, Mrs. Victor Schupp; 1 BIS, 1 GR1, 3 BOBs.

Ch. Petit Magnificent Prince (Petit Baby Dumpling ex Petite Little Doll); Breeder-owner: Goldie Stone; 1 BIS, 4 GR1, 6 GR pl, 10 BOBs.

Eng. & Am. Ch. Progress of Progresso (Eng. & Am. Ch. Don Carlos of Progresso ex Eng. Ch. Coulgorm Chloe); Owners, Bud Priser and Jim Nickerson; Breeder, Mrs. C. Hutchins (Eng.); 1 BIS, 11 GR1, 34 GR pl, 53 BOBs.

Ir. & Am. Ch. Proud Girl of Clu-mor (Herbert of Clu-mor ex Clu-mor Queen of Hearts); Owners, Wildweir Kennels; Breeders, Misses Maud and Florence Loton (Ire.); 1 BIS, 22 GR1, 19 GR pl, 49 BOBs.

Ch. Shareen Mr. Tee See (Ch. Shareen Pride of JB ex Ch. Shareen Pixie Punkin); Owner, Mrs. Margaret Spilling; Breeders, T.C. and M. L. Spilling; 1 BIS, 12 GR1, 34 GR pl, 86 BOBs.

Ch. Star Twilight of Clu-mor (Eng. & Ir. Ch. Twinkle Star of Clu-mor ex My Pretty Maid; Owner, Wildweir Kennels; Breeder, Miss Maud Loton (Ire.); 26 BIS, 81 GR1, 22 GR pl, 104 BOBs.

Ch. Trivar's Gold Digger (Ch. Trivar's Tycoon ex May Queen of Astolat); Owners, Johnny Robinson and Morris Howard; Breeder, Johnny Robinson; 2 BIS, 12 GR1, 22 GR pl.

Ch. Trivar's Princess Jervic (Ch. Trivar's Bon Vivant ex Ch. Trivar's Toffee); Owners: Victor Recondo and Jerry Vines; Breeders: Johnny A. Robinson and Morris Howard; 1 BIS, 1 GR1, 5 GR pl, 9 BOBs.

Ch. Wenscoe's Whynot of Shaumar (Ch. Wenscoe's Whizzaway of Tzumiao ex Wenscoe's Ginfizz of LaNores); Owner, Betty J. Conaty; Breeder, Wendy Anne Whitely; 1 BIS, 3 GR1, 3 GR pl, 14 BOBs.

Ch. Wildweir Contrail (Ch. Continuation of Gleno ex Wildweir Whimsy); Breeder-Owners: Wildweir Kennels; 3 BIS, 13 GR1, 26 GR pl.

Ch. Wildweir Fair N' Square (Ch. Wildweir Pomp N' Circumstance ex Ch. Rose Petal of Clu-mor); Breeder-owners, Wildweir Kennels; 3 BIS, 25 GR1, 37 GR pl, 70 BOBs.

Ch. Wildweir Moonrose (So. Am. Ch. Prince Moon of Clu-mor ex Ch. Rose Petal of Clu-mor); Breeder-owners, Wildweir Kennels; 3 BIS, 26 GR1, 30 GR pl, 59 BOBs.

Ch. Wildweir Prim N' Proper (Ch. Wildweir Pomp N' Circumstance ex Wildweir Time and Tide); Owners, Helen and Merrill Cohen; Breeders, Wildweir Kennels; 1 BIS, 16 GR1, 60 GR pl, 73 BOBs.

Ch. Wildweir Sandwich Man (Ch. Wildweir Stuffed Shirt ex My Pretty Maid of Wildweir); Owner, Frances Cohen; Breeders, Wildweir Kennels; 2 BIS, 16 GR1, 33 GR pl.

Ch. Yorkfold Bruno Bear (Rocky Royale of Winpal ex Yorkfold Koala Bear) Owner, Mr. E. E. Hitchins; Breeder, Mrs. Daphne Rossiter (Eng.); 1 BIS, 8 GR1, 14 GR pl.

Ch. Yorkfold Chocolate Boy (Buranthea's Aristocratic Pim of Johnstounburn ex Gold Dinky of Arcady); Owner, Wildweir Kennels; Breeder, Mrs. Daphne Rossiter (Eng.); 1 BIS, 3 GR1, 16 GR pl, 21 BOBs.

Ch. Yorkfold Jezebel (Eng. & Am. Ch. Yorkfold McPickle ex Ch. Bella Donna of Winpal); Breeder-Owner: Mrs. Frances C. Geraghty; 1 BIS.

OBEDIENCE

Many Yorkies have won the title of C.D. (Companion Dog), and quite a few have won C.D.X. (Companion Dog Excellent) titles, but since the beginning of Obedience trials in 1936 only the Yorkies listed below have won the coveted title of U.D. (Utility Dog). No dog of the breed, as yet, has won a Tracking title, although several have tried.

Yorkshire Terriers with the Utility Degree

	Year title was won:
Ch. Miss California of Forty-Eight, U.D. Owner, Mrs. Ruby Erickson	1951
Durgin's York of Woodlawn, U.D. Owner, George Reed	1957
Patoot's Mr. Boo of Sher-lo, U.D. Owner, Lois Noyes	1961
Patrick Emmet, U.D. Owner, Mrs. Mahne	1959

Ch. Miss California of '48, C.D., C.D.X., U.D., bred and owned by Mrs. Ruby Erickson. Miss California was the first (and to date the only) Yorkie to earn bench championship as well as all three Obedience titles.

Yorkshire Terrier graduates of Obedience school.

Mr. Rag Tag of Appline, Am. C.D., C.D.X. and U.D., Can. C.D. and C.D.X., and Berm. C.D. With a score of 197.66 at Detroit in 1974, Rag Tag became the first Toy dog to place in the Top Ten at the World Series of Obedience.

Mardel's Terrance, U.D.	1965
Owner, Merrill Cohen	
Yam Snevets, U.D.	1965
Owner, Mrs. Tepe Stevens	
Durgin's Tinkerbell, U.D.	1966
Owner, Mrs. Lewis	
Girleen of Fortfield, U.D.	1968
Owner, Edythe B. Parvis	
Donneykin's Cafe Snevets, U.D.	1968
Owner, Mrs. Tepe Stevens	
Fra-Mar's Carnaby Cricket, U.D.	1972
Owners, Marlene and Frank Schmitz	
Acee-Doucee, U.D.	1973
Owner, Miss Anita Paprota	
Henryetta Strully's Destiny, U.D.	1974
Owner, Elizabeth Strully	
Mr. Ragtag of Appoline, U.D.	1974
Owner, Judy Giddens	
Sully's Li'l Bit O' Rum, U.D.	1975
Owner, Lorraine E. Sullivan	

Quite a few Yorkies, both male and female, have won both bench and Obedience titles, and have produced champions. We can find only one Yorkie who has won both a bench Champion and an Obedience title, been a Group winner, and produced at least one champion.

She is Ch. Petite Stardust, C.D., who won her degree with scores of 199, 197 and 196.5. Besides winning her championship, Stardust was the winner of 2 Toy Groups and 3 Group placings, and was the dam of Ch. Holiday Sweet Token. Stardust, whelped in 1948 was bred by Goldie V. Stone, and owned by Mrs. Godfrey Lundberg, Winnetka, Illinois. She was shown and trained by Lee Lundberg. Through her sire, Petit Baby Dumpling, Stardust was a half-sister to BIS winner Ch. Petit Magnificent Prince.

Ch. Petite Stardust, C.D.

TOP PRODUCERS

The following honor roll of the foremost sires and dams of the breed has been compiled from the listing of champions in the offical AKC Gazette each month through the issue of July, 1975.

The lists include the sires of five or more champions, and the dams of four or more champions.

At end of the listings, there is note of the sires and dams prior to 1940 whom we feel to be deserving of recognition as top producers, even though most would not qualify under the five for sires, four for dams limitation.

Top Producing Sires

Sire of:

Ch. Wildweir Pomp N' Circumstance	95 chs.
Ch. Wildweir Keepsake	29 chs.
Ch. Gaytonglen Teddy of Mayfair	22 chs.
Ch. Wildweir Ten O'Clock Scholar	20 chs.
Ch. Wildweir Fair N' Square	17 chs.
Kelpie's Belziehill Dondi	16 chs.
Ch. Trivar's Tycoon	16 chs.
Ch. Star Twilight of Clu-Mor	15 chs.
Ch. Progress of Progesso	14 chs.
Ch. Dandy Diamond of Mayfair	13 chs.
Ch. Northshire's Mazeltov	13 chs.
Ch. Caprice of Pagham	12 chs.
Ch. Mr kipps of Grenbar	12 chs.
Ch. Wenscoe's Whizzaway of Tzumiao	11 chs.
Ch. Wildweir Darktown Strutter	11 chs.
Ch. Wildweir Dinner Jacket	11 chs.
Ch. Buranthea Doutelle	10 chs.
Ch. Wildweir Brass Hat	10 chs.
Ch. Wildweir Coat of Arms	10 chs.
Ch. Wildweir E-Major of Maybelle	10 chs.
Ch. Yorkfold McPickle	10 chs.
Ch. Yorkfold Wags to Witches	10 chs.
Ch. Bermyth Lad of Hesketane	9 chs.
Ch. Darshire's Corrigan	9 chs.
Ch. Francis Doutelle Time Bomb	9 chs.
Ch. Jolliboy of The Vale	8 chs.
Ch. Tid-le-Wink	8 chs.
Ch. Hesketane Rob of Lilactime	7 chs.
Ch. Kirnel's Topaz Medallion	7 chs.
Ch. Mayfair-Barban Mocha Mousse	7 chs.
Patoot's Jonathon	7 chs.
Ch. Ru-Gene's King Corky	7 chs.
Ch. St. Aubrey's Tzumiao's Apollo	6 chs.

Ch. Starfire Mitey Model	6 chs.
Ch. Suprema	6 chs.
Ch. Viclar's Heesa Dandy	6 chs.
Ch. Wildweir Cloud Nine	6 chs.
Ch. Yorkfold Jackanapes	6 chs.
Ch. Acama Quite-A-Bit	5 chs.
Ch. Christopher of Valleyend	5 chs.
Ch. Don Carlos of Progresso	5 chs.
Ch. Hifalutin	5 chs.
Ch. Lamsgrove Fusspot	5 chs.
Ch. Shareen Tee See	5 chs.
Ch. Toy Clown of Rusklyn	5 chs.
Ch. Trivar's Bon Vivant	5 chs.
Ch. Wildweir Cock of The Walk	5 chs.
Ch. Wildweir Doodletown Piper	5 chs.

Top Producing Dams

Dam of:

Wildweir Scarlet Ribbon	10 chs.
Daisy of Libertyhill	9 chs.
Danby's Belziehill Anya	9 chs.
Ch. Trivar's Contessa	9 chs.
Wildweir Time and Tide	9 chs.
Troubador's Germaine	8 chs.
Danby's Belziehill Abigail	7 chs.
Ch. Yorkfold Jezebel	7 chs.
Ruthie De Planta Pinta	6 chs.
Ch. Beechrise Trudy of the Vale	5 chs.
Cover Girl	5 chs.
Soham Andrea	5 chs.
Ch. Wildweir Skater's Waltz	5 chs.
BeeGee's Sue's Victory	4 chs.
Ch. Bella Donna of Winpal	4 chs.
Ch. Clarkwyn Fanciful Sue	4 chs.
Francis Picador Firecracker	4 chs.
Ch. Fro-Jo's Blue Button of Maybelle	4 chs.
Gaybrook Gladiolus	4 chs.
Little Barbie of Ramon	4 chs.
May Queen of Astolat	4 chs.
Spring Holly's Blue Shamrock	4 chs.
Ch. Trivar's Holiday Spirit	4 chs.
Wildweir Beloved Belinda	4 chs.
Wildweir Dilly Dally	4 chs.
Wildweir For-Get-Me-Not	4 chs.
Wildweir Hot Fudge	4 chs.
Wildweir Indian Magic	4 chs.
Ch. Wildweir Ticket to The Moon	4 chs.

318

Am. & Can. Ch. Haslingden Dandy Dinty, bred by Harry Smith, owned by Andre Paterson. Sire of 5 champions. Dinty weighed 3½ lbs.

Top Sires Prior to 1940

Sire of:

Ch. Haslingden Dandy Dinty	5 chs.
Ch. Petite Byngo Boy	5 chs.
Ch. Bond's Byngo	3 chs.
Ch. Armley Nicco	2 chs.
Ch. Roxy II	2 chs.
Ch. Teddy Boy	2 chs.
Ch. Clayton Wee Marvel	1 ch.
Ch. Conran Toy	1 ch.
Little Gem II	1 ch.
Ch. Senn Senn King	1 ch.

Top Dams Prior to 1940

Dam of:

Madame Be You	5 chs.
Ch. Petit Baby Snooks	2 chs.
Rose's Miss Canada	2 chs.
Senn Senn Nipper	2 chs.

BIBLIOGRAPHY

ALL OWNERS of pure-bred dogs will benefit themselves and their dogs by enriching their knowledge of breeds and of canine care, training, breeding, psychology and other important aspects of dog management. The following list of books covers further reading recommended by judges, veterinarians, breeders, trainers and other authorities. Books may be obtained at the finer book stores and pet shops, or through Howell Book House Inc., publishers, New York.

Breed Books

AFGHAN HOUND, Complete — *Miller & Gilbert*
AIREDALE, New Complete — *Edwards*
AKITA, Complete — *Linderman & Funk*
ALASKAN MALAMUTE, Complete — *Riddle & Seeley*
BASSET HOUND, Complete — *Braun*
BEAGLE, New Complete — *Noted Authorities*
BLOODHOUND, Complete — *Brey & Reed*
BOXER, Complete — *Denlinger*
BRITTANY SPANIEL, Complete — *Riddle*
BULLDOG, New Complete — *Hanes*
BULL TERRIER, New Complete — *Eberhard*
CAIRN TERRIER, Complete — *Marvin*
CHESAPEAKE BAY RETRIEVER, Complete — *Cherry*
CHIHUAHUA, Complete — *Noted Authorities*
COCKER SPANIEL, New — *Kraeuchi*
COLLIE, New — *Official Publication of the Collie Club of America*
DACHSHUND, The New — *Meistrell*
DALMATIAN, The — *Treen*
DOBERMAN PINSCHER, New — *Walker*
ENGLISH SETTER, New Complete — *Tuck, Howell & Graef*
ENGLISH SPRINGER SPANIEL, New — *Goodall & Gasow*
FOX TERRIER, New Complete — *Silvernail*
GERMAN SHEPHERD DOG, New Complete — *Bennett*
GERMAN SHORTHAIRED POINTER, New — *Maxwell*
GOLDEN RETRIEVER, New Complete — *Fischer*
GORDON SETTER, Complete — *Look*
GREAT DANE, New Complete — *Noted Authorities*
GREAT DANE, The—Dogdom's Apollo — *Draper*
GREAT PYRENEES, Complete — *Strang & Giffin*
IRISH SETTER, New Complete — *Eldredge & Vanacore*
IRISH WOLFHOUND, Complete — *Starbuck*
JACK RUSSEL TERRIER, Complete — *Plummer*
KEESHOND, Complete — *Peterson*
LABRADOR RETRIEVER, Complete — *Warwick*
LHASA APSO, Complete — *Herbel*
MINIATURE SCHNAUZER, Complete — *Eskrigge*
NEWFOUNDLAND, New Complete — *Chern*
NORWEGIAN ELKHOUND, New Complete — *Wallo*
OLD ENGLISH SHEEPDOG, Complete — *Mandeville*
PEKINGESE, Quigley Book of — *Quigley*
PEMBROKE WELSH CORGI, Complete — *Sargent & Harper*
POODLE, New Complete — *Hopkins & Irick*
POODLE CLIPPING AND GROOMING BOOK, Complete — *Kalstone*
ROTTWEILER, Complete — *Freeman*
SAMOYED, Complete — *Ward*
SCHIPPERKE, Official Book of — *Root, Martin, Kent*
SCOTTISH TERRIER, New Complete — *Marvin*
SHETLAND SHEEPDOG, The New — *Riddle*
SHIH TZU, Joy of Owning — *Seranne*
SHIH TZU, The (English) — *Dadds*
SIBERIAN HUSKY, Complete — *Demidoff*
TERRIERS, The Book of All — *Marvin*
WEST HIGHLAND WHITE TERRIER, Complete — *Marvin*
WHIPPET, Complete — *Pegram*
YORKSHIRE TERRIER, Complete — *Gordon & Bennett*

Breeding

ART OF BREEDING BETTER DOGS, New — *Onstott*
BREEDING YOUR OWN SHOW DOG — *Seranne*
HOW TO BREED DOGS — *Whitney*
HOW PUPPIES ARE BORN — *Prine*
INHERITANCE OF COAT COLOR IN DOGS — *Little*

Care and Training

COUNSELING DOG OWNERS, Evans Guide for — *Evans*
DOG OBEDIENCE, Complete Book of — *Saunders*
NOVICE, OPEN AND UTILITY COURSES — *Saunders*
DOG CARE AND TRAINING FOR BOYS AND GIRLS — *Saunders*
DOG NUTRITION, Collins Guide to — *Collins*
DOG TRAINING FOR KIDS — *Benjamin*
DOG TRAINING, Koehler Method of — *Koehler*
DOG TRAINING Made Easy — *Tucker*
GO FIND! Training Your Dog to Track — *Davis*
GUARD DOG TRAINING, Koehler Method of — *Koehler*
MOTHER KNOWS BEST—The Natural Way to Train Your Dog — *Benjamin*
OPEN OBEDIENCE FOR RING, HOME AND FIELD, Koehler Method of — *Koehler*
STONE GUIDE TO DOG GROOMING FOR ALL BREEDS — *Stone*
SUCCESSFUL DOG TRAINING, The Pearsall Guide to — *Pearsall*
TOY DOGS, Kalstone Guide to Grooming All — *Kalstone*
TRAINING THE RETRIEVER — *Kersley*
TRAINING TRACKING DOGS, Koehler Method of — *Koehler*
TRAINING YOUR DOG—Step by Step Manual — *Volhard & Fisher*
TRAINING YOUR DOG TO WIN OBEDIENCE TITLES — *Morsell*
TRAIN YOUR OWN GUN DOG, How to — *Goodall*
UTILITY DOG TRAINING, Koehler Method of — *Koehler*
VETERINARY HANDBOOK, Dog Owner's Home — *Carlson & Giffin*

General

AKC'S WORLD OF THE PURE-BRED DOG — *American Kennel Club*
CANINE TERMINOLOGY — *Spira*
COMPLETE DOG BOOK, The — *Official Publication of American Kennel Club*
DOG IN ACTION, The — *Lyon*
DOG BEHAVIOR, New Knowledge of — *Pfaffenberger*
DOG JUDGE'S HANDBOOK — *Tietjen*
DOG JUDGING, Nicholas Guide to — *Nicholas*
DOG PEOPLE ARE CRAZY — *Riddle*
DOG PSYCHOLOGY — *Whitney*
DOGSTEPS, Illustrated Gait at a Glance — *Elliott*
DOG TRICKS — *Haggerty & Benjamin*
ENCYCLOPEDIA OF DOGS, International — *Dangerfield, Howell & Riddle*
EYES THAT LEAD—Story of Guide Dogs for the Blind — *Tucker*
FRIEND TO FRIEND—Dogs That Help Mankind — *Schwartz*
FROM RICHES TO BITCHES — *Shattuck*
HAPPY DOG/HAPPY OWNER — *Siegal*
IN STITCHES OVER BITCHES — *Shattuck*
JUNIOR SHOWMANSHIP HANDBOOK — *Brown & Mason*
MY TIMES WITH DOGS — *Fletcher*
OUR PUPPY'S BABY BOOK (blue or pink)
SUCCESSFUL DOG SHOWING, Forsyth Guide to — *Forsyth*
TRIM, GROOM & SHOW YOUR DOG, How to — *Saunders*
WHY DOES YOUR DOG DO THAT? — *Bergman*
WILD DOGS in Life and Legend — *Riddle*
WORLD OF SLED DOGS, From Siberia to Sport Racing — *Coppinger*